Rethinking Second Language Learning

SECOND LANGUAGE ACQUISITION

Series Editor: **Professor David Singleton**, *University of Pannonia, Hungary* and Fellow Emeritus, *Trinity College, Dublin, Ireland* and **Dr Simone E. Pfenninger**, *University of Zurich, Switzerland*

This series brings together titles dealing with a variety of aspects of language acquisition and processing in situations where a language or languages other than the native language is involved. Second language is thus interpreted in its broadest possible sense. The volumes included in the series all offer in their different ways, on the one hand, exposition and discussion of empirical findings and, on the other, some degree of theoretical reflection. In this latter connection, no particular theoretical stance is privileged in the series; nor is any relevant perspective – sociolinguistic, psycholinguistic, neurolinguistic, etc. – deemed out of place. The intended readership of the series includes final-year undergraduates working on second language acquisition projects, postgraduate students involved in second language acquisition research, and researchers and teachers in general whose interests include a second language acquisition component.

Full details of all the books in this series and of all our other publications can be found on http://www.multilingual-matters.com, or by writing to Multilingual Matters, St Nicholas House, 31-34 High Street, Bristol BS1 2AW, UK.

SECOND LANGUAGE ACQUISITION: 98

Rethinking Second Language Learning

Using Intergenerational Community Resources

Edited by
Marisa Cordella and Hui Huang

MULTILINGUAL MATTERS
Bristol • Buffalo • Toronto

Library of Congress Cataloging in Publication Data
A catalog record for this book is available from the Library of Congress.
Names: Cordella, Marisa, editor. | Huang, Hui (Linguist) editor.
Title: Rethinking Second Language Learning: Using Intergenerational
Community Resources/Edited by Marisa Cordella and Hui Huang.
Description: Bristol; Buffalo: Multilingual Matters, [2016] | Series: Second Language
  Acquisition: 98 | Includes bibliographical references and index.
Identifiers: LCCN 2015049064 | ISBN 9781783095407 (hbk: alk. paper) | ISBN
  9781783095391 (pbk: alk. paper) | ISBN 9781783095438 (kindle)
Subjects: LCSH: Second language acquisition–Research. | Second language
  acquisition–Study and teaching–Foreign speakers. | Applied linguistics
Classification: LCC P118.2 .R478 2016 | DDC 401/.93–dc23 LC record available at
http://lccn.loc.gov/2015049064

British Library Cataloguing in Publication Data
A catalogue entry for this book is available from the British Library.

ISBN-13: 978-1-78309-540-7 (hbk)
ISBN-13: 978-1-78309-539-1 (pbk)

Multilingual Matters
UK: St Nicholas House, 31-34 High Street, Bristol BS1 2AW, UK.
USA: UTP, 2250 Military Road, Tonawanda, NY 14150, USA.
Canada: UTP, 5201 Dufferin Street, North York, Ontario M3H 5T8, Canada.

Website: www.multilingual-matters.com
Twitter: Multi_Ling_Mat
Facebook: https://www.facebook.com/multilingualmatters
Blog: www.channelviewpublications.wordpress.com

Copyright © 2016 Marisa Cordella, Hui Huang and the authors of individual chapters.

All rights reserved. No part of this work may be reproduced in any form or by any means without permission in writing from the publisher.

The policy of Multilingual Matters/Channel View Publications is to use papers that are natural, renewable and recyclable products, made from wood grown in sustainable forests. In the manufacturing process of our books, and to further support our policy, preference is given to printers that have FSC and PEFC Chain of Custody certification. The FSC and/or PEFC logos will appear on those books where full certification has been granted to the printer concerned.

Typeset by Deanta Global Publishing Services Limited.

This volume is dedicated to the memory of the late Professor Michael Clyne (1939–2010), whose distinguished achievements as a linguist, academic and author are well known internationally. Michael was the instigator of this project and inspired us to become part of his dream. Tragically, he was only able to witness its first few months of operation. With this book we hope to do justice to his visionary ideas on social inclusion and language learning in multicultural Australia.

Contents

Figures and Tables ix
Transcription Conventions xi
Acknowledgements xiii
Contributors xv

Introduction xix
Marisa Cordella and Hui Huang

Part 1: Setting the Scene: Many Cultures, Many Opportunities

1 The Immigrant Potential: Multiculturalism, Language Skills and Community Resources 3
Marisa Cordella

2 Contemporary Intergenerational Relationships 25
Susan Feldman, Harriet Radermacher and Colette Browning

3 Community Resources on our Doorstep: Language Learning in Action 37
Hui Huang and Marisa Cordella

Part 2: Constructing Identity: The Self-Presentation of Older Native Speakers

4 Taking a Stance: Older Native Speakers with Young Language Learners 51
Marisa Cordella

5 The Migration Experience and the Ethos of Self 66
   Brigitte Lambert and Marisa Cordella

6 'Who Are We?' Self-Referencing in Chinese and German
   Conversations Using the First Person Plural 85
   Hui Huang and Yanying Lu

7 Creating, Maintaining and Challenging Rapport Across
   Languages and Age Groups 110
   Marisa Cordella and Cecilia Kokubu

8 'I feel very happy that I can contribute to society': Exploring the
   Value of the Project for Older People 149
   Harriet Radermacher, Colette Browning and Susan Feldman

Part 3: Situated Learning: Enhancing the Opportunities for L2 Students

9 Gaining L2 Self-Confidence in Conversations with
   Native Speakers 171
   Hui Huang

10 Developing Interactional Competence in Dyadic Conversations:
   Cross-language Evidence 187
   Hui Huang

11 An Innovative Model for Second Language Learning and
   Social Inclusion 226
   *Hui Huang, Marisa Cordella, Colette Browning and
   Ramona Baumgartner*

Index 239

Figures and Tables

Figures

Figure 3.1 Data collection procedures — 44

Figure 5.1 Stances of German-speaking immigrants — 73

Figure 5.2 Stances of Spanish-speaking immigrants — 74

Figure 7.1 A cyclical model of rapport in verbal communication — 117

Figure 9.1 Design of the self-efficacy study — 175

Figure 11.1 An intergenerational, intercultural model of language learning and social inclusion — 227

Tables

Table 1.1 The top 14 languages other than English (LOTE) spoken at home in Victoria: Census 2011 and Census 2006 — 18

Table 3.1 Student participants in the project — 42

Table 3.2 Older participants in the project — 43

Table 3.3 Focus group questions for the students — 45

Table 4.1 Stance-taking by older L1 speakers and L2 students — 53

Table 5.1 Examples of linguistic tokens used for self-referencing — 70

Table 5.2 Examples of linguistic tokens used to indicate time and space — 71

Table 5.3 Examples of linguistic tokens used to express opinions — 72

Table 5.4 Examples of linguistic tokens used to make comparisons — 72

Table 5.5	Examples of linguistic tokens used to express feelings	73
Table 6.1	Study participants	89
Table 6.2	Use of the first person plural in 12 Chinese and German conversations	91
Table 6.3	Examples of 'we' = speaker + specified other(s)	95
Table 6.4	Examples of 我们 for ambiguous referents	97
Table 6.5	Examples of 我们 + 这 for vague alignments	98
Table 6.6	German examples of the generic use of 'we'	99
Table 6.7	Chinese examples of the aggregate use of 'we'	102
Table 6.8	German participants' use of both 'wir' and 'ich' when describing their immediate family	105
Table 7.1	RSAs that shape *mutual attentiveness*	118
Table 7.2	RSAs that shape *positivity*	121
Table 7.3	Dyadic RSA frequencies for *positivity*	133
Table 7.4	Summary of RSA frequencies for *positivity*	134
Table 7.5	RSAs that shape *coordination*	135
Table 7.6	Dyadic RSA frequencies for *coordination*	143
Table 7.7	Summary of RSA frequencies for *coordination*	144
Table 8.1	Older participants in the telephone interviews	155
Table 9.1	Self-efficacy questionnaire	176
Table 9.2	Background language of the study group	177
Table 9.3	Summary of descriptive data for each group	178
Table 9.4	Within-group comparisons	179
Table 10.1	Study participants	190
Table 10.2	Initiation and development of topics and subtopics by the student in Chinese conversations	193
Table 10.3	Initiation and development of topics and subtopics by the student in German conversations	203
Table 10.4	Initiation and development of topics and subtopics by the student in Spanish conversations	214

Transcription Conventions

Unit	Truncated syllable (first)	,
	Truncated syllable (middle and final)	-
Speakers	Speaker identity/turn start	:
	Overlapping talk begins	[
	Overlapping talk ends	]
	Latching	=
	No silence left between first speaker and second speaker's turn	
Tone	Low falling tone	\
	Rising tone	/
Pause/Silence	Pause of less than half a second	(.)
	Pause longer than half a second	(..)
	Pause longer than a second	(...)
	Pause longer than a second and a half	(....)
Vocal Noises	Inhalation	(H)
	Exhalation	(Hx)
Quality voice	Emphasis	EMPHASIS
	Perceived change based on volume or pitch change	
	Lower in volume than the rest of the talk	* *
	Laugh quality	<@ @>
Lengthening	Vowel/consonant elongation	:::
Transcribers' perspective	Researcher's comment	(( ))
	Uncertain hearing	<X X>
	Word expressed in English	<E E>

Acknowledgements

This volume is dedicated to the memory of the late Professor Michael Clyne (1939–2010) whose scholarly achievements as a linguist, intellectual and academic are well known internationally. Michael was the instigator of this project and inspired us to become part of his dream. Unfortunately, he could only witness the first few months of the project's activities. With this book we hope to make justice to his visionary ideas on social inclusion in multicultural Australia.

All the contributions to this volume are based on the cross-disciplinary research carried out by a team of linguists from the Arts Faculty and healthy ageing specialists from the Faculty of Medicine, Nursing and Health Sciences at Monash University. The project was led and guided by Associate Professor Marisa Cordella, Dr Hui Huang and Professor Colette Browning. We are thankful to all colleagues for their motivation to participate in such an innovative model of collaboration. Thank you for the initiation of this multi-disciplinary dialogue and the continuous exchange in the fields of second language acquisition, ageing and health, and discourse analysis.

The successful completion of this project could not have been achieved without the collective work of the entire research team that included Project Manager Ramona Baumgartner, Researchers Adjunct Associate Professor Susan Feldman and Dr Harriet Radermacher and Research Assistants across two faculties and three languages: Yanying Lu, Dr Brigitte Lambert, Cecilia Kokubu, Dr Victoria Gras, Jian He, Xinying Zhang, Chen Zhang, Hanzi Wu, Pei Zhou, Ye Chen and Yue Zhang; Katie Paredes, Katherine Hastings, Kavita Kaur, Hannah Lofgren, Jarrah Strunin, and Alice Whitmore; Claire Manning, David Rudman and Iris Zantop; Tiasha de Soysa, Elizabeth Greenhalgh and Clair Cullen.

We are deeply grateful for the funding support received from the Australian Research Council (LP 100100258). We also extend our thanks to four additional partner organisations for their funding, in-kind support and the help received from their dedicated and passionate Project Officers: Council on the Ageing, Department of Education and Early Childhood Development, Independent Schools Victoria and Office of Multicultural Affairs and Citizenship. We would also like to take this opportunity to thank the former Victorian Minister for Multicultural Affairs and Citizenship, the Honourable Nicholas Kotsiras, for launching our project DVD in 2012 and Professor Ed Byrne (Vice-Chancellor and President at Monash University) and Professor Rae Frances (Dean of the Faculty of Arts) for hosting the 'Golden Language Guru' award ceremony for project participants in 2010.

We feel indebted to our senior participants and Year 11 and 12 students for their loyalty and dedication to joining the research activities, cooperation with the research team and understanding of the requirements for our data collection. Our gratitude also goes to participating schools; a heartfelt thank you to the principals of Glen Waverley Secondary College (Gerry Schiller), Wantirna College (Sue Bell) and Caulfield Grammar School, Wheelers Hill Campus (Paul Runting). We thank all LOTE coordinators and language teachers across the three schools: Gerard Bate, Ting Hu, Dolores Pareta, Renate Just, Sonya Pollard, Ping Zheng, Sally Lean, Hailan Yi, Lucy Chan, Bo Chen, Jorge Leiva, Pilar Ruperti, Janet Chen, Ling Wang, Meihua Wang and Sally Wilson, for their collaboration and for sharing their passion with the research team.

The establishment and long-term implementation of the project, along with the future dissemination of research outcomes would not have been possible and will not be feasible without the fundamental support from the Monash University Arts Online Presence Programme Team (website), Teepee media video production (project DVD), Renate Just (teaching resource), the Immigration Museum Melbourne (workshop) and all teachers and schools who implemented the project in their curriculum.

Special thanks must go to the anonymous reviewers from Multilingual Matters and colleagues who were keen to provide feedback to the chapters of this volume: Alan Hatton-Yeo from the Beth Johnson Foundation in England, Dr Howard Nicholas from La Trobe University, Dr Aldo Poiani, Dr Brigitte Lambert, Dr Marc Xu, Dr Michael Henderson and Dr Robyn Spence-Brown from Monash University, Dr Leng Leng Thang from National University of Singapore, Dr Doris Schüpbach from Melbourne University, Professor Linda Tickle-Degnen from Tufts University, Dr Jianwei Xu from Vrije Universiteit Brussel and Dr Sue Fernandez from Wesley College. We are especially thankful for the invaluable editing help provided by Meredith Sherlock, who also prepared the Index.

Finally, the editor wishes to thank each of the contributors. It has been a great pleasure to work closely with one another and constantly share our ideas and insights. Mutual constructive advice on each chapter was a plus in the production of this multi-disciplinary volume. We all hope that this book may contribute to fostering social cohesion, increase language learning, well-being as well as intergenerational and cross-cultural communication in a world of constant demographic and social changes.

Contributors

Ramona Baumgartner was the Project Coordinator of the ARC Linkage Project 'Intergenerational, Intercultural Encounters and Second Language Development'. She is an experienced educational and community project manager. Her work areas include language research at Monash University as well as international education with the City of Melbourne. She has a background in language teaching and her interest lies in connecting people across cultures and generations.

Colette Browning is a Health Psychologist and Social Gerontologist. She is Director of the RDNS Institute, Honorary Professor at Peking University and Adjunct Professor at Monash University. Professor Browning is the author of more than 190 publications, including peer-reviewed papers, book chapters and monographs. Her research focuses on healthy ageing, services for older people, and behavioural and social factors in ageing and chronic disease self-management.

Marisa Cordella is an Associate Professor in Spanish linguistics at the University of Queensland. She holds a PhD in Linguistics from Monash University, an MA and Graduate Diploma in TESOL from the University of Canberra and a BA in translating and interpreting from Chile. Her area of expertise is discourse analysis and she has carried out cross-disciplinary research projects in collaboration with colleagues from Medicine and Psychology both in Australia and abroad. Associate Professor Cordella has led many research groups as well as the Spanish Programmes at Monash and the University of Queensland. She has published widely in peer-review journals, book chapters and is author of two books on discourse analysis and medical communication (one sole and one co-authored). Her research expertise and postgraduate supervision are in the areas of discourse analysis (e.g. critical discourse analysis, interactional sociolinguistics), intercultural communication, teaching methodologies, medical communication, and translation studies.

Susan Feldman is an Adjunct Associate Professor in primary health care research in the Faculty of Medicine, Nursing and Health Sciences at Monash University. For the past 30 years she has been engaged in qualitative research on ageing, with a particular interest in gender, intergenerational relations and older people from multicultural backgrounds. Associate Professor Feldman has published widely in peer-reviewed journals and book chapters and is the co-editor of five books.

Hui Huang is a Lecturer in the School of Languages, Literatures, Cultures and Linguistics at Monash University and holds a PhD in Applied Linguistics. Her research interests and publications cover the areas of second language acquisition and sociolinguistics, particularly the teaching of Chinese as a second/heritage language, ICT in language teaching, cross-cultural communication and immigrant identity. Her studies include collaboration with researchers from Linguistics, Education and Medicine in cross-disciplinary projects in Australia and overseas.

Cecilia Kokubu received her Bachelor of Arts from Monash University, majoring in Linguistics. With her background in training and development she worked as a language and communications consultant in Argentina, Mexico, the Philippines and Ukraine. After a 10-year career in the outsourcing industry, she opted for a radical change of direction and is now taking her first steps as a youth and charity worker. She currently resides in Devon, England, with her husband and twin daughters.

Brigitte Lambert holds a PhD in Linguistics and Applied Linguistics from the University of Melbourne. She advocates the benefits of multilingualism, sharing her ideas for language learning at home and in the classroom through community events and teacher conferences. She is a regular participant in the Raising Bilingual Children seminars run by RUMACCC (Research Unit for Cross-Cultural Communication) at the University of Melbourne. Inspired by the Monash project, she recently initiated a trial project for teaching German at primary school via the internet, in the role of grandmother.

Yanying Lu is currently conducting doctoral research at Monash University that explores how the self is conceptualised among Chinese immigrants and how this conceptualisation interacts with their cross-cultural experiences in Australia. Prior to this, she completed a Master of Arts in Linguistics at Monash in 2012 on the topic of conceptual metaphors. In 2011 she joined the Monash ARC project as a research assistant and continues in that role. Her research interests are cognitive linguistics, sociolinguistics, semantics and the relationship between language and social cognition.

Harriet Radermacher is a qualitative researcher whose work over the last 10 years at Monash and Victoria Universities in Melbourne has focused on the experiences of people from diverse cultural backgrounds in a range of areas including ageing, palliative care, disability and gambling. Dr Radermacher also works as a research and evaluation consultant, and is a research and policy officer at the Australian Psychological Society. She completed a doctorate in Community Psychology in 2006.

Introduction

Marisa Cordella and Hui Huang

The project described in this book offers a new approach to second language learning. Building on more than four decades of research on language teaching and policy in Australia (e.g. Clyne, 1982, 1991, 2005; Kipp *et al.*, 1955), the chapters that follow introduce a model of intergenerational, intercultural encounters that is designed to deliver a number of pedagogical and societal benefits simultaneously. Specifically, it aims to promote the utilisation of community language resources, enrich the experiences of young language learners, foster greater understanding between young and old, break down cultural stereotypes, encourage appreciation of different cultures and enhance the quality of life and community engagement of older people with a bilingual/multilingual background. The model originates from an interdisciplinary research study involving experts in second language acquisition, discourse analysis and healthy ageing.

Importantly, the model we propose can be adapted for any language or locality and the projects based on the model run for a modest cost. Australia is well known as a land of immigrants, and the new skills, new ideas and new energy they bring to their adopted country have created a culturally diverse and economically successful society. Yet the languages the immigrants speak have not yet been fully appreciated as a *resource*, and the nation's latent multilingualism remains under-exploited. At the same time, the number of hours allocated to language teaching in Australian schools is inadequate, even though an increasingly globalised world challenges us all to become proficient in more than one language, more knowledgeable about different cultures and better citizens of our region and beyond. For example, China is Australia's largest trading partner, yet in the state of Victoria where our project was based only 1456 students took Chinese as a second language at Victorian Certificate of Education (VCE) level in 2013 out of a total of more than 43,000 students.[1] This percentage is similar across Australia as a whole (see Chapter 9).

Further, being multicultural does not simply amount to recognising and accumulating the cultural knowledge of others, even though this is important. Becoming multicultural is a *process* that unfolds through the juxtaposition, comparison and interaction of different cultures (Kramsch, 2006). During such interactions, meaning and identities are negotiated, co-constructed and reconstructed. At the heart of our project therefore was a desire to create more opportunities for people from different linguistic and cultural backgrounds to meet, converse and engage in community languages and generally find out more about each other.

The intergenerational dimension of the project was realised in selecting as participants older immigrants from a non-English-speaking or a bilingual background and unrelated young language learners. This tapped into the language resources of the immigrants noted above, but also allowed us to explore the narratives of gerontology and intergenerational communication from a sociolinguistics perspective in a number of studies, and to discuss the potential for older people to remain engaged with their communities in meaningful and rewarding ways.

While all of the dimensions of the project were interrelated, the primary goal was to enhance the experience of second language (L2) learning for a group of secondary school students by complementing the formal learning environment with regular one-on-one conversations with a native speaker, recognising that young L2 learners are very rarely exposed to natural everyday use of the language they study in the classroom. Just as multiculturalism is more than a concept that can be grasped in an abstract or technical sense, but something that can only be understood through direct experience, so too is L2 learning a process of discovery of the discursive practices, cultural concepts and patterns of interaction that facilitate authentic exchange, and these can only be realised in face-to-face encounters.

The book is divided into three sections. The first part sets the scene by discussing issues around the three main themes of multiculturalism, healthy ageing and social inclusion, and second language learning in Australia. The second part presents a number of quantitative and qualitative studies that explore the stances taken by the older participants in their conversations with young language learners and their assessments of the value of the project in their lives. In the third part the focus is on the benefits of the project for the students and concludes by describing the innovative model we have developed to assist second language learning and social inclusion.

Chapter 1 discusses the idea of multiculturalism, the arguments for and against it, the history of immigration in Australia, and the various government programmes that have shaped the national character, from its 'White Australia Policy' at the beginning of the 20th century to the reforms after the Second World War that progressively ended the racial discrimination of immigration policies, introduced the term 'multiculturalism' into the vernacular, and led to a diverse and largely tolerant society. At the same time, it is noted that this state-of-affairs remains fragile, vulnerable to extremist views and to acts of opportunism for political ends, and that it is necessary to remain vigilant and to actively promote policies and programmes that ensure social harmony within ethnic diversity. The chapter then offers an overview of second language learning in Australian schools and describes the impact of various government policies on language education. The 2011 census data are used to highlight Victoria's multicultural landscape and the rich language 'resources' to be found among the older immigrant population in that State. The chapter concludes by identifying *social inclusion* as a key component of the project.

This concept is further considered in Chapter 2 in relation to the demographics of ageing and the dynamic nature of the family. It provides a critical perspective on current debates and theories about the place and role of older people in society and about intergenerational relationships. The social isolation of older people, particularly recent immigrants and those with limited English-language skills, is one area of concern, as are the 'generational gap' and ageist views that can result when young people are given limited opportunities to engage with older generations outside their immediate families. Programmes that encourage older people's participation in the civic life of their communities by sharing their skills and knowledge with young people can therefore help to break down stereotypes and enhance intergenerational understanding as well as older people's sense of well-being. Three key theoretical concepts of mentoring, generativity and reciprocity are introduced in this chapter, which, when combined, provide a useful framework for understanding the nature of the relationships between generations. These concepts help to define the longer-term benefits of conducting schools-based language education programmes such as the one outlined in this book, which include building active learning communities, creating new social relationships and networks, promoting citizenship, regenerating neighbourhoods and addressing inequality.

Chapter 3 discusses the theory of situated learning as a way of understanding L2 acquisition within a sociolinguistics framework. Situated learning theory underpins the present project, and within this conceptualisation the project is described, including its location, languages chosen, participants, data collection procedures and the various studies undertaken within the project as a whole. The intercultural dimension of the project was achieved by matching L1 speakers of Chinese, German and Spanish with students of the target language, observing the similarities and differences between the three groups, and considering to what extent cultural variables could explain some of the findings.

Stance is the focus of the next two chapters, and in particular the stances adopted by the older participants in their conversations with the young language learners. In Chapter 4, three of the stances are identified and labelled – the language instructor, the sociocultural guide and the ethical-moral adviser – and analysed in detail for each of the three language groups. Some interesting differences in topic selection between the cultural groups related to stance-taking were a feature of the transcriptions and these are considered using a sociolinguistic approach to the data to identify the wider sociocultural coordinates within which the discourse emerged. The role of language instructor quite naturally dominated the stances of the older participants in all three groups, but the stances of all participants were dynamic, allowing their self-presentation to be continually reconstructed and to emerge in new shapes throughout the interaction (Huang & Lu, 2013; Bucholtz & Hall, 2005). In addition, the fostering of 'generational intelligence' during the sessions as the older adults shared personal stories, expressed opinions and offered advice is also noted.

In Chapter 5 the stance-taking acts of the German- and Spanish-speaking immigrants are further explored in relation to the multiple identities they assigned themselves as they discussed their experiences of migration. Five non-grammatical categories of stance – expert, contextual, epistemic, comparative and affective – are identified as contributing to the older participants' *ethos of self* and analysed using examples from the recorded data. Different patterns of stance usage between the two cultural groups as well as between individual speakers are documented, and reasons for the greater emphasis on language learning by the Germans and the stronger connection with their homeland expressed by the Latin American immigrants are suggested. It is argued that the stances adopted by the older participants make them positive role models for the students, encouraging greater awareness of cultural differences and the challenges involved in making a life in a new society.

Chapter 6 is a comparative study of the self-referencing of Chinese and German native speakers using the first-person plural ('wir', wŏmen, 我们) and marks the first time these two very different languages have been studied together in this way. Analysis of the data revealed that the collective use of the pronoun and its grammatical variants (*us, ours*, etc.) was more explicit and specific in the German cohort, whereas the Chinese speakers' referential choice was very vague and referred predominantly to an unspecified or ambiguous collectivity. This cross-language comparison provides evidence that the self not only reflects and is shaped by the speaker's culture, but is also linguistically constructed and realised dynamically in the contingent moments of the interaction. The study also breaks new ground in the linguistic research of both languages by using data from verbal exchanges (the recorded conversations with young language learners) rather than written sources.

Rapport has been identified in a wide range of studies as an essential component of all successful human relationships, and those studies which focus on the importance of rapport in learning environments or in intergenerational encounters were of particular interest to our project. However, while there is an implicit understanding of what is meant by rapport, a clear definition of the concept in the field of sociolinguistics has so far remained elusive. The purpose of Chapter 7 therefore is to introduce a *model of verbal rapport*. The model draws on Tickle-Degnan and Rosenthal's

1990 model of non-verbal rapport and adapts its three essential components of mutual attentiveness, positivity and coordination for use in discourse analysis. It then supplies the verbal component missing from their model by applying the five principles of stance-taking identified by Englebreton (2007), recognising that various stances are taken to communicate rapport. The dynamic, dialogical and collaborative nature of rapport is recognised in the *cyclical* structure of the model. Examples from the recorded conversations between older Latin American immigrants and young students of Spanish are then utilised to explain and analyse the model and to offer a *taxonomy of rapport* through listing, defining, exemplifying and quantifying the rapport stance-taking acts (RSAs) of the study participants. The exploratory nature of the model is stressed and the chapter concludes by suggesting some ideas for further research.

Chapter 8 explores the concept of 'healthy ageing' and draws attention to the need for older people themselves to provide greater input into identifying how the concept should be understood, with particular reference to the value of cross-cultural perspectives in a multicultural society like Australia. The authors then analyse the indicators of health and wellbeing (self-esteem, empowerment, sense of purpose) of the older adults in the project, codifying the data obtained from their one-on-one telephone interviews with the research team at the project's conclusion. While most of the older participants identified personal benefits they had gained from their participation, an unexpected finding was the strong sense of responsibility expressed by the Chinese cohort to 'give back' to society and to provide a community service as their motivations for involvement. The theoretical tools of generativity and reciprocity introduced in Chapter 2 are drawn on again to discuss the value of the project as a vehicle for cultural and generational exchange. Finally, the authors acknowledge some of the methodological limitations of a qualitative study such as this one and suggest ways in which future studies could yield more effective results.

The next two chapters analyse performance indicators of second language learning in two quite different studies. Chapter 9 looks at the importance of self-efficacy in learning environments and considers this motivational construct in the context of L2 learning. It then offers a longitudinal analysis of the self-efficacy beliefs of 35 Chinese language students in the project to add to the small number of studies that have reported a positive relationship between an individual's self-assessment and language learning outcomes. In order to explore whether self-efficacy levels vary across cultures, the study compared two datasets – students who were background speakers of Mandarin Chinese and those who had no background in this language. The data was obtained from three questionnaires conducted over a 12 month period and subjected to statistical analysis through within-group and cross-group comparisons. A background questionnaire and focus group interviews provided supplementary qualitative data. Importantly, this is the first time that self-efficacy has been investigated for L2 *speaking*, especially in conversations with native speakers, rather than reading, writing and listening. Most of the students reported that the greatest benefit of the project for them was that it boosted their confidence in conversing with a native speaker, and the post-study questionnaire confirmed that this effect was durable. The importance of 'domain specificity' was an important finding in the analysis; that is, the students' self-efficacy levels were consistently higher when they could talk about things that were familiar to them, and this highlighted the need for topic selection to be carefully considered in other projects of the kind. Surprisingly, our assumption that background speakers would have higher self-efficacy beliefs than non-background speakers in the tested areas of speaking, listening and conversing was not confirmed, and the role of cultural expectations and norms in the rather more varied pattern of self-efficacy levels that emerged is considered for its implications for future research.

Interactional competence is explored in Chapter 10, using a conversation analysis framework to document longitudinal improvements in the students' competence in conversing with a native speaker in general and in initiating and pursuing topics in particular. The cross-language design of the study breaks new ground by enabling the dataset to be considered in relation to the possible specificity of each of the three languages (Chinese, German and Spanish). In spite of variations in each case study, however, all the student participants were shown to have improved their IC as a result of their situated learning in which both speakers in the dyad identified, interpreted and co-constructed the contingent, adaptable micro-moments of the conversation. Students learnt to model the backchannels of their partners to produce acknowledgement tokens, to take the floor and to make stepwise topic shifts, while the older participants actively promoted the students' IC by repeating and correcting lexical items, scaffolding their talk and congratulating the young learners on their progress.

The final chapter brings together all the strands of the book in a model of language learning and social inclusion that is designed to supplement formal L2 classroom teaching in primary and secondary schools. The model was developed from the Intergenerational, Intercultural Encounters and Second Language Development Project undertaken at Monash University between 2010 and 2012 and is now being adapted for use in schools more widely. The chapter discusses practical aspects of implementing the model and the benefits it offers for students, teachers, older native speakers, schools and communities alike. This innovative, empirically based model was the mastermind of the late Professor Michael Clyne, whose passionate wish it was for Australia to become a truly multilingual, multicultural and more enlightened society.

Note

(1) Victorian Curriculum and Assessment Authority. See http://www.vcaa.vic.edu.au/Pages/vce/statistics/2013/statssect3.aspx.

References

Bucholtz, M. and Hall, K. (2005) Identity and interaction: A sociocultural linguistic approach. *Discourse Studies* 7 (4–5), 585–614.
Clyne, M. (1982) *Multilingual Australia*. Melbourne: River Seine.
Clyne, M. (1991) *Community Languages: The Australian Experience*. Cambridge: Cambridge University Press.
Clyne, M. (2005) *Australia's Language Potential*. Sydney: UNSW Press.
Englebretson, R (2007) *Stancetaking in Discourse: Subjectivity, Evaluation, Interaction*. Amsterdam: John Benjamins.
Huang, H. and Lu, Y. (2013) Interactions of cultural identity and turn-taking organisation – a case study of a senior Chinese immigrant in Australia. *Chinese Language and Discourse* 4 (2), 229–252.
Kipp, S., Clyne, M. and Pauwels, A. (1995) *Immigration and Australia's Language Resources*. Canberra: Australian Government Publishing Service.
Kramsch, C. (2006) From communicative competence to symbolic competence. *Modern Language Journal* 90, 249–252.
Tickle-Degnen, L. and Rosenthal, R. (1990) The nature of rapport and its nonverbal correlates. *Psychological Inquiry* 1 (4), 285–293.

Part 1

Setting the Scene: Many Cultures, Many Opportunities

1 The Immigrant Potential: Multiculturalism, Language Skills and Community Resources

Marisa Cordella

> *Australia still has an unfinished agenda in research into community languages and the pooling of data is one way of continuing achievements in the field*
> Clyne, 2009

Introduction

For many immigrants, relocation to another place means leaving the past behind without knowing if it will ever be possible to reconnect with the country of origin. However, in an age of rapid transportation and digital communication it has become easier for most, if not all, to keep in touch with their cultural heritage. Globalisation, leading to greater permeability of national borders – even to the point of formal integration, as in the case of the European Union – has contributed to an increase in the number of people living either temporarily or permanently away from their homeland. This diaspora has generated more cultural and linguistic diversity in societies, but with it also a dynamic of both dialogue and conflict (Cuccioletta, 2001/2002) as people from a wide variety of backgrounds interact.

Multiculturalism 'is a term which has been used and disputed for four decades in various democracies in Europe, North America and Australasia', but as practised in countries like Australia it describes 'mixed populations created by international migration ... typically found in major cities living together but having different origins, religions, languages and other aspects of distinct cultures' (Clyne & Jupp, 2011: xiii). Although as a public policy it is said to be 'in retreat' (2011: xvi), it continues to play a fundamental role in many societies, being 'officially adopted' (2011: xvi) as an additional organising principle in several parts of the world.

How multicultural policies or programmes are implemented varies according to political, historical, social and economic factors. Political factors include national and international pressures on migrant intake quotas. Economic factors include locally contingent priorities such as giving preference to immigrants with specific skills. 'The multicultural political solution to ethnic diversity is, then, not universal' (Clyne & Jupp, 2011: xv) but is sensitive to the perceived benefits or drawbacks such programmes may bring to any given society.

Although countries that are linguistically and culturally diverse are not necessarily officially multilingual and multicultural, in that they possess laws and policies that ensure diversity of cultural practices – including the use of different languages in official settings (Blackledge, 2006) – they are more often than not *de facto* multicultural and multilingual. In fact, de facto multiculturalism and multilingualism often persist in spite of an official policy of monoculturalism and monolingualism and in spite of much discrimination and marginalisation. Moreover, between the two extremes there is a variety of realities that also includes the acceptance of various spoken languages within a country that has a single official language (hence the provision of translated documents for social services purposes) or the recognition and acceptance of diverse cultural practices (such as religion) within a country that is characterised by a predominant culture. Some countries, such as Canada, do have official policies of multiculturalism and multilingualism (e.g. Edwards & Chisholm, 1987) and their experience shows that such policies are perfectly consistent with a socially stable and democratic system.

Multiculturalism, whether of the de facto or the officially endorsed variety, has demonstrable benefits for a society, not only in financial terms, by facilitating commercial exchanges with the countries of origin of its immigrants, but also in terms of improving the mental flexibility (creativity, understanding of complex issues) of the population. For example, Dewaele and van Oudenhoven (2009) have shown how young immigrants settled in the United Kingdom developed higher levels of open-mindedness and cultural empathy than their monolingual/monocultural peers. Although the process of becoming familiar with a new culture can be stressful, the burden on young immigrants can be decreased by making mainstream society more aware of the very practical advantages of living in a multicultural and multilingual society. Of course, this requires real action from governments, as happens in Canada, simply because inter-ethnic tensions are easy ground for exploitation by any political party looking to reap electoral advantage. Once diverse cultural and language identities are smoothly integrated into a new construct that is socially accepted and does not trigger ostracism or discrimination by the rest of society, then positive social and psychological benefits are likely to flow (Chen *et al.*, 2008).

Joshua A. Fishman (1980) highlights the contrast between individual bilingualism and societal diglossia, alongside individual biculturalism and societal di-ethnia. Such distinctions point to the issue of social *compartmentalisation* (when diglossia and di-ethnia prevail) or social *integration* (bilingualism/biculturalism). Greater social integration retains the diversity of multicultural/multilingual societies but without the negative aspects of societal disintegration, marginalisation and ostracism that may follow from diglossia/di-ethnia. Integration within multicultural/multilingual societies is what one would expect of societies wanting to be successful in a world that is becoming not more compartmentalised but more 'globalised'.

While multiculturalism is a reality in Australian society, where nearly one in four Australian households use two or more languages (Australian Census, 2011), the monolingual mindset described by Clyne (2005) has slowed down the implementation of language programmes in schools, undermining the potential language capabilities of the nation. It is our stance in this book that immigrant language resources could be better utilised to help improve second language learning through cross-cultural communicative exchanges.

This chapter briefly discusses the history of multiculturalism in Australia and the policies that have been introduced to enhance language learning participation in secondary schools. It then examines the smorgasbord of community resources available in this area, pointing in particular to the potential contribution of first-generation immigrants to the skills development of young language learners.

Multiculturalism in Australia

In the last few years, multiculturalism has been making headlines in Europe, with British Prime Minister David Cameron declaring that 'under the doctrine of state multiculturalism, we have encouraged different cultures to live separate lives, apart from each other and the mainstream'.[1] Similarly, German Chancellor Angela Merkel told a meeting in Potsdam in October 2010 that 'this [multicultural] approach has failed, utterly failed'.[2] Despite the fact that Germany has never endorsed a multicultural public policy, the negative perception of multiculturalism that both countries share stems from a European concern linked to an increase in the number of refugees and evidence of Islamist militancy in the region (Vertovec & Wessendorf, 2010). Poor relations between immigrants and the mainstream population have had an impact on social stability and have the potential to become self-reinforcing through 'blame games' and scapegoating. As Levey states:

> The perceived trouble with multiculturalism is not – or not only – that communities do not adequately interact with each other; it is that they exist and interact as if they were monolithic, self-absorbed, and independent units. (2011: 87)

We could argue that such self-absorption might be strengthened by a social environment that is hostile to diversity, thus encouraging interactions to develop exclusively within culturally and linguistically close groups. Thus, inward-looking communities representing cultural minorities may be the result of either an internal drive towards isolation or an external push towards segregation, with both internal and external factors potentially acting in synergy.

Multiculturalism in Australia has been studied by various authors (e.g. Kipp et al., 1995; Ozolins & Clyne, 2001; Djité, 2011; Mansouri & Lobo, 2011a; Slaughter, 2011; Hajek & Slaughter, 2015, to mention a few). Although it has been a long-standing issue in countries that are historically diverse both culturally and linguistically, it has emerged as an important social concern in countries like Australia that saw themselves pretty much as extensions of the British Empire until the mass migrations that began after the Second World War. Now this mobility continues unabated, raising questions of how to include ethnic minorities in the host country. Cultural diversity represents an opportunity but also a challenge, and unfortunately it is often the case that, through the media, vested interests are keen to highlight the challenges rather than the opportunities. At the core of successful multiculturalism is the concept of *social inclusion*. This concept is discussed further below.

Cultural diversity within any given society is almost inevitable today, but social inclusion must be actively built, and can be seriously jeopardised by both culture and politics. Two opposing views have been expressed by policymakers: assimilation, whereby immigrants are expected to fully adopt and adapt to the dominant culture; and multiculturalism, in which immigrants retain their own culture, religion and language whilst abiding by the laws of the host country and freely engaging with the wider community. Within multiculturalism, integration is a dynamic process in which all are equal before the law, but customs and practices are varied and changeable and are allowed to evolve in an organic manner according to the rules of a strictly democratic process. As described by Mansouri and Lobo (2011b: 3): 'This conceptualisation of multiculturalism in Australia and indeed elsewhere was underpinned by liberal principles of democratic egalitarianism and equal citizenship that aimed to nurture cultural diversity and empower marginalised groups through affirmative measures of recognition and redistribution'.

Critics of multiculturalism point to a concern that allowing diversity to thrive may undermine social cohesion, leading to communal disharmony, while proponents of multiculturalism argue that this concern can be addressed through the development of social inclusion policies (Mansouri & Lobo, 2011b; Markus, 2011a). To achieve social inclusion in multicultural societies it is essential to foster tolerance of difference, respect for the common law and democratic institutions, and to promote the spreading of opportunities, with participation and power-sharing across different groups based on merit. Social cohesion can be achieved through the emergence of common shared values that are enriched by multiple inputs from the members of a diverse community. Social fragmentation, on the other hand, results when 'who you are' is fully determined by external factors, while an enduring sense of belonging is not possible for an individual whose input is systematically dismissed or actively rejected. This is perhaps most readily understood in the areas of religion and language, but it permeates all areas of cultural expression. In the words of Andrew Markus (2011a: 144), a cohesive community can be seen as one 'characterised by commonality of vision and shared sense of belonging across faith and ethnic groups; the appreciation and positive valuation of cultural diversity; and the development of strong and positive relationships between people from different backgrounds in the workplace, in schools and within neighbourhoods'.

In Australia, the greater emphasis on multiculturalism – which grew out of the rejection in the late 1940s and then in 1973 of the 'White Australia' Policy of a monolingual and monocultural Australia, implemented at the beginning of Federation in 1901 (Ozolins & Clyne, 2001) – suffered a serious blow during John Howard's Liberal–National Coalition Government (1996–2007), in response to the populist, anti-immigration policies of the One Nation Party led by Pauline Hanson. The debate on Australian multiculturalism is currently ongoing and embraces broader concerns about social inclusion.

Social inclusion and the spreading of opportunities across society are rooted in traditional cultural values in Australia through the concept of the 'fair go'. In the popular view, every person, no matter what background she or he may have, is entitled to a 'fair go', or equal opportunities in life. Each individual would then be able to achieve more or less in life on the basis of how well such opportunities are utilised according to capacity, interests, motivation, and so forth. Central to the 'fair go' is the role of government in providing the services and programmes that can better spread opportunities for everyone. In such an environment, diversity can be an asset rather than an obstacle.

Broadly speaking, multiculturalism in Australia has aimed at greater social inclusion and indeed has achieved a strong sense of belonging and life satisfaction, fairness and equity in the population, including among immigrants, although the latter do still report a degree of discrimination (Markus, 2011a). This affirms the view that multiculturalism can be effective in spreading opportunities within a common social/legal frame that benefits from a varied cultural input. However, as mentioned above, this equilibrium can be fragile and is exposed to the opportunism of populist politicians and ruthless power-brokers.

Historically, of course, Australia was already a multicultural country before European colonisation, with several hundred Aboriginal languages and cultures known to have existed across the continent.[3] In one sense, the establishment of the English penal colony at Sydney Cove in 1788 just added another dimension to the mosaic. De facto multiculturalism further developed in subsequent decades with the flow of immigrants from areas outside Great Britain. This historical reality was brushed aside with the implementation of the White Australia Policy, but it was recovered later as policies supporting multiculturalism were introduced. According to Ozolins and Clyne (2001: 373–374), four major stages in the process that enables acceptance of multiculturalism can be identified:

(1) Response to initial demographic pressure of immigration
 This response may include government services (e.g. language learning) to immigrants for speedier integration.

(2) Policy innovation, unevenness and drift
 Following the initial implementation of essential government policies, additional programmes can be offered by other sectors and institutions.

(3) Language initiatives across a spread of institutions
 Policies and community initiatives that strengthen the maintenance of multicultural resources and skills such as languages can be further implemented and expanded.

(4) Ideological and institutional change.

This stage is one of final cultural acceptance, across the community at large, of the concept that immigrant communities enrich our society with their varied contribution, that the transformative impetus they bring is positive, and that they help shape the national identity in a world that is itself changing at rapid speed. Achieving this final stage is an ongoing process that requires continual action at both individual and institutional levels.

Australian multiculturalism is fundamentally based on a mix of immigrant and native ethnic groups, as is also the case in Canada, New Zealand and the United States of America, just to name a few. Diverse languages, cultures and religions come together and interact in major capital cities, where the highest levels of ethnic diversity can be found. The 2011 Australian Census reveals that nearly a quarter (24.6%) of Australia's population was born overseas, 32% have both parents born overseas, and 43.1% of people have at least one parent born overseas.

To gain some insight into the notion of multiculturalism in Australia, where the dataset for our project was collected, there is a need to go back in time. The term multiculturalism was introduced in this country in 1973 by the Labor Government of Prime Minister Gough Whitlam. Later, in

1978 the Commonwealth accepted the *Report of the Review of Post-Arrival Programs and Services to Migrants,* popularly known as the Galbally Report, that proposed a set of recommendations regarding immigration. This led to the implementation of new policies and programmes that supported multiculturalism during the Liberal Government of Prime Minister Malcolm Fraser (1975–1983). A cohesive nation was seen as one in which strength was built through its unique cultural and language diversity. Fraser (1981) argued that:

> Multiculturalism is about diversity, not division – it is about interaction not isolation. It is about cultural and ethnic differences set within a framework of shared fundamental values which enables them to co-exist on a complementary rather than competitive basis.

The era marked the official end of the White Australia Policy, in which eligibility to migrate to Australia was based on race, colour and religion. It also responded to the needs of diverse language and cultural groups already present in the country, introducing multicultural television and radio broadcasting, interpreting services and language education programmes, among other initiatives available to support new immigrants and their families.

The policies of multiculturalism in 1978 were aimed at

(1) assisting new arrivals to settle in by providing services for non-English-speaking background (NESB) migrants;[4]
(2) providing egalitarian services that were available to all Australians;
(3) encouraging the maintenance of, and engagement with people of, one's own and other cultural heritage; and
(4) designing programmes to assist migrants to become self-reliant.

More explicitly, four guiding principles were laid down in the Galbally Report (Galbally, 1978: 1–2):

(a) all members of our society must have equal opportunity to realise their full potential and must have equal access to programmes and services;
(b) every person should be able to maintain his or her culture without prejudice or disadvantage and should be encouraged to understand and embrace other cultures;
(c) needs of migrants should, in general, be met by programmes and services available to the whole community but special services and programmes are necessary at present to ensure equality of access and provision;
(d) services and programmes should be designed and operated in full consultation with clients, and self-help should be encouraged as much

as possible with a view to helping migrants to become self-reliant quickly.

In the 1980s, Prime Minister Bob Hawke set up an Office of Multicultural Affairs to design diverse programmes in support of immigrants, and launched the National Agenda for a Multicultural Australia in Sydney on 2 July 1989, in which three fundamental elements were identified: cultural identity, social justice and economic efficiency. The latter was intended to

> emphasise the economic benefits of a culturally diverse society and the way that those benefits needed to be enhanced through government policy – in other words, through a promotion of immigrant languages, using immigrant networks for business purposes, providing English language to the extent that it was needed to succeed in Australian society, in making sure government services were equally accessible to all Australians ... . (Shergold, 1994/1995)

In the 1990s, however, a right-wing and nationalist political party, One Nation, led by Pauline Hanson (1997–2003), resisted the multiculturalism efforts and the developments of previous years, advocating an Anglo-Celtic framework for Australian society. John Howard's government did little to minimise the negative effects of these ethnocentric views.

In 2007 the Department of Immigration and Multicultural Affairs was renamed the Department of Immigration and Citizenship, thus replacing 'multicultural affairs', a term which had been in the name of the department for the previous 10 years in spite of various other name changes: DIMA – Department of Immigration and Multicultural Affairs (1996–2001); DIMIA – Department of Immigration, Multicultural and Indigenous Affairs (2001–2006); DIMA – Department of Immigration and Multicultural Affairs (2006–2007), with the term 'citizenship'. The change of wording appeared to be not just cosmetic but indicative of a change of attitude, especially towards recent immigrants and immigration policies. The notion of multiculturalism was devalued, with the focus being shifted towards the concept of integration that permeated subsequent policies of the Howard Government in this area. Different policies and programmes were implemented 'to protect' the nation against those who did not share 'Australian values'. The political discourse at the time warned of the significant implications of continuing large-scale immigration for both social stability and national identity (Tavan, 2008).

The terrorist attacks on the Twin Towers in New York in September 2001, which occurred while Prime Minister Howard was visiting the United States, presumably contributed further to his standing on the issue of multiculturalism. New Australian laws to combat terrorism, tightened asylum seeker procedures, reinforcement of classes on religion in the school sector, and a citizenship test were introduced (Clyne & Jupp, 2011: 195). The latter brought significant changes, and by making more stringent the processes for obtaining Australian citizenship, new immigrants were expected to integrate by adopting 'the Australian way of life'. Those applying to become Australian citizens had to satisfy the Department of Immigration and Citizenship's guidelines, which required passing not only an English-language test but also a knowledge test based on Australia's values and customs, including sections on 'Australia and its people', 'Australia's democratic beliefs, rights and liberties', and 'government and the law in Australia'.[5]

The Immigration Minister at the time, Kevin Andrews, introduced the bill into Parliament, highlighting the concept of integration as a pivotal reason for the introduction of the citizenship test:

> The test will encourage prospective citizens to obtain the knowledge they need to support successful integration into Australian society. The citizenship test will provide them with the opportunity to demonstrate in an objective way that they have the required knowledge of Australia, including the responsibilities and privileges of citizenship, and a basic knowledge and comprehension of English.[6]

Successful immigration was equated to English-language proficiency, knowledge of Australia, and recognition of the civil and social responsibilities of its citizens. Although it could be argued that having a degree of knowledge of the host country might help with forming links with locals and easing the process of integration, some sections of the citizenship test hardly provided a full picture of a multicultural society. For example, the citizenship booklet offered an extended discussion of the significance of various national symbols, including the flag, the national anthem, the national colours, Australia's floral emblem, the coat of arms and the national gemstone (Australian Government, 2007: 14–16). Critics rightly pointed out that 'good citizenship' depended on a lot more than due reverence for the wattle and the opal, or on knowing which Australian was most famous for playing cricket (Tavan, 2008).

Although there are still conflicting views about the meaning and value of multiculturalism today, some claiming that it divides the population, encourages loyalties to other nations (and even governments) and delays assimilation (Lord Parekh (2006), quoted in Jupp, 2011: 147), the idea keeps re-emerging in the political arena. Chris Bowen, Minister for Immigration and Citizenship (2010–2013) in the Labor Federal Government, reiterated in 2011 the support of his government for multiculturalism in an interview on the Australian Broadcasting Corporation (ABC) current affairs programme *7.30 Report*. He said:

> I'm not afraid to use the word multiculturalism. I'm proud of what it's meant for Australia and our way of life.... It is an indelible and irrevocable part of who we are, and without it, we would all be the poorer.[7]

Similarly, Prime Minister Julia Gillard (2010–2013) expressed the opinion, in a speech to the Australian Multicultural Council in Parliament House, Canberra, on 19 September 2012, that true multiculturalism meant something very different from the riots that sparked from time to time in cities across the Western world. For Gillard, multiculturalism was the face of

> a new migrant studying hard in an English language class, working two jobs to put their kids through school or lining up to vote for the very first time. True multiculturalism includes, *not divides, it adds more than it takes*. In the end, multiculturalism *amounts to a civic virtue* since it provides us with a way to share the public space, a common ground of inclusion and belonging for all who are willing to 'toil with hearts and hands'. And because *it always summons us toward a better future*, multiculturalism is an expression of progressive patriotism in which all Australians, old and new, can find meaning (emphasis added).[8]

'Multiculturalism' is still being used to symbolise the diversity, the inherent composition of the Australian human landscape, the shared responsibilities and enrichment, but the term 'integration' (or 'multicultural integration') (Levey, 2011) is gaining much attention at present. In the sense it is being used by conservative politicians, it is a mono-directional expectation placed mainly on immigrants to make an effort to integrate, rather than a bi-directional process in which responsibilities are mutual (multiculturalism). It is unclear how mono-directional integration can foster respect and tolerance of difference, or an appreciation of learning from diverse cultures and languages. As noted above, multicultural integration *can* be achieved without losing diversity, in exactly the same way as diverse sub-cultures can co-exist (be integrated) within a majority ethnic group (Anglo-Celtic, for instance) in spite of a variety of lifestyles, political allegiances, religious preferences, professional backgrounds and so forth. Unity in diversity is the norm in large human societies, not the exception.

We do not yet know whether changing the terminology will make any profound and significant differences to the many naturalised Australians who call Australia home. According to Clyne and Jupp (2011), the change of emphasis from multiculturalism to integration, citizenship and the attainment of shared values responds to European fears about Islamist militancy and a higher number of refugees in that part of the world. While some argue that multiculturalism in Australia has died or is on the verge of dying, the authors of this book are optimistic about its future. Australian states and territories, unlike their federal colleagues, have demonstrated a commitment to supporting the policy. Clyne and Jupp (2011: 196) argue quite clearly that 'integration, social cohesion and equity have been the overall consequence of the multicultural policies pursued in the past thirty-five years'.

How Does Australia Compare?

While governments may have their own agenda when it comes to promoting or discouraging multiculturalism, ordinary citizens also have their own views on the issue, and these may differ from the official policies. This is an important consideration, since embedded popular attitudes and beliefs regarding other ethnic groups and/or languages may have an effect on the social action of individuals and potentially predispose them (or not) to engage in language learning either at school, in other educational settings, or through day-to-day interactions with native speakers.

Markus (2011b) has investigated the perception of immigration in selected countries based on the International Social Survey Programme (ISSP) of 2003.[9] Comparisons were made between Australia, Canada, Great Britain and (West) Germany. While 39% of Australians and 34% of Canadians favoured a reduction in the number of immigrants, German and British respondents were much keener to reduce the quota, with percentages of 70% and 77% respectively. Australians (71%) and Canadians (61%) concurred that immigrants were good for the economy, but this view was not shared by Britons (22%) or Germans (29%). The proposition that immigrants bring in 'new ideas and cultures' attracted the support of Australians (75%) and Canadians (68%), but only 34% of Britons and 57% of Germans (Markus, 2011b: 92).

A series of surveys conducted during 2001 and 2008 under the Challenging Racism Project conducted by Dunn *et al.* (quoted in Markus, 2011b: 93) tested the attitudes towards immigrants in Australia. Results indicated that more than 84% of participants were in agreement with the proposition that 'it is a good thing for society to be made up of different cultures'.

More recently, the *2015 Mapping Social Cohesion* survey released by the Scanlon Foundation and carried out in collaboration with Monash University and the Australian Multicultural Foundation has shown that most people (86%) agree that multiculturalism has been good for Australia, almost the same proportion as in 2013 and 2014 (Markus, 2015: 2).

From this we might conclude that Australians overall tend to have a positive appreciation of immigrants and their cultural and linguistic diversity. This offers an encouraging starting point for building up connections between immigrant groups and local communities, thereby enhancing social relations and strengthening bonds. As Jupp indicates:

> [T]he history of policy development over the past sixty years suggests that working with ethnic diversity is more fruitful in maintaining social harmony and individual wellbeing than is working in favour of uniformity. ... Australia has built an excellent if under-funded strategy for sustaining social harmony and it would be a pity to waste it. (Jupp, 2011: 51–52)

Language Education Policies: An Overview

We turn now to the government's policies on language learning in the educational sector, mainly in schools around Australia.

A number of language education policies have highlighted the importance of learning another language and promised to increase enrolments of language learners according to specific long-term quotas. Unfortunately, these ambitions have hardly ever been realised.

Language teachers, linguists, ethnic groups, indigenous organisations and organisations for the deaf, among other groups, worked vigorously to see the first National Policy on Languages implemented at the Federal level (Lo Bianco, 1987, 1990). The main objective of this policy was to recognise the value of other languages and their complementary role in a predominantly English-language society. This was a significant step at the time since, as indicated by Ingram (2000: 3), there was a widespread belief that

> English was the national and only necessary language and that it was sufficient for international communication purposes, especially since most of Australia's international links at that time were with English-speaking countries.

A new Australian Language and Literacy Policy (LLP) was later implemented to emphasise English literacy and the languages of Australia's major trading partners (Dawkins, 1991). This policy recognised English as the 'national language' and 14 others as priority languages on the basis of their community, traditional and/or commercial importance. The priority languages included Chinese, German, Spanish (the three languages of our project), Aboriginal languages, Arabic, French, Indonesian, Italian, Japanese, Korean, Modern Greek, Russian, Thai and Vietnamese. Although the aim of the LLP was to have 25% of Year 12 students enrolled in language classes by the year 2000, this goal was thwarted by a number of factors. Among them was the 'pervasive monolingual mindset' (Clyne, 2005: 60) that has contributed to the myth that the school curriculum is too full to provide classes in languages other than English, and even in those cases where language-learning[10] classes are available the number of hours allocated to teach the language and cover the teaching material are limited. Contributing to the monolingual mindset are some further myths such as the belief that 'using another language is an indication of inability or unwillingness to speak English at all' (Clyne, 2005: xi).

Throughout the 1990s many attempts were made to respond to the national goals of introducing language programmes into schools. For example, in 1994 the report *Asian Languages and Australia's Economic Future* emphasised the teaching and learning of four Asian languages (Chinese, Japanese, Korean and Indonesian) on account of the international trade potential and specific economic value to Australia of these countries. Although an effort was made to promote these languages, the road to success proved to be harder than expected. Limited availability of qualified and trained teachers and an inadequate number of hours allocated in the curriculum to the teaching of languages were blamed for the failure to reach better results.

The principles for access to language learning have been highlighted in several Declarations for School Education (Australian Education Council, 1989; MCEETYA, 1999, 2005, 2008; ACARA, 2011: 3). For example, the *National Statement for Languages Education in Australian Schools* (MCEETYA, 2005) established an operational framework for state, territory and federal government activities. It was based on a four-year plan in which Ministers of Education would work together to achieve four main goals:

(1) establish long-term directions for languages education;
(2) advance the implementation of high quality and sustainable programmes;
(3) maximise collaboration in the use of national, state and territory resources;
(4) provide flexibility in implementation by individual jurisdictions (11).

The *Statement* sparked much discussion, research and development; however, the delivery of language programmes in schools and the commitment that they have generated in students still remain fragile (ACARA, 2011: 5). This is shown in recent national reports and statements on language learning (e.g. Liddicoat *et al.*, 2007; Nettlebeck, 2009) that demonstrate low participation, achievements and retention rates in school language programmes. According to Clyne, there is a paradox in multilingual Australia, which sees monolingualism as the norm and multilingualism as the exception, even as a problem or a deficit. This is reflected in the inadequate LOTE [Languages Other Than English] programs in schools, the low retention rates to VCE [Victorian Certificate of Education] in languages, the persistent assessment of children's early development in English only even when it is the weaker language, and, again in recent years, in the frequent failure to see the value of linguistic diversity for the individual and the nation. (Clyne, 2011: 60)

More recently the Australian Curriculum, Assessment and Reporting Authority (ACARA) has recognised the implementation of languages education as a key area to be developed in the Australian curriculum. Its paper 'The Shape of the Australian Curriculum: Languages' builds on previous language education policies and planning and provides the basis for language and cultural teaching, language learners' pathways, content and curriculum design, achievement standards and structure of the curriculum that 'will make a difference to languages learning in Australia' (ACARA, 2011: 1). The rationale for making language learning part of the Australian curriculum for all school students is rooted in the enriching opportunity that language learning brings to both individuals and the overall community in an increasingly plurilingual world. Learning languages develops intercultural capabilities, expands literacy repertoires, increases understanding of values and norms, augments processes of communication and enhances critical thinking (ACARA, 2011: 6–7).

The Shape of the Australian Curriculum: Languages recognises language learners' varying degrees of language proficiency, offering different entry points for second language learners and background learners. It also outlines the commonalities and differences of languages and the language standards that vary according to the language being learnt. The curriculum is designed utilising three interconnected strands:

(1) Communicating: using language for communicative purposes in interpreting, creating, and exchanging meaning
(2) Understanding: analysing language and culture as a resource for interpreting and creating meaning
(3) Reciprocating: reflecting upon and interpreting self in relation to others in communication as language users and language learners (self-awareness as user and learner) (pp. 23–24).

While the ACARA strategies are being developed, the *National Statement on Asia Literacy in Australian Schools 2011–2012* endorses its vision and is an advocate for the important place that Asian literacy should occupy in the Australian curriculum, recognising the growing involvement of Australia in countries such as India and China in the areas of trade, education, investment, immigration and tourism. The *Statement* points out that 'Australians need to become "Asia literate"'.

It is our hope that these initiatives, and others that will be drafted, discussed and implemented in the future, will live up to their promise and enable many more younger Australians to interpret and create meaning in a world that is ever more interconnected. The learning of languages will allow them to develop intercultural capabilities and a better understanding of and respect for diverse groups of people. As Australia moves closer to the rest of the plurilingual world, there will be further opportunities for individuals and communities to benefit from economic and cultural exchange.

> Today's Australia is a multilingual nation, in a multilingual world in which there are far more plurilinguals (those using two or more languages) than monolinguals. (Clyne, 2011: 54)

Considering the challenges we have to overcome in order to equip young students to become proficient language learners (e.g. the time allocated for language teaching, the number of qualified trained teachers and others), there is a need to start by making Australia's younger generation more engaged with language learning. One approach which has been proven to be successful (as this book will attest) is to utilise the language resources that are already available in the community.

Australia's Language Potential

Michael Clyne's monograph *Australian's Language Potential* vividly demonstrates the strange duality that exists in Australia. 'It sometimes seems as if there were two worlds, the multilingual one-third and most of the other two-thirds who are happily and proudly monolingual' (Clyne, 2005: 20). Australia's multicultural and multilingual capacity remains an under-exploited resource (Lo Bianco, 2007), and the various government policies outlined above have hampered its full potential. In particular, resources in immigrant communities that could be tapped into for language and cultural learning are currently under-utilised.

In the state of Victoria, according to the 2011 Census, 46.8% of Victorians were either born overseas or had at least one parent born overseas (Census, 2011). With regard to languages spoken, 18.2% of the population speaks a language other than English at home (SBS Census Explorer, 2011). New South Wales (32.2%) and Victoria (23.1%) are the states with the highest concentration of multilinguals (Census, 2011). Although the information in the census about languages spoken at home provides some insight into the plurilingualism of Australia, it does not fully describe the language reality in the country, as many language learners may either live alone or speak more than one language only outside the home.

The figures above do, however, reveal that multilingualism and multiculturalism constitute an important reality of Australia's social and cultural fabric. A closer look at the census data for the state of Victoria where our study was conducted reveals that the three language groups we selected are within the top 14 languages spoken at home (Table 1.1).

There is a growing presence of Chinese (Mandarin and Cantonese) in the 2011 Census data as compared with information from 2006, with an increase of 61.2% for Mandarin and 9% for Cantonese. Chinese (Mandarin) is classified as the third most commonly spoken language at home after English. Spanish is the 11th most common language, having increased to 18.4% of speakers who use the language at home. German, on the other hand, is listed in 14th place, with an increase of only 2.4% from the last Census of 2006.

Time since arrival in Australia and age of the person are also of interest as this data provides an insight into the ageing immigrant population and the likely degree of adaptation; older people who arrived recently can be compared with older people who migrated to Australia many years ago. The oldest median ages are found in European migrants: people born in Italy (68 years), Germany (62 years) and the United Kingdom (54 years)

Table 1.1 The top 14 languages other than English (LOTE) spoken at home in Victoria: Census 2011 and Census 2006

Rank 2011	Language spoken at home	Persons (2011)	As % of LOTE	Persons (2006)	Change since 2006	2011 % change
	English	3,874,862		3,668,284	206,578	5.6
1	Italian	124,856	10.1	133,327	−8,471	−6.4
2	Greek	116,802	9.5	117,873	−1,071	−0.9
3	Mandarin	103,742	8.4	64,374	39,368	61.2
4	Vietnamese	86,592	7.0	72,161	14,431	20.0
5	Cantonese	72,902	5.9	66,853	6,049	9.0
6	Arabic	68,437	5.5	55,931	12,506	22.4
7	Turkish	32,899	2.7	29,748	3,151	10.6
8	Hindi	32,704	2.6	18,181	14,523	79.9
9	Punjabi	31,068	2.5	8,202	22,866	278.8
10	Macedonian	30,945	2.5	30,771	174	0.6
11	Spanish	29,014	2.3	24,501	4,513	18.4
12	Sinhalese	28,163	2.3	16,921	11,242	66.4
13	Croatian	22,168	1.8	22,961	−793	−3.5
14	German	20,082	1.6	19,607	475	2.4

(ABS, 2012). Fewer longer-standing migrants (49%) than recent arrivals (67%) reported speaking a language other than English at home, and between 43% and 51% of these stated that they spoke English very well (ABS, 2012).

From this snapshot we can appreciate the language potential that is available in the community in various groups of older immigrants. We argue in this book that there is a tremendous opportunity in Australia for more people to learn a second language. Specifically, older immigrants could become key contributors to the intergenerational transmission of language across society, in the same way as grandparents have been shown to pass on their knowledge to younger generations within the family (Lambert, 2008). This can be achieved through their inclusion in activities that are part of language curricula.

The Potential for Social Inclusion

A number of reports indicate that many older migrants feel isolated and disengaged (Angel & Angel, 1992; Kritz et al., 2000; Lee & Crittenden, 1996; Litwin, 1995) and lack opportunities for interaction with the younger generations. Inviting them to share their language and cultural knowledge could contribute not only to creating stronger social bonds and relations with language learners – with potential positive psychological effects – but also to complementing formal classroom activities by introducing informal and naturalistic interactions that enhance the students' communicative competence.

> [T]here is a significant underutilisation of community language resources in the context of fallacious assumptions or misunderstandings about intergenerational language transmission. ... There are rich resources available to support the maintenance and transmission of community languages. (Clyne, 2005: 108)

Immigrant resources could be utilised more effectively to promote social inclusion by fostering language and cultural learning in young people. Being able to speak more than one language is an asset, not an impediment to nation building. No matter how important English remains as a *lingua franca* internationally, younger generations will inevitably be exposed to many cultures in this increasingly globalised world. Their ability to interact effectively in a multicultural and multilingual environment can only contribute in a positive way to their experience. While much language-contact research in Australia and beyond has underlined the role of grandparents as catalysts for language maintenance (e.g. Lambert, 2008), we extend this potential beyond the family environment in our project to link young language learners with older (unrelated) bilinguals.

The intergenerational dimension of this book introduces a completely new element: *social inclusion*, into the fields of language ecology, second language acquisition and gerontology. Social inclusion is a key driver of older peoples' health and well-being (Seeman & Crimmins, 2001); and social interaction, particularly in situations where older people can make a contribution, has been shown to improve both of these indicators (Newman & Brummel, 1998).

We believe that it is possible to respond effectively to the lack of participation older immigrants experience in society by inviting them to contribute to language programmes that offer oral practice to language learners. Concomitantly, the model we introduce in this book can provide the solution to the limited opportunities language learners have to converse with native speakers in natural settings. Thus, immigrant native speakers could effectively:

(1) assist students with language proficiency and cultural competency;
(2) contribute to the students' understanding and interpretation of the migration experience;
(3) provide examples from life experience of 'good' citizenship and ethical-moral standing;
(4) increase their own understanding of youth culture;
(5) increase their knowledge of how to engage effectively with younger generations.

Language learners in their turn could

(1) benefit from regular oral conversations with native speakers;
(2) improve their cultural knowledge and communicative competence;
(3) appreciate the life stories of immigrants and their contribution to society;
(4) increase their understanding of the ageing process and the culture of older people;
(5) increase their knowledge of how to engage effectively with older generations.

Later in this book, we describe the mutual benefits for upper secondary school students and older immigrants of regular conversations designed to assist language learning. On the one hand, these sessions promoted the students' language proficiency, cultural competency and self-efficacy. On the other, they gave older people the opportunity to share their life stories, to assist with language instruction in their native language, and to engage with young people in a cross-cultural exchange. We aim to show through our study that multicultural/multilingual encounters can offer many rewards.

Notes

(1) Multicultural policies in Britain a failure, says PM David Cameron. *News.com.au*, 5 February 2001. See http://www.news.com.au/world-old/multiculturalism-policies-in-britain-a-failure-says-pm-david-cameron/story-e6frfkyi-1226000767708.
(2) Merkel says German multiculturalism has failed. *uk.reuters.com*, 17 October 2010. See http://uk.reuters.com/article/2010/10/16/uk-germany-merkel-immigration-idUKTRE69F19T20101016.
(3) Indigenous 'multiculturalism' and linguistic diversity. *Our Languages* website. See http://www.ourlanguages.net.au/languages/background-information/item/28-indigenous-multiculturalism-and-linguistic-diversity.html.
(4) The term NESB was replaced by CALD (culturally and linguistically diverse) speakers in 2002 by the Howard government (1996–2007).
(5) Australian citizenship test resource, Department of Immigration and Border Protection. See http://www.citizenship.gov.au/learn/cit_test/test_resource/.
(6) The Hon. Kevin Andrews MP, Minister for Immigration and Citizenship, *House Hansard* (Parliamentary Debates, House of Representatives), 30 May 2007, 6; also quoted in Tavan (2009: 125).
(7) Multiculturalism back on the agenda. Transcript of programme broadcast on 17 February 2011. See http://www.abc.net.au/7.30/content/2011/s3141868.htm.
(8) Cited in Gillard defends nation's diversity, *The Age*, 20 September 2012. See http://www.theage.com.au/national/gillard-defends-nations-diversity-20120919-267d7.html.
(9) International Social Survey Programme (http://www.issp.org/); see National Identity II – ISPP 2003 under Archive and Data.
(10) The term 'language learning' was introduced by the national and Victorian governments and replaces the term LOTE.

References

ABS (2012) Cultural diversity in Australia: Reflecting a nation: Stories from the 2011 census. Australian Bureau of Statistics website. See http://www.abs.gov.au/ausstats/abs@.nsf/Lookup/2071.0main+features902012-2013#%29.

ACARA (2011) *The Shape of the Australian Curriculum: Languages*. Sydney: Australian Curriculum, Assessment and Reporting Authority.

Angel, J. and Angel, R. (1992) Age at migration, social connections, and well-being among elderly Hispanics. *Journal of Aging and Health* 4, 480–499.

Asia Education Foundation (2011) *National Statement on Asia Literacy in Australian Schools 2011–2012*. Melbourne: Asia Education Foundation. See http://www.eduweb.vic.gov.au/edulibrary/public/schadmin/Management/international/natstatementasialit.pdf.

Australian Census (2011) 2011 Census: A Snapshot of our Diversity. See http://www.multicultural.vic.gov.au/population-and-migration/victorias-diversity/2011-census-a-snapshot-of-our-diversity.

Australian Education Council (1989) *The Hobart Declaration on Schooling*. Hobart: AEC.

Australian Government (2007) *Becoming an Australian Citizen*. Canberra: Commonwealth of Australia.

Blackledge, A. (2006) The magical frontier between the dominant and the dominated: Sociolinguistics and social justice in a multilingual world. *Journal of Multilingual and Multicultural Development* 27, 22–41.

Chen, S.X., Benet-Martínez, V. and Bond, M.H. (2008) Bicultural identity, bilingualism, and psychological adjustment in multicultural societies: Immigration-based and globalization-based acculturation. *Journal of Personality* 76, 803–837.

Clyne, M. (2005) *Australia's Language Potential*. Sydney: University of NSW Press.

Clyne, M. (2009) Why migrant languages in the Australian National Corpus? In M. Haugh, K. Burridge, J. Mulder and P. Peters (eds) *Selected Proceedings of the 2008 HCS Net Workshop on Designing the Australian National Corpus* (pp. 44–54). Somerville, MA: Cascadilla Proceedings Project.

Clyne, M. (2011) Multilingualism, multiculturalism and integration. In M. Clyne and J. Jupp (eds) *Multiculturalism and Integration* (pp. 53–72). Canberra: The Australian National University Press.

Clyne, M. and Jupp, J. (eds) (2011) *Multiculturalism and Integration: A Harmonious Relationship*. Canberra: The Australian National University Press.

Cuccioletta, D. (2001/2002) Multiculturalism or transculturalism: Towards a cosmopolitan citizenship. *London Journal of Canadian Studies* 17, 1–11.

Dawkins, J. (1991) *Australia's Language: The Australian Language and Literacy Policy*. Canberra: Australian Government Publishing Service.

Dewaele, J.M. and van Oudenhoven, J.P. (2009) The effect of multilingualism/multiculturalism on personality: No gain without pain for Third Culture Kids? *International Journal of Multilingualism* 6, 443–459.

Djité, P.G. (2011) Language policy in Australia: What goes up must come down? In C. Norrby and J. Hajek (eds) *Uniformity and Diversity in Language Policy: Global Perspectives* (pp. 53–67). Bristol: Multilingual Matters.

Edwards, J. and Chisholm, J. (1987) Language, multiculturalism and identity: A Canadian study. *Journal of Multilingual and Multicultural Development* 8, 391–408.

Fishman, J.A. (1980) Bilingualism and biculturalism as individual and as societal phenomena. *Journal of Multilingual and Multicultural Development* 1, 3–15.

Fraser, M. (1981) Multiculturalism: Australia's unique achievement. Inaugural address on multiculturalism given by the Prime Minister, the Rt. Hon. Malcolm Fraser, to the Institute of Multicultural Affairs in Melbourne on 30 November 1981. See Transcript, http://www.unimelb.edu.au/malcolmfraser/speeches/nonparliamentary/multiculturalism.html.

Galbally, F. (1978) *Migrant Services and Programs: Report of the Review of Post-Arrival Programs and Services for Migrants, May 1978*. Migrant Services and Programs. Canberra: Australian Government Publishing Service.

Hajek, J. and Slaughter, Y. (eds) (2015) *Challenging the Monolingual Mindset*. Bristol: Multilingual Matters.

Ingram, D.E. (2000) Language policy and language education in Australia. Invited paper to students and staff of Akita University, Japan, 18 August 2000. Also published in *Akita English Studies* 1, 7–20.

Jupp, J. (2011) Religion and integration in a multifaith society. In M. Clyne and J. Jupp (eds) *Multiculturalism and Integration* (pp. 135–150). Canberra: The Australian National University Press.

Kipp, S., Clyne, M. and Pauwels, A. (1995) *Immigration and Australia's Language Resources*. Canberra: Australian Government Publishing Service.

Kritz, M., Gurak, D. and Likwang, C. (2000) Elderly immigrants: Their composition and living arrangements. *Journal of Sociology and Social Welfare* 27 (1), 85–114.

Lambert, B. (2008) *Family Language Transmission: Actors, Issues, Outcomes*. Frankfurt: Peter Lang.

Lee, M.S. and Crittenden, K.S. (1996) Social support and depression among elderly Korean immigrants in the Unites States. *International Journal of Aging and Human Development* 42 (4), 313–327.

Levey, G.B. (2011) Multicultural integration in political theory. In M. Clyne and J. Jupp (eds) *Multiculturalism and Integration* (pp. 73–87). Canberra: The Australian National University Press.

Liddicoat, A., Scarino, A., Curnow, T., Kohler, M., Scrimgeour, A. and Morgan, A.-M. (2007) *An Investigation of the State and Nature of Languages in Australian Schools*. Canberra: Department of Education, Employment and Workplace Relations.

Litwin, H. (1995) The social networks of elderly immigrants: An analytic typology. *Journal of Aging Studies* 9 (2), 155–174.

Lo Bianco, J. (1987) *National Policy on Languages*. Canberra: Australian Government Publishing Service.

Lo Bianco, J. (1990) Making language policy: Australia's experience. In R.B. Baldauf Jr. and A. Luke (eds) *Language Planning and Education in Australasia and the South Pacific* (pp. 47–79). Clevedon: Multilingual Matters.

Lo Bianco, J. (2007) Book review. Clyne, M. *Australia's Language Potential. Australian Review of Applied Linguistics* 30 (2), 25.1–25.4.

Mansouri, F. and Lobo, M. (eds) (2011a) *Migration, Citizenship and Intercultural Relations: Looking through the Lens of Social Inclusion*. Burlington, VA: Ashgate.

Mansouri, F. and Lobo, M. (2011b) Social inclusion: Exploring the concept. In F. Mansour and M. Lobo (eds) *Migration, Citizenship and Intercultural Relations* (pp. 1–10). Farnham: Ashgate Publishing.

Markus, A. (2011a) Social cohesion/Social inclusion. In F. Mansour and M. Lobo (eds) *Migration, Citizenship and Intercultural Relations* (pp. 143–158). Farnham: Ashgate Publishing.

Markus, A. (2011b) Attitudes to multiculturalism and cultural diversity. In M. Clyne and J. Jupp (eds) *Multiculturalism and Integration* (pp. 89–100). Canberra: The Australian National University Press.

Markus, A. (2015) *Mapping Social Cohesion*. See the Scanlon Foundation surveys at http://monash.edu/mapping-population (accessed 17 March 2016).

MCEETYA (1999) *The Adelaide Declaration on National Goals for Schooling in the Twenty-First Century*. Australia: Ministerial Council on Education, Employment, Training and Youth Affairs.

MCEETYA (2005) *National Statement for Languages Education in Australian Schools: National Plan for Languages Education in Australian Schools 2005–2008*. Hindmarsh, SA: DECS Publishing for the Ministerial Council on Education, Employment, Training and Youth Affairs.

MCEETYA (2008) *Melbourne Declaration on Educational Goals for Young Australians*. Melbourne: Ministerial Council on Education, Employment, Training and Youth Affairs.

Nettelbeck, C. (2009) *An Analysis of Retention Strategies and Technology Enhanced Learning in Beginners' Languages other than English (LOTE) at Australian Universities*. Canberra: The Australian Academy of the Humanities.

Neumann, K. and Tavan, G. (eds) *Does History Matter? Making and Debating Citizenship, Immigration and Refugee Policy in Australia and New Zealand*. Canberra: ANU Press.

Newman, S. and Brummel, S. (1998) *Intergenerational Programs: Imperatives, Strategies, Impacts, Trends*. New York: Haworth Press.

Ozolins, U. and Clyne, M. (2001) Immigration and language policy in Australia. In G. Extra and D. Gorter (eds) *The Other Languages of Europe: Demographic, Sociolinguistic and Educational Perspectives* (pp. 371–390). Clevedon: Multilingual Matters.

SBS Census Explorer (2011) at: http://www.sbs.com.au/censusexplorer/ (accessed 17 February 2016).

Seeman, T.E. and Crimmins, E. (2001) Social environment effects on health and aging: Integrating epidemiological and demographic approaches and perspectives. In M. Weinstein, A.I. Hermalin and M.A. Stoto (eds) *Population Health and Aging:*

Strengthening the Dialogue Between Epidemiology and Demography (pp. 88–117). New York: New York Academy of Sciences.

Shergold, P. (1994/1995) A national multicultural agenda for all Australians. Transcript of interview in the online Multicultural Research Library of Making Multicultural Australia. See http://www.multiculturalaustralia.edu.au/library/media/Audio/id/424.A-national-multicultural-agenda-for-all-Australians.

Slaughter, Y. (2011) Bringing Asia to the home front: The Australian experience of Asian language education through national policy. In C. Norrby and J. Hajek (eds) *Uniformity and Diversity in Language Policy* (pp. 157–176). Bristol: Multilingual Matters.

Tavan, G. (2008) Multiple choice time for Labor. *Age*, 10 January 2008.

Tavan, G. (2009) Testing times: The problem of 'history' in the Howard government's Australian citizenship test. In K. Neumann and G. Tavan (eds) *Does History Matter?* (pp. 125–143). Canberra: Australian National University Press.

Vertovec, S. and Wessendorf, S. (eds) (2010) *The Multiculturalism Backlash*. London: Routledge.

2 Contemporary Intergenerational Relationships

Susan Feldman, Harriet Radermacher and Colette Browning

An Ageing World

Relationships across and between generations have been the backbone of society for thousands of years. These intergenerational relationships have played a central role in the lives of individuals, groups and communities through the sharing of resources, including skills, knowledge, language, culture, attitudes and values (Feldman & Seedsman, 2005; Herd, 2010; Sánchez et al., 2007). In an ever-changing world, it remains true that positive human relationships, regardless of age, remain essential for community cohesion, as well as for individual emotional, psychological and physical health and well-being (Boström, 2011; Browning et al., 2013).

In 2002 the United Nations reaffirmed the responsibility of the world's citizens to ensure the building of societies in which the concept of 'a society for all ages' is fundamental: a society in which generations of individuals, regardless of age, are able to communicate with each other and participate in quality reciprocal relationships whilst simultaneously building a sense of interdependence and solidarity (United Nations, 2002; Sánchez et al., 2007). This comes as a clarion call in both developed and developing countries as the ageing of the world's population continues rapidly, resulting primarily from increased longevity. It is estimated that by 2050 'there will be more older people than children (aged 0–14 years) in the population for the first time in human history' (WHO, 2007: 3). The United Nations' (2013: 11) most recent edition of *World Population Ageing* reports that in the developed world almost one in every four persons (23%) is now 60 years or older, and predictions are that by 2050 the proportion will be almost one in three (32%). The oldest age group – 80 years and above – is currently the fastest-growing group, regardless of geographic region. In addition, persons worldwide are increasingly reaching the age of 100 years or more, and a large percentage of older persons reside in urban areas. In the state of Victoria, 14% of the population was aged 65 or over in 2011, and this percentage is expected to almost double by 2050.[1]

This demographic revolution presents new challenges and expectations in all aspects of society, including housing, medical care, transportation, social participation, etc. It demands that both individuals and institutions redefine the roles, relationships and responsibilities of each generation, and build a society that is truly multi-generational. We cannot assume that people of retirement age are automatically 'destined to end their lives being dependent on others for all of their care needs or living in retirement villages or nursing homes' (Feldman & Seedsman, 2005: 181). On the contrary, it is evident that many older people are adopting a range of independent lifestyles that allow them to expand their horizons through new ways of relating to and engaging with their communities, regardless of interests, expertise, generation or age. In the majority of cases, '[o]lder people want opportunities to socialize and integrate with other age groups and cultures in their communities, activities and families' (WHO, 2007: 42).

Nonetheless, there are still many older people who feel isolated and disengaged from young people. Urban design is a contributing factor. In their thoughtful work, Larkin and Newman (2013: 7) suggest that 'the segregation of groups of people by age has resulted in a serious breakdown of interaction and communication among the generations'. WHO (2007: 35) describes concerns about 'ghettoes of older people in large seniors' housing complexes'. Older people can also feel isolated in their own home if transportation and social services are inadequate.

Lack of opportunities for different generations to come together can foment a 'generational gap' and ageism, a process that routinely stereotypes and discriminates against older people, just as gender and ethnicity are targeted in sexism and racism. Ageism can be insidious, as young people 'subtly cease to identify with their elders as human beings' (Butler, 1987: 22). Sociolinguistic studies of bilingual older people, and aged care in general, have examined such phenomena as language attrition and cognition (Van der Hoeven & de Bot, 2012; Craik et al., 2010), language choice in retirement homes (Seebus, 2008), and carers' interaction with the older people (Ryan et al., 1991). Media reports predicting an increase in intergenerational mistrust abound, and entrenched notions and attitudes and negative stereotypes continue to shape contemporary ideas about each generation, whether young or old. As such there is a need for a rethink and a reassessment of the value and mutual benefit of providing opportunities for people across the generations to come together to counter ageist, sexist and racist views (Angus & Reeve, 2006; Feldman & Seedsman, 2005; Hatton Yeo, 2006).

Families and Cultures

Although it can take many forms, the family remains the dominant institution in contemporary society, and families are the primary setting in which people learn about and experience each other. It is within the family that attitudes and values – both negative and positive – are formed, and that interactions between individuals of different ages and at different life stages are possible. As Feldman and Seedsman (2005: 182) note,

> within a family structure members may give and receive care, exchange knowledge, provide economic, physical and emotional support. At the same time the extended family is seen as a support network between different generations.

Passing on knowledge from one generation to the next is pivotal in family groups (Attias-Donfut & Wolff, 2005; Lambert, 2008), and as Biggs and Lowenstein (2011: 8) have noted, 'The memory of historical events is itself shaped by the role of family members in passing the experience of social events on to younger generations'.

It is also good to recognise, however, that families are subject to complex tensions and estrangements. Relationships between and across the generations may come under pressure in families, and indeed may not be possible at all because of factors such as geographical mobility, migration and marriage breakdown (Feldman & Seedsman, 2005).

In traditional Australian Aboriginal society, Elders were accorded the highest respect both for their wisdom as teachers of the lore and culture and for their spiritual knowledge. As heads of their clan or group the Elders ensured that all members of the clan carried out their expected roles. Overall there was interdependence within the clan that gave everyone a true sense of belonging and self-worth. This system of extended family ensured that as Elders became old and frail they were respectfully cared for. For some people in our society, however, old age brings diminished family connections even as more family and community support of both a medical and a social nature is needed. On the other hand, some older people in this phase of life are the primary caregivers for an ageing spouse or other family members, including young children.

Rapid social change has placed traditional cultural values and expectations under threat, particularly among migrants from non-English-speaking countries. Australia experienced mass immigration after the Second World War and the subsequent transplanting of branches of families that have grown roots in their new country. The first generation of immigrants is now ageing, and as they age it is likely that increasing numbers will become dependent on family members. From a traditional perspective these older citizens have made their families what they are today. In many cultures gratitude and respect for the achievements of older family members are important, and are frequently reflected in genuine efforts by other family members to provide for their needs and wants during later life. It is important to understand that the extended family is seen as a support network of some significance by many cultural groups.

Within the Australian contemporary setting, two- or three-generation households can operate well, with care being provided by and for older family members. Older people in multi-generational households are integral to family life, and in most cultures they hold an important place as a spiritual and ritual leader, companion, teacher, role model and resource support for the maintenance of cultural traditions. They also provide a sense of continuity for grandchildren and younger members of the family group.

As a consequence there is a widely held, but often misleading, belief among the Anglo-Australian community that older people from culturally and linguistically diverse backgrounds necessarily receive a better quality of care in old age than those from an English-speaking background (Rowland, 1994, 1997). It is true that a higher proportion of older people born in non-English-speaking countries live in family-centred households compared with those born in Australia (VEAC, 1995), but a number of factors can influence the ability of families to care for their older members. '[W]hile the preference for caring in three generation families is strong amongst migrant families, the realities need to be de-mythologized without being devalued' (McCallum & Gelfand, 1990: 37). Just like families generally, some of those from multicultural backgrounds do not have the sustained commitment or the economic means to care for older family members.

It is also good to recognise that family tensions may develop through unrealistic cultural expectations of older members towards younger generations who were born and raised as Australian citizens. This is more likely to occur in households where older and younger family members are living together because of economic necessity. Children who have absorbed Australian values and expectations at school and at work will see life from a different, less traditional, perspective than their grandparents. Family life can also be strained by a lack of language and living skills or the absence of appropriate or alternative living options for older members. Economic dependence on adult children is one source of stress for older people who have migrated in the more recent past as part of the Australian Commonwealth Government's Family Reunion Programme. The assurance of support provision required by the government means that older people from culturally and linguistically diverse backgrounds will be financially dependent on their adult children for substantial periods of time. It is estimated that approximately 40% of these assurances break down (Russell, 1996).

Despite the negative portrayal of older and younger people in the public domain, however, relationships that value and nurture connections between individuals of all ages and generations within the family, in the community, and in learning and educational contexts continue to flourish. The work of Biggs and Lowenstein (2011: 53) suggests that 'judgements towards older adults are likely to be more positive in the private sphere than in the public', an idea supported by Feldman *et al.* (2002) and Hendricks (2004), who report that younger people in particular may think more positively about older people in their immediate family than about older people 'out there' in general.

A Community for All Ages

Building a vibrant, inclusive community demands the active engagement of individuals and groups of all ages in a wide range of settings and activities. It also requires the development of crucial networks and relationships which support and encourage individuals' feelings of trust and a sense of cohesion and belonging. Community building can take place within educational, neighbourhood, work or family settings. Within these specific settings, individuals across the age spectrum are able to learn about values and culture, give and receive care, exchange knowledge, or provide economic, physical, spiritual and emotional support (Feldman & Seedsman, 2005).

Of course, most people understand the critical importance of maintaining and building cohesive, well-functioning communities, neighbourhoods and family groups (Feldman *et al.*, 2012). Nevertheless, it must be emphasised that in the 21st century there is clear evidence of increased fragmentation in communities and families, often as the result of rapid social and economic change. Our entry into the new millennium has raised important economic and psychosocial questions about the place and role of older people in society, and many see an urgent need to address this issue and find ways of creating opportunities that will bridge the intergenerational gap (Angel & Angel, 1992; Kritz *et al.*, 2000; Lee & Crittenden, 1996; Litwin, 1995).

Many older and younger people are seeking opportunities to share their skills, knowledge and experiences with other generations, not only within the family but beyond, in a range of community settings. Older people, for example, are an invaluable source of support for young people who might need caring adults to guide and nurture them as they navigate the often difficult and complex course to adulthood (Rogers & Taylor, 1997). In addition, older people can help younger generations learn about aspects of ethics, values and culture that may not be available to them through immediate family circles. Younger people can provide older generations with specific technological skills and a window into their youthful and dynamic world, including skills around contemporary language, cultural practices and behaviour.

A New Approach to Intergenerational Studies

Intergenerational research, programmes and evaluation are multi-disciplinary by nature, drawing on a wide range of theoretical and conceptual approaches in order to better explain relationships between people in different age groups. These include scrutinising the relationships and interactions between and within generations in family, neighbourhood and institutional contexts (Kuehne, 2003a, 2003b). Unfortunately, much of the focus of intergenerational studies in the past has been based on sentiment, which 'trivializes their importance to society, and ignores their larger social and political relevance' (Kuehne, 2003b: 89; Moody & Disch, 1989).

The idea of *social capital* proposes that participation and involvement in groups can have positive outcomes for both the individual and the community. Social capital, as Coleman (1988: 98) has described it, is not one concept, but rather 'a variety of different entities, with two elements in common: they all consist of some aspect of social structures, and they facilitate certain actions of actors – whether persons or corporate actors – within the structure'. Of particular relevance to our study findings was Coleman's (1988: 119) description of how three forms of social capital may be elucidated: 'obligations and expectations, which depend on trustworthiness of the social environment, information-flow capability of the social structure, and norms accompanied by sanctions'.

Intergenerational programmes have been defined by writers including Ventura-Merkel and Liddoff (1983) as those activities which facilitate the exchange of skills and experiences by encouraging cooperative interactions between generations, especially the young with the old. Dunham and Casadonte (2009) argue commas around however that in relation to intergenerational learning projects specifically, there is in many instances a tendency for these to focus on activities outside of the formal classroom and on the experience of the older people rather than on the educational outcomes for the students. Further, as other authors have pointed out, few studies of intergenerational learning programmes have involved high school students and have focused largely on the experience of students in primary school (Dunham & Casadonte, 2009: 455; Lai & Kaplan, 2013: 426).

In our project, the educational outcomes for the high school students was a priority, specifically the achievement of clearly established formal educational objectives related to language skill and proficiency. The benefits to the older participants were also a key component, however, and these proved to be substantial, including experiencing youth culture at first hand within an educational setting. In addition, the value of older people's participation was assessed not only in relation to their role as tutors and guides but also in relation to psychosocial and health outcomes as well as specific learning outcomes with regard to their own English language proficiency. Although not necessarily a key focus of the research, understanding the attitudes of the students towards older people played a role in providing the structure for the initial phase of implementation of the project and the context for the ongoing working relationships as they developed between the multi-generational participants.

Guiding Theoretical Concepts

Valerie Kuehne (2003a: 148) posits that there has been a recent shift in intergenerational programme literature towards 'more theoretically driven studies' that seek to 'explain the ways in which intergenerational programmes operate differently from and potentially more effectively than other social programs'. A number of key concepts and critical perspectives are helpful in informing a more comprehensive understanding about relationships and interactions between people across the age groups, and these concepts were found to be particularly relevant in our own project.

Karen Vanderven (2011: 23) writes that an intergenerational theory is essential to understanding 'the real dynamics of these interactions'. Not surprisingly, there is at this time a multitude of conceptual theoretical approaches which focus on understanding how individuals and groups interact within a range of settings across and within the generations (Kuehne, 2003a). For the purpose of our research, however, we focused on the three key concepts of *mentoring*, *generativity* and *reciprocity*. While these are discussed under separate headings below, it is important to recognise that at times the boundaries between them are blurred or interconnected. These theoretical concepts have been helpful in informing the way the data generated by our project may be interpreted and understood in relation to the aims of the project. When combined, they provide a frame for our insights into the nature of the relationships between the participants as well as between the generations generally. More specifically, they offer a perspective on the longer-term value of conducting a schools-based language educational programme such as the one described in this book.

Mentoring

The role of guide or mentor has been an important one in society since ancient times (Molpeceres *et al.*, 2012). The mentoring literature is extensive, but for the purpose of our discussion mentoring is taken to be an active relationship between an experienced adult and a younger, unrelated person, 'an unrelated, younger protégé ... in which the adult provides ongoing guidance, instruction and encouragement aimed at developing the competence and character of the protégé' (Rhodes, 2002: 3).

Mentoring of younger people can take place in a range of informal community and family settings or in formal settings such as our intergenerational schools-based language programme (Molpeceres *et al.*, 2012; Rhodes, 2002). The supportive role of mentoring is reported by Kuehne (2003a: 150) as having 'positive effects on child and adolescent outcomes such as school attendance and performance, self-concept, parental relationships, and substance abuse'. Of particular relevance to our research was the notion that mentors need to be '"bi-culturally competent"

– that is, competent in both the culture of their family and in the larger community of which they are a part' (Kuehne, 2003a: 151). The mentors in our programme were well able to demonstrate these skills.

Generativity

Broadly speaking, the concept of generativity as it relates to adults, as described by Erik Erikson and colleagues (Erikson, 1964, 1980; Erikson *et al.*, 1986), is one of reaching out, giving to and guiding the next generation regardless of relationship or setting. In other words, generativity is not confined to familial relationships but extends beyond these into community, work and the broader milieu. It also implies that there is a commitment on the part of the individual that is beyond self and is associated with an inner drive to leave a legacy for society at large (Ranzijn & Grbich, 2001; Schoklitsch & Baumann, 2012). The work of Feldman Radermacher and Petersen *et al.* (2012: 98), for example, has shown that in a community of rural older men there were 'long established cultural traditions of passing on values, culture and property to following generations'.

The relevance of Erikson's theories for our own work is that generativity can also be perceived as a theme that features across the life course regardless of age (Vanderven, 2011). Many practitioners engaged with communities of older people have viewed intergenerational settings as 'an opportunity for older adults to develop themselves, and to share their accumulated knowledge and care with a younger and often eager audience' (Kuehne, 2003a: 153). This concept of generativity tends, in Kuehne's view, to be a one-way approach to intergenerational programmes, from the 'conceptual perspective of older adults fulfilling their own developmental needs while simultaneously contributing to their environments and others' development as well'. The intergenerational learning programme outlined in this book is an example of how, when applied to an educational setting, the concept of generativity allows for a broader application: that is, enrichment and achievement of prescribed educational goals for the students whilst simultaneously facilitating the needs of the older partner through a process that incorporates the ideas of mentoring and reciprocity with those of generativity.

Reciprocity

Reciprocity, social support and exchange have long been topics for investigation within discussions about the resources available to young and old across the life course. There has however, been a shift in thinking around the idea of exchange and reciprocity within relationships between these age cohorts. This shift has been coupled with discussions about the continuing desire of older people to contribute in meaningful ways to the quality of the lives of their family, friends and community. Some would argue that there may be negative consequences associated with these views, especially within familial settings. For some individuals there is a cultural expectation that older people will rely solely upon family to care for them in old age or that adult children have a duty of care to their aged parents 'because their parents brought them into existence, nurtured them, educated them and provided them with material benefits' (Bevan & Jeeawody, 1998: 323).

Intergenerational learning is based on the idea of reciprocity: that is, the two-way exchange provides 'vehicles for the purposeful and ongoing exchange of resources and learning among older and younger generations for individual and social benefits' (Hatton Yeo, 2006: 2). However, Biggs and Lowenstein (2013) remind us that reciprocity or multi-generational exchanges within family settings especially are subject to change over time. In addition, age and filial norms have an important place in the family life of each cultural group (Antonucci et al., 1990; Biggs & Lowenstein, 2013; Feldman & Seedsman, 2005). It has also been argued by some (e.g. Mannion, 2012) that the idea of 'all-age reciprocity' needs greater clarity in relation to definitions of and for practice. Other writers have described the wide range of outcomes generated by intergenerational programmes and practices, including those related to health and well-being, social inclusion and cohesion, and particularly in relation to the participation of older people or children (Martin et al., 2010; Springate et al., 2008).

In the past, intergenerational practice – particularly in educational settings – was predicated on one-way exchanges and outcomes such as 'efforts to get adults to educate the young or getting the young to support, serve, or assist older members of society' (Mannion, 2012: 388). It is further argued by Mannion (2012: 386), however, that these intergenerational exchanges, these reciprocal relationships, must always involve 'an educative element that is focused, at least in part, on the ongoing, reciprocal production of new relations between generations', particularly in an educational setting.

The effectiveness of our project was clearly measured against concrete and positive educational outcomes for the students related to their increased language proficiency, but also assessed on the ongoing and dynamic reciprocal relationships that developed between the language learners and the older participants.

Conclusion

In 2007 the World Health Organisation report on ageing specifically included the following activities in its goals of an 'age-friendly city':

- Learning about ageing and older people is included in primary and secondary school curricula.

- Older people are actively and regularly involved in local school activities with children and teachers.
- Older people are provided opportunities to share their knowledge, history and expertise with other generations. (WHO, 2007: 50)

In the following chapters we will discuss how each of these goals was addressed in our project. We will show that older people can provide a valuable source of expertise and support for young people in a purposeful and dynamic educational environment. Programmes and educational learning environments that value and foster links between people of all ages and ethnicities can also help to build active learning communities, promote citizenship, regenerate neighbourhoods and address inequality. As the global population ages, it is timely to recognise that meaningful connections between young and old are a vital part of the fabric of a healthy society.

Note

(1) The future: an ageing population. Australian Bureau of Statistics. See http://www.abs.gov.au/ausstats/abs@.nsf/lookup/2071.0main+features952012-2013; Population ageing in Victoria. Australian Bureau of Statistics. At: http://www.abs.gov.au/AUSSTATS/abs@.nsf/Lookup/1367.2Chapter3Jun+2010.

References

Angel, J. and Angel, R. (1992) Age at migration, social connections, and well-being among elderly Hispanics. *Journal of Aging and Health* 4, 480–499.

Angus, J. and Reeve, P. (2006) Ageism: A threat to 'aging well' in the 21st century. *Journal of Applied Gerontology* 25 (2), 137–152.

Antonucci, T., Fuhrer, R. and Jackson, J. (1990) Social support and reciprocity: A cross-ethnic and cross-national perspective. *Journal of Social and Personal Relationships* 4 (7), 519–530.

Attias-Donfut, C. and Wolff, F.C. (2005) Generational memory and family relationships. In M.L. Johnson (ed.) *The Cambridge Handbook of Age and Ageism* (pp. 443–454). Cambridge: Cambridge University Press.

Bevan, C. and Jeeawody, B. (1998) *Successful Ageing: Perspectives on Health and Social Construction*. South Melbourne: Mosby Publishers Australia.

Biggs, S. and Lowenstein, A. (2011) *Generational Intelligence: A Critical Approach to Age Relations*, London and New York: Routledge.

Boström, A.K. (2011) Lifelong learning in intergenerational settings: The development of the Swedish Granddad Program from project to national association. *Journal of Intergenerational Relationships* 9 (3), 293–306.

Browning, C.J., Heine, C. and Thomas, S. (2013) Promoting ageing well: Psychological contributions. In M.L. Caltabiano and L. Ricciardelli (eds) *Applied Topics in Health Psychology* (pp. 57–71). Chichester and Malden, MA: Wiley-Blackwell.

Butler, R.N. (1987) Ageism. In G.L. Maddox and R.C. Atchley (eds) *The Encyclopedia of Aging* (pp. 22–23). New York: Springer.

Coleman, J.S. (1988) Social capital in the creation of human capital. *American Journal of Sociology* 94, S95–S120.

Craik, F.I., Bialystok, E. and Freedman, M. (2010) Delaying the onset of Alzheimer disease: Bilingualism as a form of cognitive reserve. *Neurology* 75 (19), 1726–1729.

Dunham, C.C. and Casadonte, D. (2009) Children's attitudes and classroom interaction in an intergenerational education program. *Educational Gerontology* 35 (5), 455–464.
Erikson, E.H. (1964) *Insight and Responsibility*. New York: W.W. Norton & Co.
Erikson, E.H. (1980) *Identity and the Life Cycle*. New York: Norton.
Erikson, E.H., Erikson, J.M. and Kivnick, H.Q. (1986) *Vital Involvement in Old Age*. New York: Norton.
Feldman, S. and Seedsman, T. (2005) Ageing: New choices, new challenges. In M. Poole (ed.) *Family: Changing Family, Changing Times* (pp. 180–198). Crows Nest, NSW: Allen & Unwin.
Feldman, S., Mahoney, H. and Seedsman, T. (2002) Education for positive ageing: A partnership model for effecting sustainable outcomes. *Education and Ageing* 17 (1), 7–23.
Feldman, S., Radermacher, H. and Petersen, A. (2012) The vicissitudes of 'healthy aging': The experiences of older migrant men in a rural Australian community. In A. Kampf, B. Marshall and A. Petersen (eds) *Aging Men, Masculinities and Modern Medicine* (pp. 84–104). London: Routledge.
Hatton Yeo, A. (2006) *Intergenerational Practice: Active Participation across the Generations*. Stoke-on-Trent: Beth Johnson Foundation.
Hendricks, J. (2004) Public policies and old age identity. *Journal of Aging Studies* 18 (3), 245–260.
Herd, P. (2010) Education and health in late-life among high school graduates: Cognitive versus psychological aspects of human capital. *Journal of Health and Social Behavior* 51 (4), 478–496.
Kritz, M., Gurak, D. and Likwang, C. (2000) Elderly immigrants: Their composition and living arrangements. *Journal of Sociology and Social Welfare* 27 (1), 85–114.
Kuehne, V.S. (2003a) The state of our art: Intergenerational program research and evaluation: Part one. *Journal of Intergenerational Relationships* 1 (1), 145–161.
Kuehne, V.S. (2003b) The state of our art: Intergenerational program research and evaluation: Part two. *Journal of Intergenerational Relationships* 1 (2), 79–94.
Lai, A. and Kaplan, M. (2013) Intergenerational strategies for enriching the ESL education platform. *Journal of Intergenerational Relationships* 11 (4), 425–439.
Lambert, B.E. (2008) *Family Language Transmission: Actors, Issues, Outcomes*. Frankfurt am Main: Peter Lang.
Larkin, E. and Newman, S. (2013) Intergenerational studies: A multi-disciplinary field. In K. Brabazon and R. Disch (eds) *Intergenerational Approaches in Aging: Implications for Education, Policy, and Practice*. Binghampton, NY: The Haworth Press.
Lee, M.S. and Crittenden, K.S. (1996) Social support and depression among elderly Korean immigrants in the United States. *International Journal of Aging and Human Development* 42 (4), 313–327.
Litwin, H. (1995) The social networks of elderly immigrants: An analytical typology. *Journal of Aging Studies* 9 (2), 155–174.
Mannion, G. (2012) Intergenerational education: The significance of reciprocity and place. *Journal of Intergenerational Relationships* 10 (4), 386–399.
Martin, K., Springate, I. and Atkinson, M. (2010) *Intergenerational Practice: Outcomes and Effectiveness*. Slough: National Foundation for Education Research.
McCallum, J. and Gelfand, D.E. (1990) *Ethnic Women in the Middle: A Focus Group Study of Daughters Caring for Older Migrants in Australia*. Canberra: National Centre for Epidemiology and Population Health, Australian National University.
Molpeceres, M.A., Pinazo, S. and Aliena, R. (2012) Older adult mentors and youth at risk: Challenges for intergenerational mentoring programs in family-centered cultures. *Journal of Intergenerational Relationships* 10 (3), 261–275.
Moody, H.R. and Disch, R. (1989) Intergenerational programming between young and old. *The Generational Journal* 1 (3), 25–27.

Ranzijn, R. and Grbich, C. (2001) Qualitative aspects of productive ageing. *Australasian Journal on Ageing* 20 (2), 62–66.
Rhodes, J. (2002) *Stand by Me: The Risks and Rewards of Mentoring Today's Youth*. Cambridge, MA: Harvard University Press.
Ryan, E., Bhouris, R.Y. and Knops, U. (1991) Evaluative perceptions of patronizing speech addressed to elders. *Psychology and Aging* 6 (2), 442–450.
Rogers, A.M. and Taylor, A.S. (1997) Intergenerational mentoring: A viable strategy for meeting the needs of vulnerable youth. *Journal of Gerontological Social Work* 28 (1–2), 125–140.
Rowland, D.T. (1994) *Pioneers Again: Immigrants and Ageing in Australia*. Bureau of Immigration Research, Canberra: Australian Government Publication Service.
Rowland, D.T. (1997) Ethnicity and ageing. In A. Borowski, S. Encel and E. Ozane (eds) *Ageing and Social Policy in Australia* (pp. 75–93). Melbourne: Cambridge University Press.
Russell, H. (1996) *Issues for the Ethnic Aged in Victoria: An Overview*. Melbourne: Aged Care Research Group.
Sánchez, M., Butts, D.M., Hatton-Yeo, A., Henkin, N.A., Jarrott, S.E., Kaplan, M.S. Martínez, A., Newman, S., Pinazo, S., Sáez, J. and Weintraub, A.P.C. (2007) *Intergenerational Programmes: Towards a Society for all Ages*. Barcelona: 'la Caixa' Foundation, Social Studies no. 23 [PDF available online].
Schoklitsch, A. and Baumann, U. (2012) Generativity and aging: A promising future research topic?. *Journal of Aging Studies* 26 (3), 262–272.
Seebus, I. (2008) 'Dinkum Dutch Aussies': Language and identity among elderly Dutch-Australians. Unpublished PhD thesis, University of Melbourne.
Springate, I., Atkinson, M. and Martin, K. (2008) *Intergenerational Practice: A Review of the Literature*. Slough: National Foundation for Education Research.
United Nations (2002) *Political Declaration and Madrid International Plan of Action on Ageing*. New York: United Nations.
United Nations (2013) *World Population Ageing 2013*. New York, United Nations Department of Economic and Social Affairs, Population Division.
Van der Hoeven, N. and de Bot, K. (2012) Relearning in the elderly: Age-related effects on the size of savings. *Language Learning* 62 (1), 42–67.
Vanderven, K. (2011) The road to intergenerational theory is under construction: A continuing story. *Journal of Intergenerational Relationships* 9 (1), 22–36.
VEAC (Victorian Ethnic Affairs Commission) (1995) *Statistical Profile of Non-English Speaking Background Victorians*. East Melbourne, Victoria: The Commission.
Ventura-Merkel, C. and Liddoff, L. (1983) *Program Innovation in Aging: Community Planning for Intergenerational Programming*. Washington, DC: National Council on Aging.
WHO [World Health Organization] (2007) *Global Age-friendly Cities: A Guide*. Geneva, World Health Organization. See http://www.who.int/ageing/publications/age_friendly_cities_guide/en/.

3 Community Resources on our Doorstep: Language Learning in Action

Hui Huang and Marisa Cordella

Introduction

Contemporary Australian society, as we saw in Chapter 1, is both multicultural and multilingual. Its immigrants come from over 160 countries and regions, and more than 400 community languages are spoken in the home. It is also an ageing society, as we saw in Chapter 2, with many older people wanting to contribute their knowledge and wisdom to society in a meaningful way. We have already introduced the notion of these demographics as 'cultural resources' that could be better utilised. The purpose of this chapter, therefore, is to expand on this theme. Firstly, we look at the present state of second-language (L2) learning in Australia; we then discuss the theory of situated learning as it has been applied to L2 acquisition, which we adopt as the framework for our own project; and finally we introduce the project which provided the research data for this book.

Language Learning Beyond the Classroom

Despite some movement away from traditional grammar-focused approaches to language education and towards more communicative activities, few students leave Australian secondary school language courses with the ability to function successfully in an L2 environment or to carry on conversations with native speakers at more than a basic level. There is typically a disconnect between decontextualised classroom learning and the realities of authentic communication. In an attempt to bridge the gap, a number of schemes have emerged, such as the increasingly popular study abroad programmes (e.g. Regan, 1995; Dewaele & Regan, 2002; Collentine, 2004; Kinginger, 2008; Masuda, 2011), bilingual language programmes, culture projects (e.g. Allen, 2004; Byon, 2007) and more. There is no question that these activities benefit the students' language development and cultural awareness, but not all students are able to access them owing to financial limitations, clashes with curriculum arrangements, or other obstacles. However, in an immigrant country like Australia, very rich language and cultural resources already exist in local communities. The challenge is to tap into these resources so that L2 students unable to travel to other countries have the opportunity to engage with native speakers *on their own doorstep*.

A number of Australian projects have already explored the role of the L2 community as a source of input and output for language learners, with and without a home background in the language they are studying. Reports of several longitudinal studies of this nature can be found in Clyne *et al.* (1995) and Clyne *et al.* (1997). Recent American initiatives include partnership programmes (pairing 'heritage' and 'foreign' language learners for mutual enrichment) and service learning (a programme of experiential learning that allows students to work in their communities with people from diverse language, racial, economic and religious backgrounds, e.g. Valdés *et al.*, 2006).

However, much of the language contact research in Australia and beyond (e.g. Refatto, 2002; Lambert, 2008) has focused on the role of grandparents as catalysts for language maintenance. Fishman (1991) identifies the family-/community-based link with the younger generation, facilitated by extended families and demographic concentration, as a crucial factor in language transmission. Our project, on the other hand, aimed to extend this potential beyond the family and to link L2 learners with older unrelated bilinguals.

L2 Interactions and Situated Learning Theory

L2 acquisition is traditionally rendered as a cognitive process. In this view, learning is seen as 'inputting' and then 'processing' rules or units of a language. Since the 1990s, however, an increasing number of studies have been conducted in an attempt to provide a sociocultural description of L2 development (e.g. Firth & Wagner, 1997, 2007; Hellermann, 2006; Young, 1999, 2002), and specifically in a framework of 'situated learning' (Lave & Wenger, 1991; see further below) in which interactions play an essential part (e.g. Hall, 2004, 2010; Hall *et al.*, 2011; Mondada & Pekarek Doehler, 2004; Young & Miller, 2004). Ann Sfard (1998) and others have proposed a new metaphor of 'participation' to describe the acquisition process from a sociocultural perspective. According to this participation metaphor, L2 learning is a process of becoming a member of a *community*, which involves not only developing the ability to communicate through the language, but also acquiring the behaviours that are considered appropriate in that community's culture. The thinking is that language learning does not occur through the systematic command of linguistic rules or units alone; rather, it needs to be contextualised in socio-institutional settings where there are opportunities for authentic interactions with native speakers. This idea of L2 acquisition as a situated interactional process is entirely different from theories of language 'processing'. It is our stance in this book that socially situated interactions are valuable for L2 learners.

Our interactionist approach draws on several decades of theoretical and empirical work by others. In the late 1970s, Evelyn Hatch, a pioneer of discourse analysis as a tool in the study of second-language acquisition, brought together a collection of papers that made 'empirical data-based claims about the second language acquisition process' in 'natural environments' across a range of age and language groups (Hatch, 1978b: 11, 17) and identified the interactional moves in L2 student-to-student conversations by which the interlocutor sought assistance with comprehension (e.g. requests for clarification, confirmation checks) (Hatch, 1978a). Her early theoretical work was taken up by Long (1981, 1983) and Hall (1993, 1995), while Teresa Pica and her associates focused on the interactional moves of native and non-native speakers in instructional contexts, analysing the ways in which both parties modified and restructured the interaction to achieve mutual understanding (Pica 1987, 1988, 1991; Pica & Doughty 1985; Pica *et al.*, 1987, 1989, 1991; Doughty, 1991). In 1996 Long formally introduced his 'interaction hypothesis' in which a significant factor in L2 advancement is said to be face-to-face communication between the beginner and a skilled speaker as they negotiate meaning in the process of exchanging ideas and information (Long, 1996). Within this theory, interactions at the societal level are believed to play a supplementary role, contributing brief structures inside which mechanisms of acquiring knowledge are assumed to take place.

In 1999, Young took the interactionist view further by proposing that L2 knowledge does not dwell cognitively *inside* a particular contributor; rather, it comes into being when it is constructed jointly *through* the interaction (Young, 1999). This idea can be traced back to Vygotsky (1986), who maintained that higher levels of cognition, in both oral and literate traditions, can only develop through social activities, involving those of a tangible nature (e.g. paper and pencil) as well as those of a representative character (e.g. graphs, diagrams, numbers and orality). The debate is not that activities at the societal level affect cognition, but that those activities are the very *process* through which human cognition is formed. From this perspective, language is not simply a constant, resistant, rule-administered semantic system that must be mastered before a learner can begin to interact, and to some extent the theory emphasises the value of physical, linguistic, socially mediated activities that engage the student (Leontiev, 1981). Many L2 researchers aligned with this view define L2 learning as 'a highly complex and socially situated process that is dynamic and involves the negotiation of access, participation, and above all, identity' (Swain & Deters, 2007: 826). From Hall's early work on 'oral practice' (Hall, 1993) and Young on 'discursive practice' (Young, 1999, 2007, 2008, 2009) to explorations of 'interactional competence' (Hall *et al.*, 2011; Young, 2011; see further Chapter 10) and the latest conversation analysis (CA) and ethnomethodological view of interactions as the key loci of language learning and socialisation (e.g. Lantolf, 2000; Hester & Francis, 2004), studies of L2 acquisition have been necessarily interdisciplinary. Central to the multi-faceted approach, however, is the concept of *participation*: as Hall (1995: 218) put it, 'Our becoming participants involves three processes: the discovery (other- and self-guided) of interactive patterns in the practices in which we engage with others; observation and reflection on others' participatory moves and the responses to these moves; and our own active constructions of responses to these patterns'. A useful overview of the interactionist approach is given in Mackey *et al.* (2012). Emphases and hypotheses vary among scholars, but there is considerable agreement that the learning environment must include opportunities for learners to engage in meaningful social interactions with native speakers if they are to discover the linguistic and sociolinguistic rules necessary for second language comprehension and production.

Among several theories of learning that have envisioned language learning as a socialisation process in which all participants change the nature of their participation (e.g. sociocultural theory of mind, poststructuralist theories and dialogism: see Swain & Deters, 2007 for a detailed review), the most relevant and influential is *situated learning* or 'legitimate peripheral participation' (Lave, 1988; Lave & Wenger, 1991). In situated learning theory, the student acquires not only propositional knowledge, but, more significantly, as an integral part of the learning process participates in social practice and adapts continuously to the developing circumstances and activities that comprise personal interactions. It follows from this that the everyday oral practices of native speakers are a powerful resource for L2 learners. These 'culturally-mediated moments of face-to-face interaction' (Hall, 1993: 145) are the drivers of group socialisation and learning, and indeed are fundamental to the daily functioning of each individual in the group. Compared with instructional classroom learning, oral-practice immersion can help the student to understand how these resources are used by the group and learn to use these appropriately. In addition, everyday oral practices help with the development of linguistic and sociocultural competence via the provision of access to the sociocultural norms or practices of the group (Hall, 2004, 2010; Hall & Walsh, 2002; Young, 2011). In other words, interactions with a native speaker in a natural setting can assist the student not only to learn the language of the group, but also to become aware of what is involved in being a *member* of that group. Situated learning theory is particularly pertinent to our project because we believe that L2 learning should involve the *whole* person, with their sociocultural history, and that 'agent, activity, and the world mutually constitute each other' (Lave & Wenger, 1991: 33). In this holistic conceptualisation, learning the language means essentially learning how to deal with contextualised, interactionally oriented activities. That is, language learning is more than just a process of affiliation between a proficient speaker and a learner. Rather, it is implanted in the activities of: learning to organise talk through interactions, structuring participation frameworks, setting up conversation tasks, identifying personal attributes during interactions, and becoming progressively more competent members of the target language community (Mondada & Pekarek Doehler, 2004).

About the Project

The L2 classroom provides the setting for instructed language learning (see Ellis, 2002) and a comfortable practice environment for students, and enables aspects of the language to be covered that may not feature in external situations, such as in natural conversations (Schmidt, 2001). However, language practice in L2 classrooms is quite limited and artificial, and in many instances employs 'role play', in which conversations have little relation to real life. In other words, classroom learning offers students very little scope for participation in a socio-institutional context. At the same time, opportunities for young learners to approach and converse with native speakers in the community are often very restricted.

The aim of our project therefore was to supplement formal classroom learning with informal, natural interactions with native speakers of the target language. An important aspect of the initiative was that it provided students with access to the target language community without incurring significant expenses or needing to reorganise the curriculum, as would be the case with study abroad programmes and the like. In response to the call to increase the social dimension of L2 development (e.g. Firth & Wagner, 1997, 2007; Kramsch, 2002), the project drew on older bilinguals from local communities. This was a significant innovation. In this framework of legitimate peripheral participation the students were able to interact with older members of the target language community, and in so doing to develop their knowledge and ability to use the language appropriately in real-life communication.

Furthermore, these situated interactions offered the L2 learner the opportunity to learn about and communicate with another culture. Culture, in this sense, is integrated into language learning through interactions. What is achieved, then, is not merely an *accumulation* of cultural knowledge, such as is offered by traditional methods of teaching this topic, but an *intercultural capability* (Scarino, 2010). These situated learning encounters are 'a dynamic, developmental, and on-going process which engages the learner cognitively, behaviourally, and affectively' (Paige et al., 1999: 50). Our integrated approach enabled L2 learners to exchange meaning with people across languages and cultures; but also, perhaps more critically, to 'develop a reflective stance towards language and culture' (Liddicoat et al., 2003: 46). In the process, they grew in awareness that culture is not simply information *about* people and their norms, but that, more fundamentally, culture is the prism through which people exchange meaning and understand their world (Scarino, 2010).

Project participants

The project paired more than 160 upper secondary school students with 106 older participants from the local community. The students were learning either Mandarin Chinese,[1] German or Spanish, and were paired with a native speaker of the target language. Three local schools were chosen: two government secondary colleges and one independent school, between them offering the three languages. Chinese was taught at two schools, and German and Spanish at one school each. At the time of data collection, all the student participants were in Year 11 or Year 12 and aged between 15 and 17 years. They had usually started to learn the second language in Year 7 (see Table 3.1).

Each pair held a one-hour conversation in the target language every fortnight in school terms 1, 2 and 3, making nine or 10 sessions per year. The Chinese and German conversations ran for three years (2010–2012), but the Spanish conversations for only two, as the school was unable to offer the subject at VCE (Victorian Certificate of Education) level in 2012. Many students participated in the project for two years continuously, and many older participants also volunteered for more than one year.

Table 3.1 Student participants in the project

Year		*Chinese students*		*German students*		*Spanish students*	
		Male	Female	Male	Female	Male	Female
2010	School A	3	8	3	4	-	-
	School B	10	9	-	-	-	-
	School C	-	-	-	-	1	9
2011	School A	7	7	7	4	-	-
	School B	44	44	-	-	-	-
	School C	-	-	-	-	1	4
2012	School A	3	3	5	7	-	-
	School B	45	42	-	-	-	-
Total		112	113	15	15	2	13

Table 3.2 Older participants in the project

	Chinese		German		Spanish	
Year	Male	Female	Male	Female	Male	Female
2010	12	11	5	1	2	8
2011	31	56	7	4	0	5
2012	21	38	6	5	-	-
Total	64	105	18	10	2	13

Each of the three languages chosen was one of Australia's top community languages in 2006. All three have international importance. Chinese is both the most widely used L1 in the world and Australia's fastest-growing community language. Spanish is the world's third most widely spoken language, the main language of Latin America, and as the national language of two APEC (Asia-Pacific Economic Cooperation) nations is also of significance in the Pacific region. German is the European Union language with the largest number of L1 speakers. It has had and continues to have a strong presence in Central Europe.

The older participants (see Table 3.2) were recruited through ethnic community centres, churches and community clubs, following the provision of relevant information and documentation as required by the Ethics Committee of Monash University. All of the older participants were over the age of 60 and the oldest was 95 in 2012 when the collection of data was completed!

Conversation topics

During the three years of data collection, researchers worked very closely with schools and older participants to establish the conversation topics. Most were chosen in consultation with teachers at the schools in order to work with their language curriculum. However, on the basis of feedback from focus groups with students and telephone interviews with older participants, some topics were revised and adapted to better tailor them to the participants' needs. Conversation topics generally included early life experiences in the older participants' country of origin, the migration experience, work and family life in Australia, hobbies and interests, and issues concerning countries where the language is spoken. For research validity, two topics were kept the same across the three schools each year. For example, in recording 1 in 2010, the topic was the introduction to self and family. In the second recording of the year, the topic was the student's school life.

Data collection and procedures

All the conversation sessions were conducted on the schools' premises. Most were held after school hours, but in the second year of the project

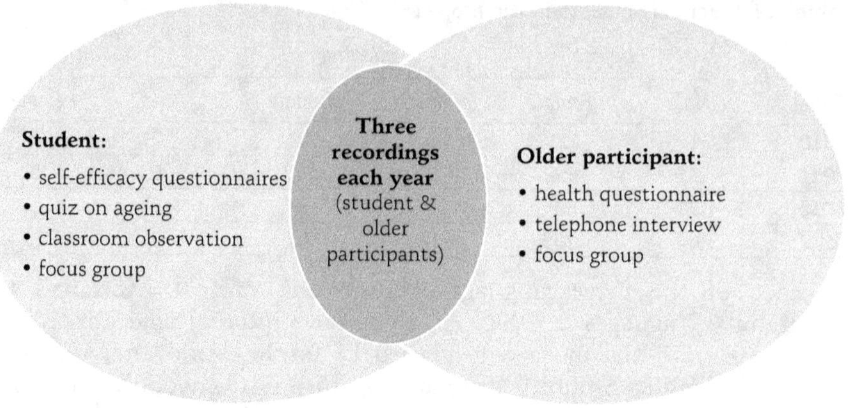

Student:
- self-efficacy questionnaires
- quiz on ageing
- classroom observation
- focus group

Three recordings each year (student & older participants)

Older participant:
- health questionnaire
- telephone interview
- focus group

Figure 3.1 Data collection procedures

two of the schools integrated the sessions into their curriculum and these then ran during class time. A combination of qualitative and quantitative measures was used to collect the data (see Figure 3.1). Older participants and student participants completed questionnaires at the beginning and end of the project each year and these were kept the same as a control measure. The information requested from the older participants incorporated standardised health questionnaires including the WHO QoL, the Kessler-10, the Reactions to Ageing Quiz, and Rosenberg's self-esteem scale as well as open-ended questions that gave them an opportunity to provide qualitative data about their experiences of ageing and the impact of the programme on their quality of life. This information was supplemented by in-depth telephone interviews with each individual, which was audio-recorded with their permission. The students were requested to complete a pre- and post-project self-efficacy questionnaire, which aimed to document changes in their degree of confidence in conducting language activities, and were also asked to fill out a quiz on ageing to help determine any modifications in their attitude to this subject. Non-participants were present during the conversations to observe what actually happened in the classroom, how the students performed linguistically, and also how they behaved around older people.

The most important data of the project came from the recordings made of the conversation sessions. Each year three sessions were recorded: the first together with the pre-project questionnaire, the third with the post-project questionnaire, and the second generally after four or five sessions. Our focus was on natural conversation as an interactional activity that transcends specific contexts, particularly with regard to L2 encounters. We adopted a primarily *emic* approach (Firth & Wagner, 1997), looking at aspects of second-language acquisition from the point of view of the learner,

Table 3.3 Focus group questions for the students

• General comments on frequency and length of the conversation meeting.
• How many times did you meet with the older participant?
• Would you like more/fewer meetings? Longer/shorter meetings?
• Benefits: What benefits do you feel you got from this project?
• Difficulties and areas to improve: What difficulties did you have during the conversations? What advice would you give us for future years?
• Topics: Were there topics during the conversations that you found uncomfortable/upsetting/difficult to approach? What advice would you give us for future years?

in order to gain an in-depth understanding of how L2 learners convey their intended meanings and communicate in the target language. We tried to note down any kind of communicative resources they deployed, shared, adapted or manipulated contingently and/or applied creatively in every micro moment (Firth & Wagner, 2007) to construct meaningful social interactions with the native speakers, in the belief that language learning is a process that takes place in the micro moments of social interaction. Following Wagner and Gardner (2004: 14), the recorded data were intended to investigate 'whether a micro-analysis of second language conversations can enhance our understanding of what it means to talk in another language, by broadening the focus beyond the sounds, structures and meanings of language to encompass action sequences, timing and interactivity'. The Year 11 students who continued their involvement with the project in Year 12 provided valuable longitudinal data for understanding the development of both L2 acquisition and social relationships in situated interactions.

Focus groups

Focus groups were held immediately after the last conversation session each year with both older participants and students (generally six to eight participants per group) in order to collect descriptive data, mainly covering what they saw as the benefits and problems of the project (see Table 3.3). This data was used partly to improve the implementation of the project at an administrative level and partly to supplement the other data of our research.

Significance and Innovations of the Project

The project sought to address a number of significant issues, including the lack of opportunities for L2 acquisition in natural settings, the lack of connection between monolingual and multilingual Australians, and the isolation of older migrants, and offered a framework for engaging with each of these simultaneously. We examined which aspects of L2 development were enhanced during the conversation sessions: attitudinal (e.g. self-efficacy), cognitive (e.g. intercultural, lexical, morphosyntactic, phonological, prosodic knowledge) and behavioural (e.g. interactional competence). We also documented how the conversations fostered intergenerational empathy, promoting the quality of life and self-esteem of the older migrants, and positive attitudes to ageing and older people among secondary school students. These findings are explored in detail in the following chapters.

Note

(1) Henceforth referred to simply as 'Chinese'.

References

Allen, L. (2004) Implementing a culture portfolio project within a constructivist paradigm. *Foreign Language Annals* 37, 232–239.

Byon, A. (2007) The use of culture portfolio project in a Korean culture classroom: Evaluating stereotypes and enhancing cross-cultural awareness. *Language, Culture and Curriculum* 20 (1), 1–19.

Clyne, M., Jenkins, C., Chen, I., Tsokalidou, R. and Wallner, T. (1995) *Developing Second Language from Primary School: Models and Outcomes*. Canberra: National Languages and Literary Institute of Australia.

Clyne, M., Fernandez, S., Chen, I. and Summo-O'Connell, R. (1997) *Background Speakers*. Canberra: Language Australia.

Collentine, J. (2004) The effects of learning contexts on morphosyntactic and lexical development. *Studies in Second Language Acquisition* 26, 227–248.

Dewaele, J. and Regan, V. (2002) Maîtriser la norme sociolinguistique en interlangue française: Le cas de l'omission variable de 'ne'. *French Language Studies* 12, 123–148.

Doughty, C. (1991) Making it happen: Interaction in the second language classroom. From theory to practice. *Studies in Second Language Acquisition* 13, 93–94.

Ellis, R. (2002) The place of grammar instruction in the second/foreign language curriculum. In E. Hinkel and W. Fotos (eds) *New Perspectives on Grammar Teaching in Second Language Classrooms* (pp. 17–34). Mahwah, NJ: Lawrence Erlbaum Associates.

Firth, A. and Wagner, J. (1997) On discourse, communication, and (some) fundamental concepts in SLA research. *Modern Language Journal* 81, 285–300.

Firth, A. and Wagner, J. (2007) Second/foreign language learning as a social accomplishment: Elaborations on a reconceptualized SLA. *Modern Language Journal* 91 (Supplement s1), 800–819.

Fishman, J. (1991) *Reversing Language Shift: Theoretical and Empirical Foundations of Assistance to Threatened Languages*. Clevedon: Multilingual Matters.

Hall, J.K. (1993) The role of oral practices in the accomplishment of our everyday lives: The sociocultural dimension of interaction with implications for the learning of another language. *Applied Linguistics* 14, 145–166.

Hall, J.K. (1995) (Re)creating our worlds with words: A sociohistorical perspective of face-to-face interaction. *Applied Linguistics* 16, 206–232.

Hall, J.K. (2004) Language learning as an interactional achievement. *Modern Language Journal* 88, 607-612.

Hall, J.K. (2010) Interaction as method and result of language learning. *Language Teaching* 43, 202–215.

Hall, J.K. and Walsh, M. (2002) Teacher–student interaction and language learning. *Annual Review of Applied Linguistics* 22, 186–203.

Hall, J.K., Hellermann, J. and Pekarek Doehler, S. (eds) (2011) *L2 Interactional Competence and Development*. Bristol: Multilingual Matters.
Hatch, E. (1978a) Acquisition of syntax in a second language. In J.C. Richards (ed.) *Understanding Second and Foreign Language Learning* 34–70. Rowley, MA: Newbury House.
Hatch, E. (1978b) Discourse analysis and second language acquisition. In E. Hatch (ed.) *Second Language Acquisition: A Book of Readings* (pp. 401–435). Rowley, MA: Newbury House.
Hellermann, J. (2006) Classroom interactive practices for developing L2 literacy: A microethnographic study of two beginning adult learners of English. *Applied Linguistics* 27, 377–404.
Hester, S. and Francis, D. (2004) *An Invitation to Ethnomethodology: Language, Society and Interaction*. London: Sage Publications.
Kinginger, C. (2008) Language learning in study abroad: Case studies of Americans in France. *Modern Language Journal* Monograph Series, Volume 1. Oxford: Blackwell.
Kramsch, C. (2002) 'How can we tell the dancer from the dance?'. In C. Kramsch (ed.) *Language Acquisition and Language Socialization: Ecological Perspectives* (pp. 1–30). London: Continuum.
Lambert, B. (2008) *Family Language Transmission: Actors, Issues, Outcomes*. Frankfurt: Peter Lang.
Lantolf, J. (ed.) (2000) *Sociocultural Theory and Second Language Learning*. Oxford: Oxford University Press.
Lave, J. (1988) *Cognition in Practice: Mind, Mathematics and Culture in Everyday Life*. Cambridge: Cambridge University Press.
Lave, J. and Wenger, E. (1991) *Situated Learning: Legitimate Peripheral Participation*. Cambridge: Cambridge University Press.
Leontiev, A.A. (1981) *Psychology and the Language Learning Process*. London: Pergamon.
Liddicoat, A.J., Papademetre, L., Scarino, A. and Kohler, M. (2003) *Report on Intercultural Language Learning*. Canberra: Australian Government Department of Education, Science and Training.
Long, M.H. (1981) Input, interaction, and second – language acquisition. *Annals of the New York Academy of Sciences* 379, 259–278.
Long, M.H. (1983) Native speaker/non-native speaker conversation in the second language classroom. In M. Clarke and J. Handscombe (eds) *On TESOL '82: Pacific Perspectives on Language Learning* (pp. 207–225). Washington, DC: TESOL [Teachers of English to Speakers of Other Languages, Inc.].
Long, M.H. (1996) The role of the linguistic environment in second language acquisition. In W. Ritchie and T. Bhatia (eds) *Handbook of Second Language Acquisition* (pp. 413–468). San Diego: Academic Press.
Mackey, A., Abbuhl, R. and Gass, S.M. (2012) Interactionist approach. In S.M. Gass and A. Mackey (eds) *The Routledge Handbook of Second Language Acquisition* (pp. 7–23). London: Routledge.
Masuda, K. (2011) Acquiring interactional competence in a study abroad context: Japanese language learners' use of the interactional particle *ne*. *Modern Language Journal* 95, 519–540.
Mondada, L. and Pekarek Doehler, S. (2004) Second language acquisition as situated practice: Task accomplishment in the French second language classroom. *Modern Language Journal* 88, 501–518.
Paige, R.M., Jorstad, H., Siaya, L., Klein, F. and Colby, J. (1999) Culture learning in language education: A review of the literature. In R.M. Paige, D.L. Lange and Y.A. Yeshova (eds) *Culture as the Core: Integrating Culture into the Language Curriculum* (pp. 47–113). Minneapolis: University of Minnesota. Reprinted in Lange, D.L. and Paige, R.M. (eds) (2003) *Culture as the Core: Perspectives on Culture in Second Language*

Learning. A Volume in Research in Second Language Learning, Research in Second Language Learning (pp. 173–236). Greenwich, CT: Information Age Publishing.

Pica, T. (1987) Second-language acquisition, social interaction, and the classroom. *Applied Linguistics* 8, 3–21.

Pica, T. (1988) Interlanguage adjustments as an outcome of NS-NNS negotiated interaction. *Language Learning* 38, 45–73.

Pica, T. (1991) Classroom interaction, negotiation, and comprehension: Redefining relationships. *System* 19, 437–452.

Pica, T. and Doughty, C. (1985) Input and interaction in the communicative language classroom: A comparison of teacher-fronted and group activities. In S. Gass and C. Madden (eds) *Input in Second Language Acquisition* (pp. 115–132). Rowley, MA: Newbury House.

Pica, T., Young, R. and Doughty, C. (1987) The impact of interaction on comprehension. *TESOL Quarterly* 21, 737–758.

Pica, T., Holliday, L., Lewis, N. and Morgenthaler, L. (1989) Comprehensible output as an outcome of linguistic demands on the learner. *Studies in Second Language Acquisition* 11, 63–90.

Pica, T., Holliday, L., Lewis, N., Berducci, D. and Newman, J. (1991) Language learning through interaction. *Studies in Second Language Acquisition* 13, 343–376.

Refatto, A. (2002) Contact Phenomena between Veneto, Italian and English in the Third Generation in Australia. PhD thesis, Monash University.

Regan, V. (1995) The acquisition of sociolinguistic native speech norms: Effects of a year abroad on L2 learners of French. In B. Freed (ed.) *Second Language Acquisition in a Study Abroad Context* (pp. 245–267). Amsterdam: John Benjamins.

Scarino, A. (2010) Assessing intercultural capability in learning languages: A renewed understanding of language, culture, learning and the nature of assessment. *Modern Language Journal* 94, 324–329.

Schmidt, R. (2001) Attention. In P. Robinson (ed.) *Cognition and Second Language Instruction* (pp. 3–32). Cambridge: Cambridge University Press.

Sfard, A. (1998) On two metaphors for learning and the dangers of choosing just one. *Educational Researcher* 27 (2), 4–13.

Swain, M. and Deters, P. (2007) 'New' mainstream SLA theory: Expanded and enriched. *Modern Language Journal* 91 (Supplement s1), 820–836.

Valdés, G., Fishman, J., Chávez, R. and Pérez, W. (2006) *Developing Minority Language Resources: The Case of Spanish in California*. Clevedon: Multilingual Matters.

Vygotsky, L.S. (1986) *Thought and Language*. Cambridge, MA: MIT Press.

Wagner, J. and Gardner, R. (2004) Introduction. In R. Gardner and J. Wagner (eds) *Second Language Conversations* 1–17. London: Continuum.

Young, R. (1999) Sociolinguistic approaches to SLA. *Annual Review of Applied Linguistics* 19, 111–128.

Young, R. (2002) Discourse approaches to oral language assessment. *Annual Review of Applied Linguistics* 22, 243–262.

Young, R. (2007) Language learning and teaching as discursive practice. In Z. Hua, P. Seedhouse, L. Wei and V. Cook (eds) *Language Learning and Teaching as Social Interaction* (pp. 251–271). Basingstoke and New York: Palgrave Macmillan.

Young, R. (2008) *Language and Interaction: An Advanced Resource Book*. London and New York: Routledge.

Young, R. (2009) *Discursive Practice in Language Learning and Teaching*. Malden, MA and Oxford: Wiley-Blackwell.

Young, R. (2011) Interactional competence in language learning, teaching, and testing. In E. Hinkel (ed.) *Handbook of Research in Second Language Teaching and Learning 2* (pp. 426–443). New York: Routledge.

Young, R. and Miller, E. (2004) Learning as changing participation: Discourse roles in ESL writing conferences. *Modern Language Journal* 88, 519–535.

Part 2
Constructing Identity: The Self-Presentation of Older Native Speakers

4 Taking a Stance: Older Native Speakers with Young Language Learners

Marisa Cordella

Introduction

As people interact with each other, they take up stances, positioning themselves discursively through their selection of words and texts taken from the discourse repertoire. The speakers operate within a sociocultural matrix that invests the individual performance with social meaning (Jaffe, 2009a; Bucholtz, 2009; Kiesling, 2009). Stances are thus both linguistic and social acts construed through a set of utterances or sentences that shape the discourse.

Stance theory posits that subjects position themselves in a social sphere through dialogical means, evaluate the linguistic object at one level or another, and engage in a sociocultural dimension. In Du Bois's model, stance is described as

> a public act by a social actor, achieved dialogically through overt communicative means, of simultaneously evaluating objects, positioning subjects (self and others), and aligning with other subjects, with respect to any salient dimension of the sociocultural field. (2007: 163)

While multiple and complex positions can be enacted throughout a conversation, the position adopted by one person in a given instance simultaneously also positions the other; and such 'other stance attribution' – 'the attributing of stances to others' – (Coupland & Coupland, 2009: 229) is maintained if it remains uncontested. In this case the 'interactional calibration' is a 'collaborative and consensual' activity (Jaffe, 2009a: 8), although non-resistance may not necessarily imply consent or compliance (Wodak, 1996, 1999). A health clinic is a good example to illustrate this point. Here doctors assign the role of non-expert to the patients while they take on the role of expert in the medical field (Cordella & Poiani, 2014; Cordella, 2004; Sarangi, 2001). Similarly, in a teacher–student relationship, knowledge is imparted and the differentiation between expert (i.e. teacher) and novice (i.e. student) is made explicit discursively in the selection of content material and forms of talk used in the classroom. The differentiation of knowledge is manifested within the epistemic knowledge frame that is 'culturally grounded, because claims to know are embedded in and index particular regimes of knowledge and authority' (Jaffe, 2009: 7).

The position that participants occupy, assign to others, contest or accept, relates to the performative nature of stances where the interactional work is constructed and negotiated discursively. Stance-taking provides an insight into the speakers' world views and reveals the unfolding relationships, expressed within forms of talk, that may respond, for example, to the prior turns (Jefferson *et al.*, 1977; Sacks *et al.*, 1974), or show traces of textual features constituted with elements from other texts (i.e. intertextuality), or present a combination of other language elements (i.e. interdiscursivity) that provide a framework for the interpretation and meaning of discourse (Jaffe, 2009a: 21). The communicative work is also made feasible within a sociocultural field that allows expressions of alignment, disalignment or realignment to the other's position, thus maintaining, contesting or restoring the dialogical performance between/among individuals while the social order is tested.

Stances that Instruct, Guide and Advise

In this chapter we analyse some of the conversations recorded during our project, using a sociolinguistic approach, to identify how individuals from different generations position themselves and others during their discourse, respond to each other's linguistic needs, and learn from each other. Our interpretation of the data is based on stance theory and applies a social gerontology perspective.

As described in Chapter 3, the topics of conversation in our recorded data were suggested by the schools' language teachers and researchers. However, no guidance was given to the participants as to how they should conduct these conversations or how they should position themselves in the discourse. Stances were identified according to the predominant positioning of either party and recurrent themes arising from the conversations (e.g. first language (L1) and second language (L2) clarification requests, sociocultural information statements, advice statements).

To maximise accuracy in the taxonomy of stances, a second researcher independently confirmed the language strategies used within a stance (Cordella & Huang, 2012, 2014).

In the natural conversations between each pair, three main stances were identified: the stance of *language instructor*, the stance of *sociocultural guide*, and (notably among the older participants) the stance of *ethical-moral adviser*.

Table 4.1 Stance-taking by older L1 speakers and L2 students

Older L1 speaker	direction	L2 student
L2 instructor (Chinese, German or Spanish)	→	L2 learner (Chinese, German or Spanish)
English learner	←	English instructor
sociocultural guide	↔	sociocultural guide
ethical-moral adviser	→ ←----	ethical-moral confirmer

The older participants adopted all three stances (Table 4.1), with that of *language instructor* predominating, as one might expect in a school classroom setting. The stances of *sociocultural guide* and *ethical-moral adviser* were employed by them to a lesser degree, but they represented a unique opportunity for the students to learn about older people's culture, values and beliefs. Although the students tended not to act as moral-ethical advisers themselves, some evidence of alignment with the older participants' moral perspective was evinced in the third year of recordings through verbal agreement or acknowledgement markers, pointing to their ability to be actively engaged with, if not initiators of, this particular stance (see Chapter 5).

The language instructor

Language instructors do more than model usage of a specific language: they also bring with them the cultural experiences embedded in the utterances they make and the strategies they adopt. Thus,

> Intercultural language learning involves developing with learners an understanding of their own language(s) and culture(s) in relation to an additional language and culture. It is a dialogue that allows for reaching a common ground for negotiation to take place, and where variable points of view are recognised, mediated, and accepted.
>
> Learners engaged in intercultural language learning develop a reflective stance towards language and culture, both specifically as instances of first, second, and additional languages and cultures, and generally as understandings of the variable ways in which language and culture exist in the world ... (Liddicoat *et al.*, 2003: 46).

The first two examples below show two pedagogical strategies adopted by the older participants. In Example 4.1, Mrs Fischer[1] encourages Ben to speak German by asking questions about a popular film and a book he has read. This requires comprehension and production skills on the part of Ben, who understands the questions and can easily respond with the yes/no format, but eventually needs assistance to elaborate more fully on the book. The cultural convention in each of Mrs Fischer's questions is the formal 'Sie' form of address.

Example 4.1 'Can you comment on the book?'
German conversation: Mrs Fischer, Ben

105	Mrs Fischer	und haben sie den film gesehen/
		and have you seen the film/
106	Ben	oh ja
		oh yes
107	Mrs Fischer	ja und haben sie das buch schon fertig gelesen/
		yes and have you already finished reading the book/
108	Ben	oh ja
		oh yes
109	Mrs Fischer	ja (..) können sie kommentar (.) machen (.) über das buch ganz kurz/
		yes (..) can you make (.) comments (.) about the book very briefly/
110	Ben	<E like [<xxx>] E>
		<E like [<xxx>] E>
111	Mrs Fischer	[es ist von einem] amerikanischen schriftsteller
		[it is by an] american writer
112	Ben	ja
		yes

Example 4.2 illustrates how the older participant models the target language and elicits a response from the student.

Example 4.2 'Mathematics: you say it once more'
Chinese conversation: Ms Li, Rebecca

117	Ms Li	数学 (..) 你再讲一遍
		shùxué (..) nǐ zài jiǎng yī biàn
		mathematics you say it once more
118	Rebecca	好
		hǎo
		ok
119	Ms Li	数学
		shùxué
		mathematics
120	Rebecca	数学
		shùxué
		mathematics

Many of the strategies utilised by the older participants in their interactions with the students resembled those found in classroom settings (Long, 1996; Lynch, 1990; Saville-Troike, 1988), where attention is given to assisting and encouraging students with the language acquisition process. Asking questions, responding to learners' queries, negotiating meaning, repetitions, clarification, corrections and extension of lexical items were prominent in the display of the *language instructor* stance.

The stance of *language instructor* was also evident among the L2 learners, though to a much smaller extent. This stance emerged when it was necessary to clarify the meaning of an English term that had been mispronounced or misused by the older person, who had switched languages in order to make a point or to try and help the student understand the target language. Limited English proficiency on the part of the older migrant could lead to miscommunication and prompt the student to provide language assistance in turn.

In the example below, Mr Diaz is trying to explain the meaning of 'train to the clouds', a scenic railway that attracts many visitors to Salta Province in Argentina. It connects the Argentine northwest with the Chilean border in the Andes, crossing at 4200 metres above sea level.

Example 4.3 'The train to the clouds'

Spanish conversation: Mr Diaz, Maddy

544	Mr Diaz	tengo::: (.) e::: (.) como es/
		i ha:::ve (.) e::: (.) how to say it/
545		mensajes que me mandan en computadora/ (.) de argentina (.) tengo el
		chain messages sent online/ (.) from argentina (.) i have the
546		tren de las nubes (.) el tren es <E rai E> (.) el::: (.) cómo es el tren/ tren
		train to the clouds (.) train is <E rai E> (.) the::: (.) how do you say train/ train
547		tren tren tren en inglés (.) el:: <E <r> <re> <reiway> E> o <E reilai/ E> (.)
		train train train in english (.) el:: <E <r> <re> <reiway> E> o <E reilai/ E> (.)
548		tren <E reilai/ E> (.) tren [por ejemplo]
		train <E reilai/ E> (.) train [for example]
549	Maddy	(.) ummm [<E train E>]=
		(.) ummm [<E train E>]=

Mr Diaz asks for lexical confirmation in English (lines 546–547). In his attempts to correctly pronounce 'railway', he produces 'reɪwaɪ' (547) and 'reɪɫaɪ' (547, 548) instead, until the student assists. Maddy again takes the *language instructor* stance in lines 552 and 555 by providing the desired lexical item and the right pronunciation for 'clouds' in response to Mr Diaz's rising tone.

550	Mr Diaz	<E yeah E> (.) que va (.) por ejemplo que va a la <E flinder E>
		<E yeah E> (.) one (.) for example that goes to <E flinder E>
551		(.) el tren=
		(.) the train=
552	Maddy	=ah <E train station/ E> (.) aha
		=ah <E train station/ E> (.) aha
553	Mr Diaz	(.) pero va (.) muy alto (.) va entre ver de
		(.) but it travels (.) very high (.) it travels between the
554		<E clodi E> (.) <clu> <E clodi/ E> <E clous/ E> nubes/=
		<E clodi E> (.) <clu> <E clodi/ E> <E clous/ E> clouds/=
555	Maddy	=<E clouds/ E> (.) clouds/

The student's verbal action is a response to the older person's enquiry, but concomitantly contests her 'assigned' position as language learner, creating a dialogical exchange where the negotiation of meaning is central to the interaction and where learning is a collaborative and mutual activity not purely centred on the L2 learner but shared between each party interacting in the event.

The sociocultural guide

This stance opens a window to historical events that have shaped individual lives and outlooks on life. It is through such intercultural and intergenerational exchanges that both parties can become better equipped to understand their own and other groups and to be more open and reflective about language and culture.

As *sociocultural guides*, the older participants deploy memories of the past to recount their life stories drawn from decades of accumulated knowledge and experience. In their reflections they often return to their countries of origin or places they had lived in or visited over the years. These reflections acquire a particular blend of wisdom and introspection as they reformulate the past, while recounting past and present becomes a seamless narrative of giving meaning and shape to their lives.

The older people's reminiscences reveal personal experiences of global events. In the following example (4.4), Mr Diaz explains to the student why many people from Latin America decided to migrate to Australia. Migration was seen as a way of overcoming the limited financial opportunities available on that continent at a time of military oppression, and of providing children with a good education. This social value, which is still held in high regard (OECD/World Bank 2009), was seriously jeopardised in the older person's country of origin, impacting on the future of his whole family.

Example 4.4 'A chance to give them a future'

Spanish conversation: Mr Diaz, Maddy

15	Maddy	/por qué immigraron a australia/
		/why did you migrate to australia/
16	Mr Diaz	emigré a australia por la situación económica (.) e::: (.) el
		i migrated to australia because of the economic situation (.) e::: (.) the
17		gobie::rno/ había (.) problemas de gobierno/ (.) e:::m::: (.) el
		go:::vernment/ had (.) problems of government/ (.) e:::m::: (.) the
18		dinero o la plata/ e::: no alcanzaba para vivir/ (.) tenía (.) tengo dos
		money or cash/ eh::: wasn't enough to live on/ (.) i had (.) have two
19		hijos a la cual (.) no le podía dar un estudio/ (.) no podían ir a un::: (.)
		children whom (.) i couldn't educate/ (.) they couldn't go to a::: (.)
20		y::: (.) ahí a un::: <xxx> a la <E high eschool E> a la:: *esto::* la
		and::: (.) then to a::: <xxx> to the <E high eschool E> to the:: *this::* the
21		secundaria/ como se dice allá/ (.) (H) y::: (.) entonces no había
		secondary/ as it is called there/ (.) (H) and::: (.) then there was no
22		de darle en el futuro <xx> (.) que siguieran estudiando
		chance to give them a future <xx> (.) that they could continue with their studies
23		(.) 'tonce emigré (.) a australia/ (.)
		(.) so i migrated (.) to australia/ (.)

Example 4.5 shows how the older participant, as *sociocultural guide*, can cross space and time: here Nicola is taught about Christmas in Germany when Mrs Fischer was a child. Such stories also summon the *language instructor* to explain special vocabulary and to make sure the student has

58 Part 2: Constructing Identity: The Self-Presentation of Older Native Speakers

Example 4.5 'We sang Christmas carols'
German conversation: Mrs Fischer, Nicola

133	Mrs Fischer	und in früheren zeiten (.) als ich kind war (.) da hatte jeder KERZEN (.) am weihnachstbaum (..)
		and in earlier times (.) when i was a child (.) everyone had CANDLES (.) on the christmas tree (..)
134	Nicola	<E CULTURES E>/
		<E CULTURES E>/
135	Mrs Fischer	<E CANDLES E>/
		<E CANDLES E>/
136	Nicola	oh
		oh
137	Mrs Fischer	ja (..) u:nd (..) auch (.) LAMETTA (.) das sind so silber so aus folie/ <E like foil strips you know long strips and you hang them over E>=
		yes (..) a:nd (..) also (.) LAMETTA (.) they're silver made from foil/ <E like foil strips you know long strips and you hang them over E>=
138	Nicola	=a:h ok=
		=a:h ok=
139	Mrs Fischer	=<E the branches E> (.) und die kerzen und das lametta (.) ahm ja sehen sehr hübsch aus ja (.) zusammen ja ahm (..) es gibt eine ganz besondere atmosphäre (.) ja/ <E you can understand that/ and (.) that was when I was a child E> ahm (..) und bei uns wurde immer (.) die weihnachtsgeschichte vorgelesen aus der bibel/ (..) u:nd wir haben weihnachtslieder gesungen
		=<E the branches E> (.) and the candles and the lametta (.) ahm yes look very pretty yes (.) together yes ahm (..) it makes a very special atmosphere (.) yes/ <E you can understand that/ and (.) that was when I was a child E> ahm (..) and at our house always (.) the christmas story was read to us from the bible/ (..) a:nd we sang christmas carols

understood. Mrs Fischer also tries to convey the special atmosphere of the German Christmas celebrations, leaving the impression that this was an enjoyable experience for her.

For the older participants, sharing their life stories can be a rewarding experience, particularly if they are able to recount them in their native language. But acquiring first-hand knowledge of the lives and interests of young students can be an enriching experience too, as many older people have had limited contact with younger generations outside their own families. In the following extract (Example 4.6), Mr Wu learns about work experience practices of Australian school students. His responses in lines 947 and 950 suggest that this was new and perhaps surprising information.

Example 4.6 'Can you work now?'

Chinese conversation: Mr Wu, Shane

945	Mr Wu	你今年十六岁了可以做工吗
		you are 16 years old this year can you work
946	Shane	可以十:::五岁就可以开始做工
		i can i could start working when I was fif:::teen
947	Mr Wu	哦
		oh
948	Shane	因为有些人在我在麦当劳他们在好像9年级他们都可以去做工但是大部分都
		because some working at mcdonald's are in year 9 but most of them are
949		是10年级
		year 10
950	Mr Wu	哦哦
		oh oh

The ethical-moral adviser

The stance of *ethical-moral adviser* arises from a desire to pass on advice and guidance to others that will better equip them as they make decisions about their lives. One person's wisdom attained over the years can be a *resource* for others, helping to make their lives easier. In our study, ethical-moral positioning was a feature of the L1 speakers, who were able to draw on decades of life experience in their conversations with the students. Further, the older participants may have perceived these encounters as an opportunity to mould young people outside their family domain, and indeed, may have considered it their duty to do so. The students presented as a fresh audience for the older people, whose families may well have heard the proffered advice many times before. This stance can be an indicator of the quality of the relationship that has developed between the pair: that is, it suggests that the older person cares about the student's future.

Mrs Wang's moral guidance in Example 4.7 centres on the value of studying literature in the wider context of gaining a good education.

The student voices strong support for her stance on the subject and is rewarded with approval for having expressed his alignment in correct Chinese (line 130).

Example 4.7 'Studying literature enriches your ideas'

Chinese conversation: Ms Wang, Dario

123	Ms Wang	所以呢 (.) 你::: 你说你小就喜欢看书
		so (.) you::: you said since you were little you liked to read
124		这样呢 (.) 你就能 (.) 有可能把文学学好 ehm 是吧/=
		in this way (.) you can (.) have the possibility of studying literature well ehm right/=
125	Dario	=是
		=right
126	Ms Wang	这 (.) 文学呢 (.) 你就一 (.) 就要依靠你平常多看书
		the (.) about literature (.) you must (.) rely on reading lots of books as part of your normal life
127		是吧 (.) [书看得多] (.) 那么你那个思想呢 (.) 比较丰富
		right (.) [if you read a lot of books] (.) then your ideas (.) will be richer
128	Dario	[对对对]
		[yes yes yes]
129	Ms Wang	那么你那个文学呢 (.) 就能学[好]
		then literature (.) you can learn [very well]
130	Dario	[mm] 你说的对
		[mm] what you said is right
131	Ms Wang	很好 (.) 你说的很好
		very well (.) you said it very well
132	Dario	谢谢
		thank you

In Example 4.8, Mr Günther is trying to determine Adam's position on smoking and drug-taking before revealing his own stance that drugs do not fit with a healthy lifestyle. The student denies any involvement with drugs, and then aligns with the older participant's stance by agreeing with the directive not to engage in such activities.

Example 4.8 'Never take drugs'

German conversation: Mr Günther, Adam

241	Mr Günther	(..) rauchst du/ (.) zigarette/
		(..) do you smoke/ (.) cigarette/
242	Adam	*wie bitte/*
		pardon/

Example 4.8 Continued

243	Mr Günther	RAUCHST du/
		do you SMOKE/
244	Adam	nein/
		no/
245	Mr Günther	nein/
		no/
246	Adam	*nein*
		no
247	Mr Günther	und auch keine DROGen (..) <E try oeh (.) you you do not try any drugs or something E>
		and also no DRUGs (..) <E try oeh (.) you you do not try any drugs or something E>
248	Adam	*mm: (.) [nein]*
		mm: (.) [no]
249	Mr Günther	<E [no] (.) never do this (.) yeah/ E>
250	Adam	*yeah*

In contrast to our earlier findings (Cordella & Huang, 2012, 2014), the overall dataset contained only a few instances where the students aligned with the ethical-moral stance of the older people, either through silence or verbal agreement. On the other hand, there were no instances in our data of the student challenging, negating or diverging from the older person's position.

Discussion of the Findings

All of the L1 speakers strongly favoured the stance of *language instructor* when interacting with the students. This finding accords with the data analysed during the first two years of recordings (Cordella & Huang, 2012, 2014). The older participants clearly saw themselves as instructors in the target language and as providing a useful service to the school community. The classroom setting was conducive to this self-attributed role, providing an educational framework for the questions, clarifications, explanations and assistance with language and grammatical forms sought by the student and/or offered by the older person in the exchange. The same strategies for teaching the language were used by all three language groups, but with some specific differences which are discussed in Chapter 5.

As *sociocultural guides*, the older participants utilised a number of themes, allowing individual self-reflection to be expressed at its fullest, and thereby revealing clear differences between the language groups as well. Chinese and German older participants covered a variety of topics – from homeland culture to family pets – whereas the Spanish older participants tended to focus on the political turmoil and financial problems that led to their migration to Australia (e.g. Example 4.4 above). In the Chinese data, the talk focused on different aspects of China – sightseeing, school management and education, social issues, the economy, food and drink, history, culture and major events, and more generally, sport, health and well-being. The German older participants compared aspects of life in Germany and Australia – language learning, sociocultural traits, home life and family core values – and raised topics such as the re-unification of Germany and travel experiences within and outside Australia. The differences in the themes chosen by the migrants may be explained in terms of their life experience, including education level, socio-economic status, and reasons for leaving their homeland.

The stance of *ethical-moral adviser* highlights more specifically the social and cultural expectations of a given group as well as the particular personal circumstances of individuals that have shaped their outlook on life. Instilling in the students the value of education was more prominent among the Chinese and Spanish older participants than it was for the German cohort, for whom access to education was perhaps taken for granted, political upheavals in that part of the world notwithstanding. However, this latter group did highlight the importance of learning a language. Advice on family relationships and maintaining respect for one's elders featured in the Spanish and Chinese conversations but was only infrequently provided by the Germans.

It is a cultural norm in Australia (and elsewhere) for older people to pass on the wisdom of their life experience to the next generations in the form of advice and guidance. As we saw in Chapter 2, however, intergenerational relations in a contemporary multicultural society are sometimes strained. It is worth observing that the stance of *ethical-moral adviser* was not challenged by the students in our study, perhaps because they did not know their older partner well enough and were constrained by politeness.

Pedagogical and Personal Benefits

Our findings indicate that the stances adopted during the conversations were beneficial for both groups of participants in all three spheres: linguistic, social and affective. The *language instructor* supported the student's efforts to learn the language in an informal and natural manner, while conversing in their native tongue with a fresh audience gave the older participants a sense of purpose as well as the emotional satisfaction of observing young people interested in learning their language. As *sociocultural guides* the older participants increased the students' awareness of different cultures and social practices, and as *moral-ethical advisers* used examples from their own experiences to offer valuable life lessons.

The students responded to the stances of their conversational partners by correcting or improving their use of the target language as directed, by reciprocating with language instruction in English, by sharing sociocultural information about youth, or by listening to the guidance offered by the older people. As language students who had shown an interest in participating in such a project, they demonstrated their ability to be ambassadors for youth culture. In the first instance, they benefited scholastically from exposure to the target language, but they also acquired skills in conversation management (see Chapter 10), and at a deeper level the stances adopted by them in return signalled engagement with the other. Through dynamic positioning in interactive and dialogical verbal exchanges, the native speakers and students were able to construct a positive and enriching learning experience for each other.

Beyond the narrow focus of language learning, the programme has been shown to assist with what Biggs and Lowenstein (2011) call 'generational intelligence' – that is, an awareness by different age groups of each other's needs:

> The surrounding environment, the discourses that shape people's understanding of themselves and others in social space, are key to the relative capacity to place oneself in the position of the age-other and thereby, understand their thoughts, feelings and actions. (2011: 42)

There is also a recognised need among social thinkers 'to strengthen solidarity between generations and intergenerational partnerships, keeping in mind the particular needs of both older and younger ones, and encourage mutually responsive relationships between generations' (United Nations Second World Assembly on Ageing, Madrid, 2002, quoted in Biggs & Lowenstein, 2011: 3). Exchanges such as those described in this chapter can help to validate, alter or refute preconceived or stereotypical ideas about each generation, as described by Jaffe (2009a: 14):

> patterns in the cumulative results of speaker stancetaking shape both what is understood to be indexed by particular linguistic forms or practices and, potentially, the language ideologies that underpin how people look at the connections between language forms and practices and the social world.

In the next chapter we look further at these stances adopted by the older participants, and examine what they reveal about them as they discuss their identity as immigrants in contemporary Australian society.

Note

(1) All participants' names have been changed.

References

Biggs, S. and Lowenstein, A. (2011) *Generational Intelligence: A Critical Approach to Age Relations*. London: Routledge.

Bucholtz, M. (2009) From stance to style: Pender, interaction, and indexicality in Mexican immigrant youth slang. In A. Jaffe (ed.) *Stance: Sociolinguistic Perspectives* (pp. 146–170). Oxford: Oxford University Press.

Cordella, M. (2004) *The Dynamic Consultation: A Discourse Analytical Study of Doctor–Patient Communication*. Amsterdam: John Benjamins.

Cordella, M. and Huang, H. (2012) Adultos mayores inmigrantes y estudiantes de ELE: Los roles de participación que surgen en conversaciones intergeneracionales e interculturales. *Signo y Seña* [Argentina] 22, 13–33.

Cordella, M. and Huang, H. (2014) L1 and L2 Chinese, German and Spanish speakers in action: Stancetaking in intergenerational and intercultural encounters. In J. Hajek and Y. Slaughter (eds) *Challenging the Monolingual Mindset* (pp. 97–112). Bristol: Multilingual Matters.

Cordella, M. and Poiani, A. (2014) *Behavioural Oncology: Psychological, Communicative and Social Dimensions*. New York: Springer.

Coupland, J. and Coupland, N. (2009) Attributing stance in discourses of body shape and weight loss. In A. Jaffe (ed.) *Stance* (pp. 227–250).

Du Bois, J.W. (2007) The stance triangle. In R. Englebretson (ed.) *Stancetaking in Discourse: Subjectivity, Evaluation, Interaction* (pp. 139–182). Amsterdam: John Benjamins.

Feldman, S., Radermacher, H. and Petersen, A. (2012) The vicissitudes of 'healthy ageing': The experiences of older migrant men in a rural Australian community. In A. Kampf, B. Marshall and A. Petersen (eds) *Aging Men: Masculinities and Modern Medicine* (pp. 84–104). London: Routledge.

Jaffe, A. (2009a) Introduction. In A. Jaffe (ed.) *Stance: Sociolinguistic Perspectives* (pp. 3–28). Oxford: Oxford University Press.

Jaffe, A. (2009b) Stance in a Corsican school: Institutional and ideological orders and the production of bilingual subjects. In A. Jaffe (ed.) *Stance: Sociolinguistic Perspectives* (pp. 119–145). Oxford: Oxford University Press.

Jefferson, G., Sacks, H. and Schegloff, E. (1977) *Preliminary Notes on the Sequential Organization of Laughter*. Cambridge: Department of Linguistics, University of Cambridge.

Kiesling, S.F. (2009) Style as stance: Stance as the explanation for patterns of sociolinguistic variation. In A. Jaffe (ed.) *Stance: Sociolinguistic Perspectives* (pp. 171–194). Oxford: Oxford University Press.

Liddicoat, A.J., Papademetre, L., Scarino, A. and Kohler, M. (2003) *Report on Intercultural Language Learning*. Canberra: Department of Education, Science and Training.

Long, M.H. (1996) The role of the linguistic environment in second language acquisition. In W.C. Ritchie and T.K. Bhatia (eds) *Handbook of Second Language Acquisition* (pp. 413–468). New York: Academic Press.

Lynch, T. (1990) Researching teachers: Behaviour and belief. In C. Brumfit and R. Mitchell (eds) *Research in the Language Classroom* (pp. 117–143). London: Modern English Publications.

OECD/World Bank (2009) *Tertiary Education in Chile*. Reviews of National Policies for Education, Paris, OECD/World Bank.

Sacks, H., Schegloff, E. and Jefferson, G. (1974) A simplest systematics for the organization of turn-taking for conversation. *Language* 50, 696–735.

Sarangi, S. (2001) Editorial. On demarcating the space between 'lay expertise' and 'expert laity'. *Text: An Interdisciplinary Journal for the Study of Discourse* 21 (1/2), 3–11.

Saville-Troike, M. (1988) Private speech: Evidence for second language learning strategies during the 'silent' period. *Journal of Child Language* 15, 567–590.

WHO [World Health Organization] (2007) *Global Age-friendly Cities: A Guide*. Geneva, World Health Organization. See http://www.who.int/ageing/publications/age_friendly_cities_guide/en/.

Wodak, R. (1996) *Disorders of Discourse*. London: Longman.

Wodak, R. (1999) Discourse and racism: European perspectives. *Annual Review of Anthropology* 28, 175–199.

5 The Migration Experience and the Ethos of Self

Brigitte Lambert and Marisa Cordella

Introduction

Human migration can be understood as both *geographical relocation* (to a new *physical* environment) and *identity negotiation* (within a new *cultural* environment); together these constitute the *migration experience* (Kerswill, 2006). This experience has been extensively documented in various disciplines. Anthropological perspectives have noted different experiences based on gender (Kofman, 2000; Espin, 1997), language and identity adjustments, and issues such as unemployment (Miller, 2007; Junankar & Mahuteau, 2005). Sociological studies have examined child and adult migrants (e.g. Hofstetter, 2001), while a European study has probed issues for young migrants and the retirement and social policies for older people (Warnes & Williams, 2006). Migration is recognised as a process of adjustment, acclimatisation, appropriation, assimilation or incorporation that is influenced by a range of social, economic and psychological factors. Personal narratives detail the push-and-pull factors behind the migration decision, the subsequent associations with the culture of origin, and the losses and gains that have marked resettlement.

In the field of sociolinguistics there have been studies on bilingualism, language maintenance and identity (e.g. Piller & Takahashi, 2011; Lambert, 2008; Norton, 2000; Clyne, 1991), and in long-standing bilingualism research, older migrants are acknowledged for their role in language maintenance (Lambert, 2008; Clyne, 2005; Clyne, 1991). Although our study concentrates on presentation of personal identity rather than any specific challenges facing immigrants, the above research orientations do link to the themes our participants discussed with the students.

In this chapter we examine the multi-layered and complex positioning (stance-taking) of older immigrants during their interactions with young language learners, and quantify the linguistic stance acts which index migration and identity in past and present social contexts. The social identity that the older people construct for themselves in a specific social setting is captured in the notion of the *ethos of self*, defined as 'the projection of knowledge and moral authority derived from one's life history' (Johnstone, 2009: 34) which informs the manner of personal presentation of an individual to an audience. Our research aims to offer a deeper and broader understanding of what the 'migration experience' and identity adjustment entail.

Accordingly, the following specific research questions expand on the previous chapter:

(1) How do older participants from German- and Spanish-speaking backgrounds choose to portray themselves?
(2) How does an ethos of self reveal commonalities and differences in the two language groups?

Older migrants want to share their life experiences with others for many reasons. As discussed in the previous chapters, some feel a duty to educate and inform the younger generation so that their specific knowledge of events and personal transformation is not lost. Others have a need to pass on their acquired wisdom to help improve the lives of family members, turning past experiences into a learning opportunity. Others may just enjoy the opportunity to talk about their lives in a social setting. Whatever the motivation, such individuals have abundant knowledge that can be shared with the wider community.

Identity and the Self

Historical (Markus & Sims, 1993) and sociolinguistic (Piller & Takahashi, 2011; Schüpbach, 2009) research on migration using narrative or ethnographic approaches has allowed for personal reflection on issues of identity, language, change and belonging for members of immigrant communities. Often the concept of multiple identities is linked to language learning (Norton, 2000), but can also be applied to other social and psychological experiences across time and space.

A background of changing social environments contributes to the formation of multiple identities which are internalised and presented to the world overtly and covertly, depending on the context (Abes *et al.*, 2007; Jones & McEwen, 2000). The purpose of the interaction and activity type are pragmatically relevant here (Ehlich & Rehbein, 1986), as are the social relationships enacted in the event, the opportunities offered by generational encounters (Coupland & Coupland, 2009; Giles, 1991) and the dialogical participation in the verbal exchange (Jaffe, 2009). Narrative, for young and old alike, is an important way of integrating or coping with the diverse facets of identity (Sears, 2011; Meinhof & Galasiński, 2005). Many of the identities emerging in the interaction, such as 'immigrant', invest older people with authority and expertise in their L1 language proficiency and in the topics they choose to discuss.

We draw on the notion of *positionality* to interpret the stance work of our immigrant participants, following Jaffe (2009: 3), who defines stance-taking as 'taking up a position with respect to the form and content of one's utterance'. In our study, the terms 'stance-taking' and 'positioning' are used as synonyms. This approach focuses on the identities emerging from the immigrants' stance-taking acts in conversation with the students, those 'brought-along' (Williams, 2008: 39) from life experience across many decades and those developed for the fulfilment of the immediate conversational task. As mentioned above, to explain this phenomenon more fully we have turned to the ethos of self as posited in Johnstone (2009), which foregrounds the speakers' authority, expertise and credibility on the topics being discussed. In particular, Johnstone's study shows how the research subject's linguistic output as a politician can be interpreted as persuasive tactics designed to underscore personal credibility and authority, and notes that a stance style indexes a 'personal identity, a particular lingual biography' (2009: 46). The words and their manner of usage in combination thus create an individual and recognisable identity through an interactional stance and style which impact on the listener in positive, negative or neutral ways. While the notion of credibility has some relevance to our research, we are more concerned with the overall image of themselves the immigrants present during biographical accounts and how this contributes to an understanding of self within an intercultural learning setting. With this conceptualisation, we place the immigrants at the centre of the conversation as they talk about their life experiences, knowledge and feelings.

Methodology

Fifty-one conversations between older migrants and secondary students (32 in German and 19 in Spanish) contributed approximately 45 hours of the recorded data which informs this chapter.

Most of the German immigrants came to Australia by ship during the migration boom in the 1950s and 1960s, having lived in Europe during the Second World War. A few arrived after 1980. Many of the Germans had experienced social hardship as well as forced or unforced relocations in Germany before deciding to migrate to Australia. As a group they were generally well-educated and financially secure, travelling regularly within Australia, back to Germany and elsewhere. All of them were proficient bilinguals, fluent in Standard German and English, and several were multilingual, including German dialects.

Latin American immigrants had generally found political or financial refuge in Australia. In the 1970s they left Argentina, Chile or Peru, in the 1980s El Salvador, and, in the five years prior to the study, Colombia, searching for a country that could provide a stable and better future for their children and themselves. Their education levels varied: some had not completed secondary schooling while others had attained a technical diploma. Those who found jobs in Australia worked mainly in factories, using English for instrumental purposes but lacking the proficiency in the language to aspire to a professional career. Their opportunities to travel in Australia and overseas in older age had been limited and were mostly restricted to the occasional special offers of the market.

Despite these differences in background, however, the German and Latin American immigrants had several characteristics in common:

- They had left one cultural community and become part of a new one, able to pass their knowledge of this experience onto the younger generation.
- As individuals, they complied with the main conversational task requirement of the project, being native speakers of the target language. As members of that language group, they were also able to act as language instructors, and this role was complemented significantly by the roles of sociocultural guide and moral-ethical adviser (see Chapter 4).
- Their stories were personal, but also reflections on historical events and times.
- Their experiences were unique, but also a part of the broader migration movement.
- Age lent the older participants experience, which the students lacked.
- They demonstrated authority and spoke as experts on their language and life, as opposed to the students, who were novices (Cheng, 2010; Sarangi, 2001).

The conversations were either structured around a set of questions provided by language teachers or developed naturally within a prescribed theme. This allowed all participants an opportunity to discuss the same topics in the course of the school year and for most recorded conversations to be based on a common topic across language groups, although the conversations do not necessarily reflect identical content. Thus we make no claims or generalisations about topic preferences for German and Spanish native speakers. The older participants were allowed to adopt any stance they wished, or thought was appropriate or expected of them, on the topics of age, migration, leisure activities, health and so on.

Analytical Framework

Du Bois's (2007) stance triangle initially facilitated an overview of the types of grammatical stance work undertaken by the immigrants in the two languages. However, in order to better accommodate differences in German and Spanish, we devised five non-grammatical categories to code the recorded data provided by the native speakers by noting the predominant interest area of their talk as revealed by the linguistic tokens and expressions they used. This method highlighted references to self, the world, spatial and temporal contexts, comparisons and affect. In our classification, no item was taken as the exclusive expression of a particular stance or position, but was allocated to a relevant category each time it appeared. The older participants did not necessarily use the same linguistic items within these categories even if they came from the same language group, e.g. 'in meiner Kindheit' (*in my childhood*) and 'ich als Kind' (*I as a child*). We therefore suggest that non-grammatical categorisation can be more easily transferred to analyse datasets from different languages.

Our data coding covered linguistic tokens, utterances and routines whose social meanings were mapped to the five stances described below.

1. Expert stance

The immigrants' expert stance was determined from their talk about themselves, covering what they have done and achieved and know about life and language. We noted self-reference pronouns, self-assigned social identity labels and the language practice strategies that were applied to the students, as shown in Table 5.1.

Self-references included singular, plural, reflexive and possessive pronouns and descriptive identity markers, and were collapsed into one group. These linguistic tokens were accompanied by verb constructions (e.g. 'ich habe ... gespielt', *I have ... played*) which described mental or observable lived actions (Rehbein, 1977) and experiences that were and

Table 5.1 Examples of linguistic tokens used for self-referencing

Linguistic tokens	Self-reference	Social identity	Language instructor
German	ich, mich, mir, mein, wir, uns, unser *I, me, me-reflexive, mine, we, us, our*	als Sechzehnjähriger *as a 16-year-old*	Asking questions, etc.
Spanish	yo mío/a, reflexivo (me lo dijo), nosotros, nuestro *I, mine, mine-reflexive (he told me), verb ending (1st person singular), we, reflexive (he told us), verb ending (1st person plural)*	cuando era joven, emigrante *when I was younger, a migrant*	Correcting students, etc.

continue to be part of their world, both as individuals and group members. The immigrants' social identity at different life stages and in various social environments was identified by nominal labels and synonyms, which also indexed group membership. Evidence of the language instructor, the fundamental expert role of immigrant participants in the study, was coded according to verbal strategies identified by Cordella and Huang (2012, 2014) and Cordella (see Chapter 4), such as corrections of student utterances, explanations of vocabulary and use of English to facilitate comprehension.

2. Contextual stance

We applied the past, present and future markers coded for temporal position to personal historical events such as migration, daily activities and future plans. *Here* and *there* in the spatial category were taken to be synonymous with Australia and elsewhere in the immigrants' recollections. The appearance and frequency of these linguistic items provided links to the importance and relevance of events and places in their lives.

Temporal and spatial contexts will also be addressed in no. 4. *Comparative Stance* below (see Table 5.2).

Table 5.2 Examples of linguistic tokens used to indicate time and space

Linguistic tokens	Temporal	Spatial
German	damals, 1954, im Krieg, jetzt, heute, lange Zeit her, nächstes Jahr	in Deutschland, in Australien, hier, da, in China, nach dem Westen
	then, 1954, during the war, now, today, a long time ago, next year	*in Germany, in Australia, here, there, in China, to the West*
Spanish	antes, anteriormente, en el pasado, cuando + imperfecto o pretérito, atrás, en el futuro	en + lugar, aquí, acá allí/ahí, allá
	before, previously, in the past, when + imperfect or preterit, ago, in the future	*in + place, here nearby, there less near, there farther*

3. Epistemic stance

Life experience provided the immigrants with information and beliefs that, in turn, influenced the type of advice they gave to the students. Our analysis accounted for three aspects of an epistemic stance, as shown in Table 5.3.

World references were categorised according to impersonal pronouns and stative verbs which indexed general knowledge deemed to be factual by the immigrants. Their own belief actions were coded for epistemic verbs;

Table 5.3 Examples of linguistic tokens used to express opinions

Linguistic tokens	World reference	Belief actions	Advice markers
German	es ist, wie gesagt, man *it is, as said, one*	glaube, meine, denke, finde *believe, mean, think, find*	kann, muss, wenn *can, must, if*
Spanish	uno, todo el mundo, ellos *one, everybody, they*	creer, pensar, saber/conocer *believe, think, know*	tiene que, debe que, hay que *have to, must, there is a need to*

and verbs plus negation, indicating uncertainty or a lack of knowledge, were counted as a single item. Stronger beliefs expressed as advice were coded for modals and hypothetical markers which indexed the ability or necessity of an action to achieve preferred outcomes.

4. Comparative stance

Our analysis accounted for the immigrants' evaluation of changes from the past to the present and differences between people and places. Our coding targeted temporal and spatial pairs; however, sometimes time and place overlapped (see Table 5.4).

The comparison of spatial differences was particularly salient when evaluating the migration experience.

Table 5.4 Examples of linguistic tokens used to make comparisons

Linguistic tokens	Temporal changes	Spatial differences
German	damals, jetzt *then, now*	da ist es anders als in Australien/China/Melbourne *it is different there than in Australia/China/Melbourne*
Spanish	antes, ahora *before, now*	es diferente allá/allí/en mi país *it is different there/in my country*

5. Affective stance

The affective stance indexed the migrants' feelings about their life experiences, their preferences and satisfaction with decisions made, and their orientation towards the students' interests. The coded linguistic tokens included nouns, adjectives, verbs and adverbs that showed both positive and negative evaluations (see Table 5.5).

Table 5.5 Examples of linguistic tokens used to express feelings

Linguistic tokens	Verbs, adjectives, expressions
German	mag nicht, fantastisch, das ist Schade
	don't like, fantastic, that's a pity
Spanish	lindo, hermoso, bien, bueno, pena, lástima
	lovely, beautiful, okay, good, shame, pity

We used a data-driven approach to categorise the linguistic items of the dataset, and these were checked regularly with other researchers to maximise accuracy and consistency during this process. The chosen categories were also evaluated by an independent researcher.

Discussion of the Findings

How do older participants from German- and Spanish-speaking backgrounds choose to portray themselves?

Figures 5.1 and 5.2 quantify the migrants' stance-taking as demonstrated in their conversations with the students. All of the five main stances (expert, contextual, epistemic, comparative and affective) were adopted and interacted with each other simultaneously throughout the conversations as follows:

Among the Germans, the expert stance emerged as the most prominent in all conversations, ranging from 50+% to 80+% of all stances in the recorded interactions. This was accompanied most often by epistemic positioning, but with a wide range of between approximately 5% and 40%.

In the conversations of the Latin American immigrants, the expert stance fluctuated between 15% and 70%, and was strongly supported by the epistemic stance, which varied from approximately 10% to 60%.

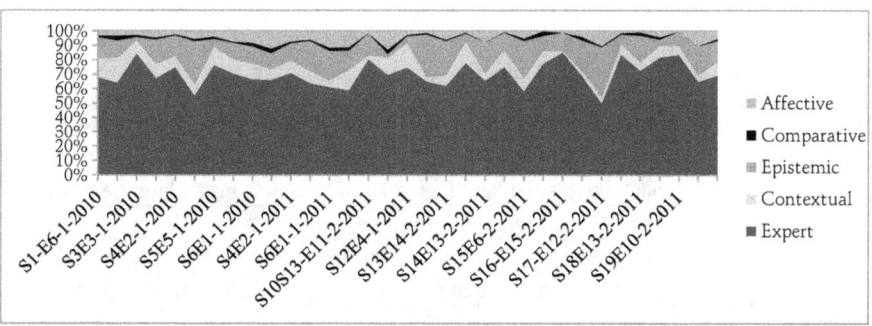

Figure 5.1 Stances of German-speaking immigrants

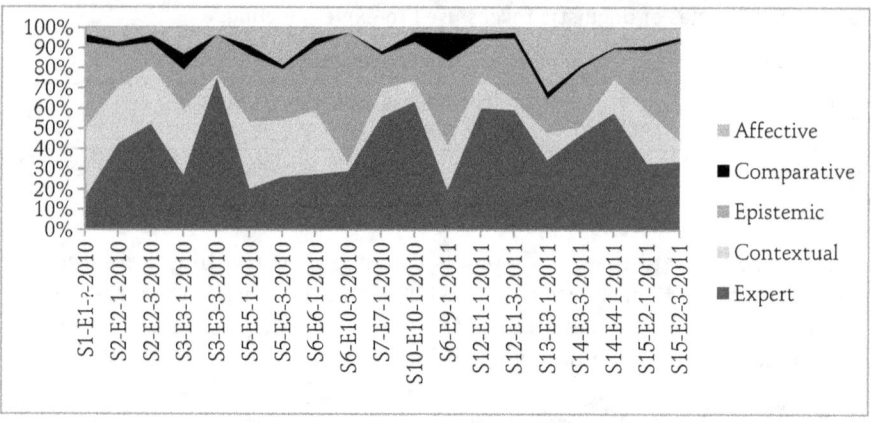

Figure 5.2 Stances of Spanish-speaking immigrants

The two graphs show that the expert stance was adopted by all the German- and Spanish-speaking participants but predominated in the German conversations, whereas the contextual, epistemic and affective stances were in greater evidence in the Spanish. The comparative stance generally featured least for both groups. However, we make the point that while all the stances emerged in both language groups, their frequency varied considerably in the individual conversations between each of the pairs of older participants and students, depending on such factors as language proficiency, attitudes towards the conversational task and perhaps even their feelings about each other (see Chapter 7).

We next examined how the immigrants chose stances that presented specific images of themselves. These emerged directly from the topic under discussion and tended to occur in various combinations, but also to accumulate in the course of the conversation. Indeed, certain images were emphasised or invoked more frequently and may have left thereby a vivid impression on the student.

Example 5.1 'I helped many young Australians'
German conversation: Mr Schmidt, Jane*

1	Mr Schmidt	ja ja dann äh (.) in meiner \<E experience E\> ich hab äh wenn ich
		yes yes then ah (.) in my \<E experience E\> i did ah when i
2		nach australien kam (.) ich hab äh damals einen klub geleitet (..)
		came to australia (.) i managed a club at that time (..)
3		und ich hab viele junge australier (.) und australierinnen (..) äh
		and i have many young australian men (.) and women (..) ah
4		vermittelt
		linked up

* All participants' names have been changed.

The expert stance here clearly draws on personal experience, which is often emphasised when talking with the student. In Example 5.1, the temporal expression *when I came to Australia* establishes a contextual position to complement the underlying authority of self-references and actions – *I managed, I helped*. This fosters an appreciation of the migration experience and presents a capable individual who enjoys being of assistance.

Example 5.2 'I had a beautiful job in Chile'
Spanish conversation: Mrs Morales, Christopher

1	Mrs Morales	=muchos años que no trabajo/ (.) yo tuve:::m (.) un trabajo muy
		=*i haven't been working for a while/ (.) i had::: (.) a job very*
2		lindo en chile/
		beautiful in chile/

Reference to a *beautiful* job in Chile in Example 5.2 invokes contextual, comparative and affective positioning alongside the expert position in the aftermath of migration to Australia, foregrounding Mrs Morales' social identity as a worker who is currently unemployed (see Miller, 2007).

Example 5.3 'I've still got my "ute"'
German conversation: Mr Weber, John

1	Mr Weber	ich hab kein deutsches auto ich hab ein australisches auto [a:]
		i don't have a german car i have an australian car [a:]
2	John	[a] holden oder ford
		[a] holden or a ford
3	Mr Weber	einen rodeo
		a rodeo
4	John	ah rodeo=
		ah rodeo=
5	Mr Weber	=aber ein ich war früher ein (.) ich hab häuser gebaut (.) ein bauherr
		=*but a before i was a (.) i built houses (.) a builder*
6		<E i was a builder E>\=
		<E i was a builder E>\=
7	John	=ah ok
		=ah ok
8	Mr Weber	so ich hab immer noch mein <E ute E> nicht ganz neu aber fast neu so
		so i've still got my <E ute E> not completely new but almost new so
9	John	yep @@ @@
		yep @@ @@

The self-references detailing ownership of an iconic Australian vehicle (a utility, or pick-up truck), combined with the colloquialism *ute* in

Example 5.3, present the image of an Australian tradesman with whom the student can readily identify, as indicated by the response *yep* and laughter. Mr Weber's expert stance suggests that immigrants can establish a secure existence in their new country and perhaps call it 'home'.

Example 5.4 'Teach me about the music young people listen to today'
Spanish conversation: Mrs Valdez, Alice

1	Mrs Valdez	(..) y esa cuál es esa/ ay me tienes que enseñar esa porque es música
		(..) and which one is that one/ oh you need to teach me about the music
2		de gente joven y yo estoy VIEJA
		young people listen to today i i am OLD

In Example 5.4 Mrs Valdez highlights the age difference between them, a generational gap that is indexed further by an increase in volume of the word *old* when referring to herself and young people's music of today. The older participant in effect adopts a novice stance on what she does not know. Directives like *teach me* indicate a willingness to engage with youth culture and to learn from her student partner.

Example 5.5 'You can still try'
German conversation: Mrs Fischer, Christopher

1	Mrs Fischer	versuchen sie einen ganzen satz (.) zu sagen\ (..) <E a whole sentence E>
		try to say (.) a whole sentence (..) <E a whole sentence E>
2		öhm (..) was finden sie besonders schön wenn sie zusammen sind
		um (..) what do you think is especially nice when they are together
3	Christopher	ahm:: <E *don't know how to say it* (.) sorry i'm very bad at speaking E>
		ahm:: <E *don't know how to say it* (.) sorry i'm very bad at speaking E>
4	Mrs Fischer	<E yes: (..) öhm: (..) but don't make it an excuse\ E>
		<E yes: (..) öhm: (..) but don't make it an excuse\ E>

In Example 5.5 Mrs Fischer encourages Christopher to answer a question about activities that old and young people can do together. A formal distance between them is maintained by the use of 'Sie'. This linguistic convention seemingly places both parties on an equal social footing, but also foregrounds the older person's positioning as an expert on German who knows the appropriate form of address and who facilitates the student's practice of this as part of the language. Mrs Fischer brooks no excuse for at least not trying, and therefore appears as a stricter type of language instructor. We do not know the effect of this approach on the student's language learning, but learners are regularly confronted with diverse teaching styles, and their achievements may not always be directly correlated with the teaching style or method (Charkins et al., 1985).

Example 5.6 'There are challenges in life: I have to begin again now'
German conversation: Mr Schmidt, Jane

1	Mr Schmidt	meine partnerin die starb am sonntag morgen/ und da war ich nicht (.)
		my partner she died on sunday morning/ and then i wasn't (.)
2		zufrieden und ich hab- mich nicht WOHL gefühlt nachher auf-n Montag
		settled and i didn't feel WELL afterwards on the monday
3	Jane	ja=
		yes=
4	Mr Schmidt	=<dae:::m mich> (.) hierhin zu kommen und mich zu unterhalten über bestimmte dinge nich-/ ich muß jetzt wieder anfangen
		=<so:::for me> (.) to come here and to talk about certain things you know/ i have to start again now

Example 5.6 illustrates the contextual and affective positioning of the German man as he discusses the recent death of his partner, and demonstrates to the student that existence in older age is not static. He has experienced a significant change, and actions must be taken to continue living. We note that Mr Schmidt explains that he did not feel like talking to the student the previous week, possibly because he would not have been able to fulfil the language teaching task.

Example 5.7 'Life was hard thirty years ago'
Spanish conversation: Mrs Fernandez, Daniel

1	Mrs Fernandez	=y era muy este:: muy del- muy:: (.) muy peligroso vivir en
		=and it was this:: very very very:: (.) very dangerous to live in
2		argentina en esa época (.) *bueno* (.) nos vinimos (.) -tamos acá de
		argentina at that time (.) *well* (.) we migrated (.) we've been here
3		que:: (.) treinta años
		for:: (.) thirty years

While Example 5.6 refers to an event that occurred recently and Example 5.7 to one that happened 30 years ago, they both add to the student's understanding of the life experiences of older people. Reference to past conflicts in Argentina in Example 5.7 also links to the older participant's reasons for migrating.

Example 5.8 'We used to bottle the wine'
Spanish conversation: Mr Diaz, Maddy

1	Mr Diaz	[e:::] (.) bodega si porque::: (.) el vino/ <E wine E> el vino (.) viene de
		[e:::] (.) winery yes because::: (.) the wine/ <E wine E> the wine (.) comes from
2		mendoza (.) a rosario donde es mi provincia donde yo vivía (.) (H)
		mendoza (.) to rosario which is the province where i used to live (.) (H)
3		y allí nosotros la poníamos en botella
		and there we used to bottle the wine

Locative positioning in Example 5.8 reveals the immigrant's knowledge about geographical and historical features, sociocultural conventions and traditions in the place he was born and in places he has travelled.

In the next two examples, the immigrant's contextual and epistemic stances inform the student about the past status of German in the United States (Example 5.9) and social conditions in Chile (Example 5.10). This type of knowledge may be linked to background factors like social class and the level of education of the older participant.

Example 5.9 'German was widely spoken in the United States'
German conversation: Mr Weber, John

1	Mr Weber	ähm ursprünglich zum beispiel in den ich glaub das war in
		ah originally for example in the i think that was in
2		den zwanziger dreißiger jahren (.) deutsch das war sehr so
		the twenties or thirties (.) german that was very so
3		viel viel in den vereinigten staaten in <E the usa E> viel gesprochen
		widely widely in the united states in <E the usa E> widely spoken

Example 5.10 'Nowadays people are very impoverished'
Spanish conversation: Mr Diaz, Maddy

1	Mr Diaz	(.) y::: <en ar y en> actualmente está muy pobre la gente muy
		(.) a:::nd <in ar and in> nowadays people are very impoverished very
2		pobre\ (.) no tienen trabajo/ (.) no tienen moneda/
		impoverished\ (.) they don't have a job/ (.) they don't have currency/
3		(.) plata (H) ROBAN mucho (.) MATAN mucho (.) ASALTAN asaltan es
		(.) money (H) they STEAL a lot (.) KILL a lot (.) ROB rob is to
4		robar (.) [con arma]
		steal (.) [by threatening with weapons]
5	Maddy	[hm] <E yeah E>
		[hm] <E yeah E>

The immigrants regularly stressed their belief in the value of language learning, and this epistemic positioning also translated as practical advice to the student. In Example 5.11, imperative modals like 'must' index a strategy for oral practice, which draws on the older participant's experience of learning English as a second language in Australia.

Example 5.11 'You must speak how it comes out of your mouth'
German conversation: Mr Schmidt, Jane

1	Mr Schmidt	<du mußt> du mußt so reden wie der wie dir der mund gewachsen
		<you must> you must speak how it comes out of your mouth
2		[ist] nich-/
		see/
3	Jane	[*ja*]
		[*yes*]

Indirect advice is often marked by impersonal referencing and may be accompanied by affective positioning, as shown by Mrs Ramos's attitude to life expressed in the next example (5.12).

Example 5.12 'Life should not be taken so seriously'
Spanish conversation: Mrs Ramos, Sarah

1	Mrs Ramos	[la] vida no hay que
		life should not be
2		tomarla tan serio cuando no se necesita
		taken so seriously unless there is a need to
3		[@@ <E that's what we do best E> @@]
		[@@ <E that's what we do best E> @@]

The comparative stance, seen in Example 5.13, draws on lived experiences, observation and evaluation. Here Mrs Fischer tells Nicholas about differences in Christmas traditions. She appears to be neutral when making the comparison, though the use of 'schon' (*already*) in line 5 may hint at a criticism of the Australian tradition.

Example 5.13 'Christmas was celebrated a bit differently'
German conversation: Mrs Fischer, Nicholas

2	Mrs Fischer	(.) ah wurde weihnachten ah im gegensatz zu weihnachten
		(.) ah christmas in contrast to christmas
3		in australien ein bißchen anders gefeiert zum beispiel wurde
		in australia was celebrated a bit differently for example

Example 5.13 (Continued)

4		der weihnachtsbaum erst am weihnachstag aufgestellt
		the christmas tree wasn't put up till christmas eve
5		ja nicht schon vier wochen vorher
		you know not four weeks earlier already

In our final example (5.14), the older participant's expert stance on the migration experience is complemented by affective positioning, demonstrating to the student that major life changes can be positive and, as suggested by the word 'boom', that challenges like language learning can be treated with a sense of humour.

Example 5.14 'We liked the country'
Spanish conversation: Mrs Fernandez, Rachel

1	Mrs Fernandez	este::: y nos gustó el país nos quedamos
		thi::::s and we liked the country we stayed
2		yo no no volvía a mi a mi (.) a mi país no volví por diez año- (..)
		i didn't i didn't return to my to my (.) to my country i didn't return for ten years (..)
3		viví acá estaba contenta
		i lived here i was happy
4		me gustaba (.) conocí a mucha gente (..)
		i liked it (.) i met a lot of people (..)
5		empecé a estudiar inglés (..) pero mi inglés (..) iba por acá boom
		i began to study english (..) but my english (..) went down here boom

As native speakers and migrants from countries in which German and Spanish are spoken, it is a given that the older people have something to offer students in respect of language practice, knowledge and advice, and this value emerges particularly in stories about the circumstances of migration and the ageing process. Their stance-taking strategies are not concerned with 'proving' credibility, although a persuasive tone may be detected in some of the offered advice. On the basis of life experience extending up to eight decades, the older participants are held to be experts and their authority is not challenged by the student 'novices', who are only in their late teens.

How does an ethos of self reveal commonalities and differences in the two language groups?

Although both the German- and Spanish-speaking groups shared a distinct preference overall for adopting the expert stance, the data revealed many individual differences (Figures 5.1 and 5.2). Contextual, epistemic, comparative and affective positioning added to the personal identities chosen by the older people during the conversations.

Each older individual's ethos of self has been shaped by his or her cultural and social background, among other variables. Accordingly, stance acts and positioning were essentially individual and fed into the teaching and advice, conscious and unconscious, which they presented to the students.

The diverse social identities acquired by the older people during their lives and in different locations added to the authenticity of the information and recommendations they offered to their student partners. While the German and Latin American migrants shared identities such as 'child', 'worker', 'migrant' and 'old', a significant difference was manifest in the area of language experience. Germany has many national and regional boundaries and these create an awareness of language and dialect variety among the population. Thus language learning for the German group emerged as a fact of life, a process that is found at the centre of their identity as individuals, as Germans and later as migrants to an English-speaking country. In contrast, the Spanish-speaking migrants in the project had no experience of regional and national language variation (although this does also exist in Latin America).

When adopting the expert and contextual stances, the older participants described the many activities and events in which they have been and are engaged, before and since coming to Australia. Notably, the German speakers were still making plans for the future, whereas this was not mentioned by the Spanish-speaking group.

The lessons imparted from the epistemic position, by both groups, were intended as life-improving examples for the students. Here the type of knowledge and advice that was proffered was, in part, influenced by the level of education the older people had been able to attain both before and after migration, and, related to this, their socio-economic background. The Germans were able to connect with the students through shared travel experiences, which was not the case for the Spanish-speaking group. However, a common thrust of both groups was the promotion of language learning and ideas for connecting the younger and older generations.

An important component of the older participants' talk was their comparative positioning when discussing changes and developments over time and across place. This conveyed to the students how they evaluated life transitions such as migration. Here the German men and women, who in the main represented an earlier wave of migration, demonstrated positive adjustments to living in Australia, whereas many of the more recently arrived Spanish speakers still showed a strong orientation to their birth lands.

Affective positioning demonstrated the immigrants' general attitude towards their own lived experiences and to the experiences of the students.

Both groups revealed personal likes and dislikes, but were invariably interested in the students, expressing approval and freely offering support.

All of these stances interacted and complemented one another to reveal older people as individuals who could benefit the students' personal, cultural and linguistic development.

Conclusion

Stance research on body image (Coupland & Coupland, 2009) has commented on aged appearance and the negative impression often left on the young, pointing to the ideologies that are fostered by stance constructions of older speakers themselves and by stances attributed to them by others, including the media. Here we have demonstrated that when older people are provided with the opportunity to take up an expert stance, they can be an instructive and cultural resource for young people. Their expertise in their native language and their willingness to share it with young language learners can help to neutralise negative generational and cultural stereotypes. This ethos of self opens the door to young people becoming more aware of the issues around ageing that older people face, and in turn encourages them to be more receptive to the other stances the older participants take up, particularly the affective stance through which they share their personal stories and feelings.

Although we have not attempted in this chapter to quantify the effectiveness of the five different stances adopted by the older participants on the students' language development, cultural understanding or level of engagement with the older generation, we can report that the focus groups conducted with the students at the end of each year highlighted their appreciation of the contributions made by the older participants about their language and culture. The older partner's talk was essentially unchallenged by the students, for reasons including respect for the older person and limited ability to express themselves in the target language. The degree of rapport existing between any two individuals must also play a part. The students may have been able to engage more readily with the German speakers, who felt more settled in Australia and could talk on topics of interest to young people, such as travel, because of their higher socio-economic status. Nonetheless, all of the older participants were invariably interested in the students, and the stances they adopted were intended to offer education and support. We look at the question of rapport in detail in Chapter 7.

The five stances classified in this study provided an analytical framework for identifying the multi-layered identities constructed by older immigrants as they discussed their experiences of migration and resettlement, and demonstrated that their positioning as storytellers and advice-givers makes them positive role models for the students.

References

Abes, E.S., Jones, S.R. and McEwen, M.K. (2007) Reconceptualizing the model of multiple dimensions of identity: The role of meaning-making capacity in the construction of multiple identities. *Journal of College Student Development* 48 (1), 1–22.

Butler, R.N. (1987) Ageism. In G.L. Maddox and R.C. Atchley (eds) *The Encyclopedia of Aging* (pp. 22–23). New York: Springer.

Charkins, R.J., O'Toole, D.M. and Wetzel, J.N. (1985) Linking teacher and student learning styles with student achievement and attitudes. *The Journal of Economic Education* 16 (2), 111–120.

Cheng, B. (2010) 'Reassuring' during clinical examinations. Novice and expert talk in dentistry. *Journal of Asian Pacific Communication* 20 (2), 185–206.

Clyne, M. (1991) *Community Languages: The Australian Experience*. Cambridge: Cambridge University Press.

Clyne, M. (2005) *Australia's Language Potential*. Sydney: UNSW Press.

Cordella, M. and Huang, H. (2012) Adultos mayores inmigrantes y estudiantes de ELE: Los roles de participación que surgen en conversaciones intergeneracionales e interculturales. *Signo y Seña* [Argentina] 22, 13–33.

Cordella, M. and Huang, H. (2014) L1 and L2 Chinese, German and Spanish speakers in action: Stancetaking in intergenerational and intercultural encounters. In J. Hajek and Y. Slaughter (eds) *Challenging the Monolingual Mindset* (pp. 97–112). Bristol: Multilingual Matters.

Coupland, J. and Coupland, N. (2009) Attributing stance in discourses of body shape and weight loss. In A. Jaffe (ed.) *Stance: Sociolinguistic Perspectives* (pp. 227–250). Oxford: Oxford University Press.

Du Bois, J.W. (2007) The stance triangle. In R. Englebretson (ed.) *Stancetaking in Discourse* 139–181. Amsterdam: John Benjamins.

Ehlich, K. and Rehbein, J. (1986) *Muster und Institutionen*. Tübingen: Narr.

Espin, O.M. (1997) The role of gender and emotion in women's experience of migration. *Innovation. Journal of European Social Science Research* 10 (4), 445–455.

Giles, H. (1991) Gosh, you don't look it! A sociolinguistics of ageing. *The Psychologist* 4, 99–106.

Hofstetter, E.O. (2001) *Women in Global Migration, 1945–2000. A Comprehensive Multidisciplinary Bibliography*. Westport, CT: Greenwood Press.

Jaffe, A. (ed.) (2009) *Stance: Sociolinguistic Perspectives*. Oxford: Oxford University Press.

Johnstone, B. (2009) Stance, style and the linguistic individual'. In A. Jaffe (ed.) *Stance: Sociolinguistic Perspectives* (pp. 29–52). Oxford: Oxford University Press.

Jones, S.R. and McEwen, M.K. (2000) A conceptual model of multiple dimensions of identity. *Journal of College Student Development* 41, 405–414.

Junankar, P.N. and Mahuteau, S. (2005) Do migrants get good jobs? New migrant settlement in Australia. *The Economic Record* 81, August, 34–46.

Kerswill, P. (2006) Migration and language. In K. Mattheier, U. Ammon and P. Trudgill (eds) *Sociolinguistics/Soziolinguistik. An International Handbook of the Science of Language and Society* 3 (2nd edn) (pp. 1–27). Berlin: De Gruyter.

Kofman, E. (2000) The invisibility of skilled female migrants and gender relations in studies of skilled migration in Europe. *International Journal of Population Geography* 6, 45–59.

Lambert, B.E. (2008) *Family Language Transmission: Actors, Issues, Outcomes*. Frankfurt: Peter Lang.

Markus, A. and Sims, E. (1993) *Fourteen Lives: Paths to a Multicultural Community*. Clayton, Vic.: Dept of History, Monash University.

Meinhof, U.H. and Galasinski, D. (2005) *The Language of Belonging*. Basingstoke: Palgrave MacMillan.

Miller, R. (2007) *Researching Life Stories and Family Histories*. London: Sage.
Norton, B. (2000) *Identity and Language Learning: Gender, Ethnicity, and Educational Change*. Harlow: Longman/Pearson.
Piller, I. and Takahashi, K. (2011) Linguistic diversity and social inclusion. *International Journal of Bilingual Education and Bilingualism* 14 (4), 371–381.
Rehbein, J. (1977) *Komplexes Handeln. Elemente zur Handlungstheorie der Sprache*. Stuttgart: Metzler.
Sarangi, S. (2001) Editorial: On demarcating the space between 'lay expertise' and 'expert laity'. *Text: Interdisciplinary Journal for the Study of Discourse* 21 (1/2), 3–11.
Schüpbach, D. (2009) *Shared Languages, Shared Stories, Shared identities? An Exploration of Life Stories of Swiss-German Immigrants in Australia*. Frankfurt/M.: Peter Lang.
Sears, C. (2011) Integrating multiple identities: Narrative in the formation and maintenance of the self in international school students. *Journal of Research in International Education* 10 (1), 71–86.
Warnes, A.M. and Williams, A. (2006) Older migrants in Europe: A new focus for migration studies. *Journal of Ethnic and Migration Studies* 32 (8), 1257–1281.
Williams, A.M. (2008) Brought-along identities and the dynamics of ideology. Accomplishing bivalent stances in a multilingual interaction. *Multilingua* 27, 37–56.

6 'Who Are We?' Self-Referencing in Chinese and German Conversations Using the First Person Plural

Hui Huang and Yanying Lu

Introduction

Over the last few decades there has been considerable research interest in the uses of *we* and its grammatical variants (*us, our, ours*) to self-reference speakers (e.g. Brown & Gilman, 1960; Kitagawa & Lehrer, 1990; Lerner & Kitzinger, 2007). In this chapter we offer new directions for this research as we compare the ways in which the first person plural is used by older Chinese and German native speakers to self-reference in conversations with young language learners. Using extracts from the recordings described in Chapter 3, we analyse the variety of applications of *we* used by the speakers, with a particular interest in how the data identifies different usage patterns in the two languages in cross-cultural oral settings.

The Self, Group Membership and the First Person Plural

The concept of 'self' has different meanings in different cultures, and is reflected in the way in which people converse in daily communications. Brown and Gilman's (1960) pioneering study was among the first to show that pronominal choice is affected by the perceived relationship between the speaker and the hearer. The use of personal references in an interaction reveals how the individuals perceive themselves, both within society generally and in relation to their interactive partner(s) (Bourdieu, 1991; Mühlhäusler *et al.*, 1990; Ochs, 1992). In addition, the culturally appropriate use of personal references is a manifestation of the reciprocal and inseparable relationship between linguistic convention and sociocultural practice (Mühlhäusler *et al.*, 1990; Ting-Toomey, 1999).

The actual words speakers choose to use, either consciously or subconsciously, are closely related to how individuals identify themselves in the culture that shapes them and influences their daily activities, including in their conversations with others (e.g. Lerner & Kitzinger, 2007).

Among the cross-cultural definitions of self, some scholars identify the self in terms of its relationship to others. Markus and Kitayama (1991), for example, in their seminal paper, posit that Asian cultures emphasise the concept of self as being inextricably linked to others, while independence is more valued in Western (particularly American) culture. The degree of connectedness between the self and others is fundamental to how the self is construed and perceived. From this viewpoint, Brewer and Gardner (1996) identified three levels of self-representation: individual (personal self), interpersonal (relational self) and group (collective self), all of which, they argue, may coexist within the same individual and can be stimulated at different times or in different contexts. When collective identities are activated, the distinctive feature of the self will be shared with others in the group. The nuances between these various aspects of the self are the level of inclusiveness in the construal of the self.

Recognising the intrinsically cultural and societal features of the self, many sociolinguistic researchers argue that the self can be analysed and accessed from a social constructionist perspective. In particular, they emphasise that the social positioning of the self-and-others and self-conceptualisation are constituted when people interact (Bucholtz & Hall, 2005; Holland & Quinn, 1987). Conversation analysts also support the view that the self emerges from conversations and is constructed by the interactants (e.g. Schegloff, 2007; Lerner & Kitzinger, 2007). The self, therefore, is conceptualised as an inherently *social product* jointly created by each individual within the conversational context, rather than a pre-determined, psychological construct within each individual's mind (Bucholtz & Hall, 2005). The speaker's perceived connectedness with the listener or others is thus available for analysis because it is revealed in their use of pronouns, as identified by Brown and Gilman (1960) in their early work. In other words, personal pronouns reflect the speaker's identified self and his/her relationship with other people in the given context. However, it is important to recognise that the self that emerges from the interaction should not be understood as an objective reality, but is influenced by the individual's subjective disposition that varies according to different social conventions and occasions. Individuals may change their alignment within the group during the course of an interaction in order to present the self more positively; that is, the individual self can be modified if it clashes with the collective self.

Like English, the first person plural 我们 (wǒmen, *we*) in Chinese and 'wir' (*we*) in German are referential and deictic. They suggest a partial collectivity that includes the speaker or the writer plus one or more others.

The 'one' can be the listener(s) (*you and me*), specified or unspecified others (e.g. *the people in the room with us, Australian residents*), or a generic third party (as in *We all need a hobby*). However, these pronouns need not imply collectivity: as Postoutenko (2009) has argued, *we* can mean a single person, a couple, a religion or all of humanity. The choices made between a singular and a plural marker of personal self-identification are said to be associated with the perceived roles of the speaker and hearer as they locate themselves on the continuums of status and solidarity (Brown & Gilman, 1960), or as a result of 'a complex interrelation between discursive rules and social hierarchies of a given time and place' (Postoutenko, 2009: 200).

Moreover, the choice of pronoun may be decided by culturally and even politically oriented conventions. For example, in her study of the social and communal dimensions of the first person plural in Chinese, Mao (1996) was the first in modern Chinese literature to argue that the boundary between我 (wǒ, *I*) – the singular form – and 我们 (wǒ men, *we*) – the plural form – can be blurred. The author attributed this phenomenon to the traditional Chinese ethos that values the communal over the individual, whereby我们 evokes a sense of modesty and/or politeness as well as neutralising conflict and enhancing the power of the collective. Mao's study became the cornerstone for construing the 'social-implicature aspect' (1996: 126) of the first person plural in Mandarin Chinese: that 我们 not only obeys grammatical rules but also respects sociocultural norms. Surveys of first person pronoun use in classical literature suggest that this feature is inherited from classical Chinese in which the use of the plural form to refer to an individual is a feature of the discourse (e.g. Lee, 1999, 2012; Lai & Frajzyngier, 2009). According to Lee (2012), a description of how pronouns index different types of self can be obtained by approaching the historical Chinese first person pronominal system from an interactional perspective. Using modern Chinese corpora, a number of researchers have investigated how the self is constructed through the use of self-reference in written discourse (Kuo, 1999; Xiang, 2003) and in conjunction with forms of address (e.g. Chao, 1956; Biq, 1991; Hsiao, 2011), by examining the first person singular 我 (*I*) and/or 你 (nǐ, *you*). However, none of these studies have focused on how the plural pronoun 我们 is used in Mandarin Chinese in self-referencing or construction, nor has the intriguing mixture of first person plural and singular forms in modern Chinese been explored in the recent literature.

Studies of 'wir' (*we*) in German by researchers like Whitt (2014) and Baumgarten (2008) have focused on the intersubjective meanings of the first person plural in the written corpora. According to these authors, the intersubjective and constructive meaning-making of 'wir' can be explored by looking at its co-occurrence with verb types (see also Vassileva, 1998). Analysis of 'wir' in these constructions, with their close relationship to English usage (Baumgarten, 2008: 435; Whitt, 2014: 62), offers a range of interpretations. The use of 'wir' allows the writer to both indicate authorship and channel his/her readership to a larger community. However, no studies of how 'wir' is used in oral communication have been found, especially one that considers how the speaker identifies him- or herself in relation to others.

In fact, all previous studies of 'wir' have drawn on written data and have compared first person pronoun use in German with that of other European languages (e.g. Vassileva, 1998 – English, French, Russian and Bulgarian; Whitt, 2014 and Baumgarten, 2008 – English). A recent collection by Pavlidou (2014) examines first person plural pronoun use in English, German, Norwegian, Italian and Polish from semantic, pragmatic, interactional and genre-specific perspectives. However, no study hitherto has attempted to compare German and Chinese usage, particularly in relation to self-referencing. The purpose of the present study, therefore, is to fill these gaps.

About the Study

Our data is drawn from two recordings (R1, R2) of dyadic conversations between three older Chinese native speakers and three older German native speakers and their student partners, a total of 12 conversations conducted in the target language as part of the project described in Chapter 3. R1 was made in mid-March 2011 on the topic of work and jobs, while R2 was made in September 2011 on the topic of attitudes towards different generations. The study aimed to provide answers to the following research questions:

(1) What types of 'we' emerge from the Chinese and German data?
(2) What does pronoun use reveal about a speaker's group membership?
(3) What are the differences or similarities between the two languages?

Table 6.1 reveals a large variation in the length of stay in Australia of the older immigrants, from 57 years (Mrs Fischer)[1] to just three years (Ms Liu) at the time the data was collected. Overall, the Chinese participants in the project were recent immigrants compared with their German counterparts. This may be one reason why all the German speakers were English and German bilinguals, while the Chinese participants only spoke Chinese (Mandarin and Cantonese). All the older participants in Table 6.1 were living in stable family households, and indeed all except Ms Bai had a long-term partner or husband. Except for Ms Liu, who conversed with two students, the other older participants had the same partner over the two recorded conversations. The ethnic and linguistic diversity of the student participants, summarised in the last column of the Table, is a snapshot of the multiculturalism of contemporary Australia discussed in Chapter 1.

Table 6.1 Study participants

Older participant	Age in 2011	Gender	Linguistic background	Family background	Student partner & their background
Ms Liu*	66	F	Mandarin and Cantonese	A recent immigrant to Australia (2008), lives with her husband and children.	Lucy, a Cantonese and English bilingual girl with some Chinese cultural background at home.
					Daisy, an English monolingual girl whose mother was born in Singapore and father in Australia
Ms Bai	67	F	Mandarin	Joined her child in 1977 in Australia and lives with her children and grandchildren.	Phuc, a Vietnamese and English bilingual boy with a Vietnamese family background.
Ms Wen	79	F	Mandarin and Cantonese	Arrived in Australia in 1985, lives with her husband and children.	Chrissie, an English monolingual girl whose mother was born in Singapore and father in Australia.
Mr Schmidt	81	M	German and English	Immigrated to Australia in 1954. He was divorced from the mother of his son and has been living with a different partner for a long time.	Michelle, an English monolingual girl. Her parents are both from Australia.
Mr Günther	64	M	German and English	Arrived in Australia five years ago. He was divorced from his first wife with whom he has a few children. He currently lives with his second wife and their son.	Adam, a multilingual boy who was born in Brazil with Portuguese as his first language and English as his second language.
Mrs Fischer	79	F	German and English	Immigrated to Australia at the age of 24 in 1956. She and her partner have four children. She has always lived with her partner.	Nicholas, a multilingual male with a Malaysian mother. He claims English as his first, Chinese as his second, German as his third, and Japanese as his fourth language.

* All participants' names have been changed.

Data Collection and Analysis

After the recorded conversations had been carefully transcribed, all uses of *we* and its variants were identified and judiciously analysed. As the purpose of the study was to investigate how *we* is used to self-reference, the different grammatical forms were not the focus and consequently all forms were collapsed. In German, *we* includes 'wir' (*we*, nominative), 'uns' (*us*, accusative and dative) and 'unser/e/es/en' (*our/s*, possessive). Every individual occurrence of the pronominal form was carefully examined and assigned to one of the following four groups: (1) speaker + listener; (2) speaker + other(s) (with two sub-groups, 2a: specified other(s) and 2b: unspecified other(s)); (3) everyone (speaker + listener + others); and (4) other uses, including speaker only (*me, myself, I*).

Table 6.2 shows how many times the first person plural was used by each of the older participants in the four different senses described above.

The numbers show that in both the Chinese and German conversations *we* referred to all three possibilities: (1) speaker + listener; (2a) speaker + specified other(s); and (2b) speaker + unspecified other(s); but it is notable that the third group was strongly favoured by the Chinese (44 out of 90) and the second by the Germans (35 out of 80). Most striking, however, was the finding that all three of the Chinese older participants used the first person plural in the singular sense of *I* (group 4) 16 out of 90 times, a usage not found in the German; but, equally distinctive, one of the Germans used 'wir' in a generic way four times to refer to everyone (group 3), a usage not recorded in the Chinese data. All of these results will be discussed in detail below.

(1) 'We' = Speaker + Listener

We in this sense welcomes the listener as a member of an in-group of two. It offers the interactant the opportunity to align with the speaker in the conversational 'here and now' as well as in events that are outside the situated present. This 'inclusive use' (Scheibmann, 2004) was found to be more common in the German data, and was the preferred usage of Mrs Fischer (12 times). Ms Liu and Ms Bai used 我们 in this sense a total of 3 and 9 times respectively, but Ms Wen did not use it at all.

Example 6.1 'Today we are going to discuss'
Chinese conversation (R2): Ms Liu, Daisy

1	Ms Liu	今天**我们**要讨论的就是 (.)
		jīn tiān wǒmen yào tǎo lùn de jiù shì (.)
		today what we are going to discuss is (.)
		today what we are going to discuss is (.)
2	Daisy	有:::啊 明白
		yǒu :::a míng bai
		there :::uh i see
		there :::uh i see

'Who Are We?' Self-Referencing in Chinese and German Conversations 91

Table 6.2 Use of the first person plural in 12 Chinese and German conversations

	Chinese data					German data				
		Older participant + other(s)					Speaker + other(s)		
Recording no. and dyad	Older participant + student	specified other(s)	unspecified other(s)	Referring to self	Recording no. and dyad	Older participant + student	specified other(s)	unspecified other(s)	Referring to everyone
R1, Ms Liu / Lucy	0	4	8	6	R1, Mr Schmidt / Michelle	0	9	3	0
R3, Ms Liu / Daisy	3	0	1	0	R3, Mr Schmidt / Michelle	6	11	14	4
R1, Ms Bai / Phuc	7	2	7	6	R1, Mr Günther / Adam	6	2	0	0
R3, Ms Bai / Phuc	2	10	17	0	R3, Günther / Adam	0	3	0	0
R1, Ms Wen/ Chrissie	0	2	7	3	R1, Mrs Fischer / Nicholas	5	7	0	0
R3, Ms Wen / Chrissie	0	0	4	1	R3, Mrs Fischer / Nicholas	7	3	0	0
Totals	12	18	44	16		24	35	17	4

Example 6.2 'We love football'
German conversation (R1): Mr Günther, Adam

45	Mr Günther	mei- (.) mein heimatland ist deutschland\ (.) <E your E> heimatland ist brasilien\
		my (.) homeland is germany\ (.) <E your E> homeland is brazil
46	Adam	ja
		yes
47	Mr Günther	(..) ah **wir** haben etwas zu- öh gemeinsam\ (..) **wir** lieben fussball\
		(..) ah we have something in oh in common\ (..) we love football

In these two examples (6.1 and 6.2) the pronouns refer to the speaker and the listener in the present context. By including their student partners in the self-reference, the older participants fashion the dialogue in a cooperative manner so that the younger person feels engaged. The inclusive use of 'we' in line 47 suggests a symmetrical relationship between them. However, we find that in the Chinese data some inclusive use of the first person plural form is extended to membership of a group in which the hearer was not originally incorporated (Example 6.3). Here 我们 is used inclusively, bypassing the differences between the speaker and the hearer (e.g. in age, region, culture) and engaging the hearer as an in-group member of the speaker with whom he has something in common.

Example 6.3 'We have many that work'
Chinese conversation (R1): Ms Bai, Phuc

333	Ms Bai	就是在**我们**国家跟在这:::这澳大利亚是一样的*要*电脑要求他
		jiùshì zài **wǒmen** guójiā gēn zài zhè:::zhè àodàlìyà shì yīyàng de*yào* diànnǎo yàoqiú tā
		just is in our country and in here::: here australia same *need* request him
		in our country and also here::: in australia the *need* request for him is the same
334		一定对电脑熟悉的 (.) 啊对吧/要求 <xx> 你像**咱们**好多那个::: <E work E>
		yīdìng duì diànnǎo shú xi de (.) a duì ba/ yāoqiú <xx> nǐ xiàng zánmen hǎoduō nà gè::: <E work E>
		must to computer familiar (.) right/ request <xx> you like we many that <E work E>
		must be familiar with computers is it right/ you see we have many that <E work E>
		...

Example 6.3 (Continued)

338	在澳大利亚 (.) 好像:::工作的品种没什么区别
	zài àodàlìyà (.) hǎoxiàng::: gōngzuò de pǐnzhǒng méi shénme qūbié
	in australia (.) seems work type no much difference
	in australia (.) it seems there is not much difference between types of work
339	我觉得这里好多
	wǒ juéde zhèlǐ hǎo duō
	i feel here better
	i feel it's better here

In the first part of the extract, Ms Bai separates the student from her own group when she refers to *our country* (我们国家, wǒmen guójiā), meaning China, when she compares China and Australia in line 333. In the very next line, however, she explicitly self-references speaker + listener by using 咱们 (zánmen), a more inclusive form of *we* in Chinese that is intended to engage the listener. This switch to inclusive use seems a bit stilted at first, but in lines 338 and 339 it becomes clear that the older participant's intention is to create a stronger connection between the pair by alluding to their shared status as Australian residents when she comments that Australia is a much better place to live than China (line 339).

(2) 'We' = Speaker + Specified or Unspecified Other(s)

The second group includes the speaker plus any other individual(s) or group(s) with which the speaker identifies. The 'others' in this group could be the speaker's spouse or family, or the other participants in the project (i.e. identifiable individuals), or a collective 'other' such as Australian Chinese immigrants, or older people in the community. *We* functions in this sense to place the speaker within an identified referent group, and gives a biographical context to the *I* of the speaker that can help the listener to establish rapport. Use of the pronoun in the plural also allows the speaker to speak *on behalf of the group* on topics requiring knowledge and moral authority (see 'the moral-ethical adviser' in Chapter 4 and 'the ethos of self' in Chapter 5). As such, it strengthens the stance of the speaker at the same time as it softens the assertion of the individual's beliefs and opinions. Not included directly in this 'exclusive use' of the pronoun (Scheibmann, 2004), however, is the listener him/herself: the speaker's interactant is excluded from *we* when the topic is the 'other-than-here/now'. The first person plural can also be effective when the speaker wants to establish a distance between them or to index a hierarchy in the relationship.

In Table 6.2 we saw a major difference between the Chinese and German data regarding the frequency of 我们 or 'wir' in the sense of speaker + other(s). Speaker + specified other(s) was much more prominent among the Germans (35 out of 80) than among their Chinese counterparts (18 out of 90), while the latter showed a strong preference for speaker + unspecified other(s) (44 out of 90, compared with 17 out of 80 for the Germans). All the older participants used 'we' to refer to family, friends, old school peers, acquaintances, or the people they have met in their lives, but the Chinese much less frequently. Nonetheless, speaker + other(s) was the most frequently used of the four groups overall. Examples from the recorded data can be found in Tables 6.3 and 6.4.

(2a) 'We' = Speaker + Specified Other(s)

The purpose of using the first person plural in these cited cases (see Table 6.3) is to maintain a certain boundary of the in-group, especially in the German data where this boundary is used with respect to other groups that occur in the same utterance: 'if you [students] don't understand' (Mr Schmidt), 'my parents' (Mr Günther), and 'my Dad and my Mum' (Mrs Fischer). By comparison, the Chinese use is more deictic without specifying any second group. We observe, however, that in all of the above examples the first person pronoun does not include the hearer, who is spatio-temporally separate from the events being discussed (Baumgarten, 2008).

(2b) 'We' = Speaker + Unspecified Other(s)

Table 6.2 quantified our finding that the Chinese data is biased towards the use of 我们 to refer to the speaker + unspecified other(s). Closer examination of the transcripts reveals that this group generally fell into two categories: (1) an ambiguous usage that does not identify any particular individuals or group; and (2) a vague reference to a group with which the speaker aligns.

All of these examples of我们 are used in a very inexplicit sense: that is, they leave who the 'others' are very open. The speaker may find it unnecessary to identify the referent group because the purpose of using 我们 might just be to establish an in-group with which the speaker can identify. In other words, these older Chinese participants perhaps prefer to view themselves as one of a group and to talk about the self through a relationship with others (Markus & Kitayama, 1991).

The second category includes the interesting finding that 我们 is used together with another deictic pronoun 这 (zhè, *here, this*) as a linguistic chunk to create a boundary for the group where 我们 does not refer to the speaker and some specified other. Instead, it refers to everyone in the group to which the speaker belongs.

我们这 may sometimes include the listener when the conversation is contextualised (Examples 1 and 4), or may be exclusive of the hearer

Table 6.3 Examples of 'we' = speaker + specified other(s)

R1	550	Ms Liu	::: 嗯::: 我先生 (.) **我们**两个 (.) 我女儿 我女婿 ::: èn::: wǒ xiānsheng (.) wǒmen liǎng gè (.) wǒ nǚer wǒ nǚxu *::: um::: my husband (.) we two (.) my daughter i son in law* *:::um::: my husband (.) and i the two of us (.) my daughter and my son in law*	refers to my husband and I
R1	389	Ms Bai	香港 **我们**从香港:::从中国到香港 (.) xiānggǎng wǒmen cóng xiānggǎng::: cóng zhōngguó dào xiānggǎng (.) *hong kong we from hong kong::: from china to hong kong (.)* *we went to hong kong::: from china we went to hong kong (.)*	refers to my family and I
R1	183	Ms Wen	所以**我们**就都到*那里*(.) 几姊妹都到*那里*读书啊 suǒyǐ wǒmen jiù dōu dào*nàlǐ* (.) jǐ zǐmèi dōu dào *nàlǐ* dú shū a *so we then all went *there* (.) sisters all went *there* study ah* *so we all went *there* (.) all the sisters went *there* to study ah*	refers to my sisters and I
R2	47	Mr Schmidt	daß ah **wir wir uns** wird gesacht **wir** sollen nur deutsch sprechen aber wenn hier wenn de wenn de nich verstehst ((was **wir**)) *that ah we we were told we should only speak german but if here if you if you don't understand ((what we))*	refers to the German participants in the project
R2	154	Mr Günther	*öh* ich kann mich an meinn groß-vater noch erinnern\ und (.) das war ein guter freund (.) ja/ (..) **wir** haben alles das gemacht was die eltern nicht gemacht haben **oh* i can still remember my granddad\ and (.) he was a good friend (.) yes/ (..) we did everything our parents didn't do*	refers to my granddad and I

(Continued)

Table 6.3 (Continued)

R1	396	Mrs Fischer	ich habe (..) ich kann mich erinnern daß (.) mein vater und meine mutter (..) **uns** alle (.) kinder (.) lieb gehabt haben (..) <E they <x> E> (.) sie haben **uns** (.) immer (..) versorcht <E they looked after us (.) in a lovely way E> (.) das ist was ich ver- versuche zu sagen (..) und ich kann mich erinnern (.) an eine harte zeit (.) am ende des krieges/	refers to all the children in the family
			i have (..) i can remember that (.) my dad and my mum (..) all of us (.) kids (.) were loved (..) <E they <x> E> (.) they always (.) cared (..) for us <E they looked after us (.) in a lovely way E> (.) this is what I tr- try to say (..) and i can remember (.) a hard time (.) at the end of the war/	

(Examples 2, 3 and 5). Like the inclusive use of 我们 discussed above, Examples 1 and 4 are statements intended to engage the listener affectively and cognitively in the conversation: the pronominal phrase conveys 'you, I and everyone living in Australia'. In contrast, in Examples 2, 3 and 5 the group boundary indicator excludes the listener, who is a young student, not an older person like the speaker. But whether the intention is to include or exclude the listener, the vague use of 我们这 is still fundamentally collective in nature; that is, all of these 我们 do not specify any particular individual but index a group of which the speaker identifies him/herself as a member (Table 6.4).

Example 6.5 'You have to form an opinion'
German conversation (R2): Mr Schmidt, Michelle

116	Mr Schmidt	alles alles was **wir** alles was **wir** machen können ist **wir** können **uns** nur mit euch
		everything everything that we everything that we can do is we can only
117		dadrüber unterhalten und ihr müßt euch die müßt die meinung <x abmachen x>
		talk to you about this and you have to <x form x> an opinion
118		was ihr machen wollt und was machen könnt (.)
		what you want to do and can do (.)

Table 6.4 Examples of 我们 for ambiguous referents

R1	481	Ms Liu	我们用 老百姓的讲就是 (.) 自己要有 很多 (..) 知识 wǒmen yòng lǎobǎixìng de jiǎng jiù shì (.) zìjǐ yào yǒu hěnduō (..) zhīshi
			we use common people talk is (.) self need have a lot of (..) knowledge
			in common people's words we say (.) that we need to have a lot of (..) knowledge
R2	169	Ms Liu	老人老的年纪大的**我们**叫 老人 lǎorén lǎo de niánji dà de wǒmen jiào lǎorén
			old people old age big we can call old people
			we call old people old people
R1	505	Ms Bai	=**我们**也经常用这句话 <@@> =wǒmen yě jīngcháng yòng zhè jù huà <@@>
			=we also often use this sentence <@@>
			=we also often use this sentence <@@>
R2	78	Ms Bai	一定要功夫不像**我们**现在喝茶似的一下就完了 yídìng yào gōngfu bú xiàng wǒmen xiànzài hē chá shìde yí xià jiù wán le
			must have time not like what we now drink tea very soon complete
			it must have a lot of time unlike now we complete drinking tea very quickly
R1	182	Ms Wen	像**我们**就不需要劳动力 (.) xiàng wǒmen jiù bù xūyào láodòng lì (.)
			like us no need labour force (.)
			for example we do not need labour force (.)
R2	917	Ms Wen	那**我们**那个都读俄文哪 (.) 我现在连那几个字母我都不认识了 nà wǒmen nàge dōu dú éwén na (.) wǒ xiànzài lián nà jǐ gè zìmǔ wǒ dōu bú rènshi le
			then we then all read russian (.) i now even several alphabets i cannot recognise
			then we studied russian (.) but now i cannot even recognise several alphabets

This vague usage of the pronoun was employed by all three Chinese older participants in each of their conversations (Table 6.2), and was particularly frequent in Ms Bai's second session with Phuc (17 times). In contrast, it was absent from the conversations of Mr Günther and Mrs Fischer, but featured 14 times in Mr Schmidt's second conversation with Michelle. Even with the lower overall totals for the Germans, however, it was the most frequently used form by a speaker in a single conversation (17 and 14 times). It is also interesting to note that the next-highest totals were

Table 6.5 Examples of 我们 + 这 for vague alignments

1	R1	758	Ms Liu	我们这里呢 *就比* 在中国呢就 这一点呢
				wǒmen zhèlǐ ne *jiù bǐ* zài zhōngguó ne jiù zhè yì diǎn ne
				we here *just like* in china this point
				we here *compared with* china on this point
2	R2	53	Ms Bai	就算我们这老一代
				jiùsuàn wǒmen zhè lǎoyídài
				if counted we this old generation
				even our old generation
3	R2	231	Ms Bai	我们这样老年人
				wǒmen zhèyàng lǎoniánrén
				we this kind old people
				old people like us
4	R1	640	Ms Wen	我们这里 (.) 唉还是北京好呀
				wǒmen zhèlǐ (.) ài háishì běijīng hǎo ya
				we here (.) well still beijing good
				we are here (.) well beijing is still better
5	R2	279	Ms Wen	我们这些老人
				wǒmen zhèxiē lǎorén
				we these old people
				we these old people

by the same speakers in the other sub-group of the same category, speaker + specified other(s) (10 and 11 times). To put it another way, Ms Bai and Mr Schmidt drew attention to their alignment with the broader community and the 'world out there' very frequently in their talk (Table 6.5).

In Example 6.5 Mr Schmidt uses 'wir' and 'uns' to refer to himself and others who are unspecified in the context. As he talks to the student he adopts the stance of ethical-moral adviser that we discussed in Chapter 4. Instead of using a singular form, the use of the plural adds more weight to Mr Schmidt's authority as he pronounces that the student 'has to' do something. In other similar examples in the German data, 'wir' refers to Australian society or to older German people as a group. All of these instances of vague plural pronoun use can be understood as an appeal to an institutional authority that the listener is supposed to respect or obey.

(3) 'We' = Everyone (Speaker + Listener + Others)

This category did not feature in the Chinese data at all, and among the Germans was only identified in Mr Schmidt's second conversation with Michelle (4 times). This generic use is different from the vague use of the previous category where there is always some boundary of in-groupness by

Table 6.6 German examples of the generic use of 'we'

R1	223	das is das ist das problem das **wir** heutzutage haben
		that is that is the problem we have nowadays
R2	80	und so ist das mit mit vielen andern lebewesen *nich*/ und ah (.)
		*and that's the way it is with with many other living creatures *no*/ and ah (.)*
	81	da haben **wir** noch viel viel viel zu tun um um **uns** weiter (.) zuentwickeln
		we still have lots lots lots to do to for us for us to further (.) evolve
	82	und ahm (.) die luft ist dreckig das atmen wird schwerer (..) ah <xx>
		and um (.) the air is polluted breathing gets more difficult (..) ah <xx>
	83	**wir** haben ungefähr fast fast sieben <E billion people on earth E> (...)
		we have about nearly nearly seven <E billion people on earth E> (...)
R2	116	und ah darum haben **wir** ja soviele <E demonstrations E> über die in der ganzen welt
		and ah that's why we have so many <E demonstrations E> about it in the whole world

way of excluding people outside the group (which may include the listener in other-than-here/now cases) (Kitagawa & Lehrer, 1990).

Mr Schmidt is the speaker in all of the extracts in Table 6.6. In the lines prior to line 223 he is discussing the students from the previous year of the programme and the challenges they faced as they learnt another language. He then generalises in line 223 that 'we' all have this issue nowadays. His use of 'wir' rather than the more formal 'man' (*one*) here may be intended to present a warmer and more inclusive manner to the student. In lines 81–83 and 116 of R2 he includes himself and the student in a universal humanity of 'wir' that must take action for a sustainable planet, using the first person plural to make the student feel that the world's problems are her responsibility too, but also to de-emphasise his subjectivity and to offer his views as statements of fact (Budwig, 2000).

Although this generic use did not occur in the Chinese data, Chinese people do use 我们 to refer to 'one' in general. Its absence from the conversations in our study may be explained by the participants' deliberately greater emphasis on cultural norms, behaviours and material goods in their talk with the students. Mr Schmidt was the exception in our study with his interest in more philosophical discussions.

(4) 'We' = I, Myself

The singular understanding of the 'royal we' in English was not found at all in the German data, but featured quite strongly in the Chinese (16 out of 90 times). Specifically, we found that the plural 我们 was employed as a self-reference by the participants in places where the singular 我 (wǒ, *I*) would normally have been used. This particular strategy of substituting individuality with collectivity was coined 'aggregating' by Lerner and Kitzinger (2007) and has the function of broadening the scope of responsibility from the speaker alone to the collective (2007: 546–547).

Example 6.6 'We do volunteer work'
Chinese conversation (R1): Ms Liu, Lucy

613	Ms Liu	(.) *所以* 我觉得标准是 一样的 (..) 不管 全世界 选择工作的标准
		(.) *suǒyǐ* wǒ juéde biāozhǔn shì yíyàng de (..) bùguǎn quán shìjiè xuǎnzé gōngzuò de biāozhǔn
		(.) *so* i think standard is the same (..) no matter whole world choose work standard
		(.) *so* i think the standard is the same (..) no matter where it's standard to choose the job
614		都一样 <E money E> 要多 <@ 钱要多@> 为的是要养 (.)
		dōu yíyàng <E money E> yào duō <@qián yào duō@> wèide shì yào yǎng (.)
		all same <E money E> need a lot <@money need a lot@> in order to raise (.)
		it's the same for everyone <E money E> we need a lot <@money need a lot@> in order to raise (.)
615		好像就是说 我们早年 我们 就要 养 家 要养 养家 要养父母
		hǎoxiàng jiù shì shuō wǒmen zǎonián wǒmen jiù yào yǎng jiā yào yǎng yǎng jiā yào yǎng fùmǔ
		like it is to say we in early years we also raise family need raise family need raise dad and mum
		for example in our early years we needed to raise a family support parents
616		当然我们做义工 这是一个 对社会的 贡献 要养孩子 对不对
		dāng rán wǒmen zuò yìgōng zhè shì yígè duì shèhuì de gòngxiàn yào yang háizi duì bú duì
		of course we do volunteer work this is to society contribution need raise children is it right
		of course we do volunteer work this is a contribution to society children need to be raised is it right
617		那我肯定要有钱 没有钱 我怎么这是要的 (H) 但是你不可能说
		nà wǒ kěngdìng yào yǒu qián méiyǒu qián wǒ zěnme zhè shì yào de (H) dànshì nǐ bù kěnéng shuō
		then i must have money no money i how this is want (H) but you cannot say
		then i must have money if no money how can i say what i want (H) but you cannot say

Example 6.6 (Continued)

618		我不要钱 我永远不要钱 工作 那是 那是 不行的
		wǒ búyào qián wǒ yǒngyuǎn búyào qián gōngzuò nà shì nà shì bùxíng de
		i don't want money i forever don't want money work that that is not alright
		i don't want money i don't want money forever and just to work that is not alright
619	Lucy	嗯
		èn
		um
		um

In this extract, Ms Liu may seem very inconsistent in her choice of self-referencing personal pronouns. The singular form 我 is supported by words with emotional force, such as 觉得 (juéde, *feel, think*), 肯定要 (kěng dìng yào, *must have*), which reflect intrinsic attitudes and are used particularly in the communication of 'sincerity' (Coppieters, 1982). Interestingly, Ms Liu either aggregately repairs or tends to use the collective self 我们 when talking about the importance of raising children (line 615) and the social value of the 'volunteer work' she is doing (line 616), i.e. participating in the research project. We would argue that institutional engagement plays a very important role in her self-referential choice. When 我们 is used, she seems to imply an issue of shared concern or value. Her use of 我们 is 'accidentally' associated with a sense of obligation and engagement. 我, however, is selected when the topic has a clearly individual orientation, as in her assertion (speaking from personal experience) that everyone needs to earn money to survive. Her use of the singular and plural is not inconsistent, therefore, but deliberate, serving to separate her social being from her individual self. She is trying to be equally 'sincere', if not more 'sincere', when she speaks in the plural. However, her main concern in such a choice might be to maintain the boundaries of the organisation she feels she belongs to. The group membership emerges when 'the collective cover' (Lerner & Kitzinger, 2007: 550) is adopted to speak for a group rather than a single individual, as discussed earlier. This is also reflected in the other Chinese participants' conversations examined below.

Example 6.7 'At that time we had no choice in China'
Chinese conversation (R1): Ms Bai, Phuc

65	Phuc	什:::么是好工作
		shén::: me shì hǎo gōngzuò
		what:: is a good job
		what:: is a good job

(Continued)

Example 6.7 (Continued)

66	Ms Bai	为什么
		wèishénme
		why
		why
67		我们那时候呢就没有选择 在中国
		wǒmen nà shíhou ne jiù méiyǒu xuǎnzé zài zhōngguó
		we at that time had no choice in china
		we had no choice in china then

Here Ms Bai does not answer the student's question directly; instead, she starts her story as a member of a group rather than as simply herself. Her preliminary utterance in line 66 seems at first to be an absent-minded reply to the student's question, but is in fact a strategy to take the floor and outline the cultural context by self-inquiring *why*. In doing so, she is able to continue smoothly with her answer as she tells her story, but from the perspective of the group (i.e. millions of Chinese in that context and period) with which she identifies herself as a member.

Another observation of the aggregate use of *we* in the Chinese data is its use in the description of past events. Many such instances of 我们 occur in the Chinese conversations when the older participants are recalling some early experience or suggesting a purposeful action they took years ago. Some examples of this are given in Table 6.7.

All of the occurrences of 我们 in these examples are used by the Chinese participants instead of the usual singular 我. One reason for this might be that it is polite in Chinese to avoid expressing personal feelings or opinions too openly and to mediate such utterances through the voice of the implied

Table 6.7 Chinese examples of the aggregate use of 'we'

1	R1	559	Ms Liu	(..) 好像**我们** 早年 我们这个年龄
				(..) hǎoxiàng wǒmen zǎonián wǒmen zhège niánlíng
				(..) seem we in early time we this age
				(..) it seems that back then people of our age
2	R1	136	Ms Bai	**我们**那时候呢就没有的选择
				wǒmen nà shíhou ne jiù méiyǒu de xuǎnzé
				we at that time have no choice
				at that time we didn't have a choice
3	R1	147	Ms Wen	(..) 那以前说起**我们**:::读书的时候啊
				(..) nà yǐqián shuō qǐ wǒmen::: dú shū de shíhou a
				(..) then previously talking about we::: studying when
				(..) speaking of when we::: studied back then

group (Xiang, 2003). Another reason might relate to the 'strong preference for past-time orientation' in Chinese culture (Yau, 1988: 53) whereby the past experiences of an individual cannot be conceived as separate from the experiences of the group as a whole. Thus, as the three Chinese older participants tell their stories they tend to choose the collective rather than the singular form to self-reference even though their story might be quite personal.

Example 6.8 'At that time we were teachers'
Chinese conversation (R1): Ms Liu, Chrissie

234	Ms Liu	那时**我**::: 很多很多 有 有的给我寄 di 有的给我寄 卡::: 问候
		nà shí **wǒ**::: hěn duō hěn duō yǒu yǒude gěi wǒ jì di yǒude gěi wǒ jì kǎ::: wènhòu
		at that time i::: many many there some send me some send me ca:::rd to greet
		at that time many many people sent me:::sent me greeting ca:::rds
235		那就是**我 我**觉得 我这个选择工作**我**觉得很开心 (H)
		nà jiùshì **wǒ wǒ** juéde wǒ zhègè xuǎnzé gōngzuò **wǒ** juéde hěn kāixīn (H)
		that is i i feel i this choice work i feel very happy (H)
		that is i feel my choice of this work is good i feel very happy
236		当时**我们**做老师 工资 薪水 非常 非常 得 低 (H)
		dāngshí **wǒmen** zuò lǎoshī gōngzī xīnshuǐ fēicháng fēicháng de dī (H)
		at that time we being teacher salary payment very very low (H)
		at that time we were teachers and the salary was very very low
237		大学毕业 只有 人民币 四十 (.) 二 块
		dàxué bìyè zhǐ yǒu rénmínbì sì shí (.) èr kuài
		university graduate only have renminbi forty (.) two
		after graduation from university our salary was only forty (.) two yuan
238	Chrissie	噢::: (H)
		ò::: (H)
		oh::: (H)
		oh::: (H)
239	Ms Liu	<E veli veli E>
		<E veli veli E>
		<E veli veli E>
240	Chrissie	=很少
		=hěn shǎo
		=very little
		=very little

(Continued)

Example 6.8 (Continued)

241	Ms Liu	少 很:::少 但是**我们**一样做得 很开心 对不对 但是 现在不同了
		shǎo hěn::: shǎo dànshì wǒmen yíyàng zuò de hěn kāixīn duì bú duì dànshì xiànzài bùtóng le
		little very::: little but we same do very happy is it right but now it is different
		very little::: however we were very happy is it right but now it is different
242		我现在的工资是 论 万::: 计 **我**的退休金有 (.) 九千 退休金
		wǒ xiànzài de gōngzī shì lùn wàn::: jì wǒde tuìxiūjīn yǒu (.) jiǔ qiān tuìxiūjīn
		my current salary is counted by ten thousand::: my retirement pension have (.) nine thousand retirement pension
		my current salary is worth ten thousand::: my retirement pension is (.) nine thousand
243		都有九千
		dōu yǒu jiǔ qiān
		all have nine thousand
		up to nine thousand
244	Chrissie	=噢
		=ò
		=oh
		=oh
245	Ms Liu	所以不一样了 那 当时**我们**参加的时候 没有那么 好::: 哇:::
		suǒyǐ bù yíyàng le nà dāngshí wǒmén cānjiā de shíhòu méiyǒu nàme hǎo::: wà:::
		so not same then at that time we join in not that good::: wow:::
		so it is not the same at that time when we went to work it was not that good::: wow:::
246		[对吧
		[duì ba
		[is it right
		[is it right
247	Chrissie	嗯]
		èn]
		um]
		um]

In this example we can see that Ms Liu seems to be speaking on behalf of people from her past even as she tells the student that she was a teacher on a low salary but was very happy nonetheless (lines 236, 241). This is especially interesting when the present is intertwined with the past: we can detect the change of lens from singular to plural in lines 236, 241 and 245.

The shift from 我 to 我们 and back to 我 might be a way to get the hearer's attention, as the student may be less able to relate to the experiences of a group she is not familiar with. The collective form 我们 may also reflect the nostalgic feelings aroused in the speaker as she remembers her past (Yau, 1988), particularly a past in a country and culture she has left behind. In terms of affective engagement, we can see that Ms Liu is more engaged when the collective pronoun is used and more detached when she is speaking in the singular about certain facts in her present life. Apart from its role in self-distancing or authority-distribution, the use of 我们 evokes the social aspect of identity, the belonging to a group, and thinking about this referent group can 'trigger emotions' (Smith, 1993: 303). This, in fact, also reveals the emergent and context-dependent nature of the speaker's identity in talk-in-interaction (Huang & Lu, 2013). The practice of pronoun switching was not specific to this example but was common among the three Chinese participants.

Even though German has no equivalent usage of 'wir' in the sense of 'ich' (*I*) we did notice some variable uses of the singular and plural forms when the participants were describing their immediate family, in contrast to the consistent use of the plural in references to their extended family (i.e. relatives in Germany) (see Table 6.8).

A careful look at the profiles of the speakers and the topics being discussed may help to explain these findings. Mr Schmidt's and Mr Günther's use of the singular to describe their immediate family (e.g. 'mein Sohn' (*my son*)) are reasonable because of their marriage history and family status (Table 6.1). Mr Schmidt divorced the mother of his son a long time ago and has been living with a new partner for many years; 'mein Sohn' therefore indicates that his present partner (the most usual co-referent of his 'wir') is not the mother of his son. In the case of Mr Günther, who also separated from the mother of his older children a long time ago and now lives with his second partner and their son, his use of the singular 'mein Sohn' may be an attempt to avoid any confusion between

Table 6.8 German participants' use of both 'wir' and 'ich' when describing their immediate family

	Mr Schmidt (R1)	Mr Schmidt (R2)	Mr Günther (R1)	Mr Günther (R2)	Mrs Fischer (R1)	Mrs Fischer (R2)
Use of 'ich' (*I*) and 'mein' (*my*) when talking about immediate family	7	3	3	1	4	1
Use of 'wir' (*we*) and 'unser' (*our*) when talking about immediate family	0	0	0	0	3	2

his first and second families. On the other hand, the use of the possessive 'mein' may simply be a way for these men to show paternal pride in their sons.

Mrs Fischer's case, however, is intriguing. This German participant, who has a very stable marriage and four children with her husband, used 'ich' and 'wir' interchangeably in talking about her immediate family. In particular, she showed a consistent mixed use of *my* and *our* in referring to her children or grandchildren, and this happened constantly.

Example 6.9 'I have four children'
German conversation (R1): Mrs Fischer, Nicholas

111	Mrs Fischer	nich-/ ja/ ja gut (..) und hier in australien (...) ist **unsere** familie (..) gewachsen
		isnt it/ yes/ yes good (..) and here in australia (...) our family (..) grew up
112		**mein mann und ich** haben zwei töchter (.) und zwei söhne wie viel sind das/
		my husband and i have two daughters (.) and two sons how many is that
		....
125	Nicholas	<E as in (..) like whose whose children/ E>
126	Mrs Fischer	**ich** ich habe vier kinder=
		i have four children
127	Nicholas	=oh
128	Mrs Fischer	verstehen sie des/=
		do you understand that/=
129	Nicholas	=ja=
		=yes=

In this extract Mrs Fischer uses 'unsere' for her immediate family, probably to distinguish them from her family back in Germany, which she refers to as 'mein' (*my*) family. In the same sentence she uses 'mein Mann und ich' (*my husband and I*) to explain what 'unsere' refers to. Ten lines later, she switches to 'ich' in response to the student's question in English rather than repeating the phrase 'mein Mann und ich' or 'unsere Familie'. Her focus now seems to be on the number of children she and her husband have – not on the fact that they are hers or her husband's children. We can see that in order to get her meaning across to Nicholas there is negotiation of meaning between them. Mrs Fischer may feel that the use of 'ich' or 'mein' is comparatively easier and more explicit for the student. As we can see, she has been checking the student's comprehension, and the simpler statement could well be a conscious language strategy to help her interlocutor, in this case a second language student, understand what she is saying. Unlike Mr Schmidt and Mr Günther, who focus more on the topics, Mrs Fischer pays much more attention to the student's language use and comprehension. That is, her use of 'ich' rather than 'wir' may have facilitated comprehension and interaction rather than signalling any actual change of alignment.

Conclusion

Self-referencing has been widely accepted as a useful indicator of the social realities and cultural norms of a particular society (Mühlhäusler et al., 1990; von Wiese, 1965). This chapter has examined how the first person plural was employed in self-referencing by native speakers of Chinese and German in dyad conversations with non-native speakers. We found that collective self-referencing was more explicit and specific in the German data: that 'wir' and its variants were used in a very deictic way and created a clearer in-group boundary with respect to other referent groups. In contrast, the Chinese speakers' referential choice of the first person plural was very vague and referred predominantly to an unspecified or ambiguous collectivity. Such vague use of *we* in the Chinese data might nonetheless open up more opportunities for the speaker to move between different groups with greater ease: with a blurred boundary, the speaker can simultaneously be a member of the older generation, an immigrant to Australia, a spokesperson for a people with a great culture, and an actor in China's past – all of these memberships intertwined and overlapping.

This cross-language comparison also provides evidence that the self not only reflects and is shaped by the speaker's culture, but is linguistically constructed and realised dynamically in the contingent moments of the interaction. On the one hand, the referential choice of *we* is the result of the speaker's interactional patterns shaped by his or her original culture. The Chinese self is primarily collectively oriented, which imposes a greater influence on Chinese participants to choose the first person plural. Their wide ranging use of 我们 to refer to the speaker and to unspecified people or groups, as well as to replace the singular 我 in describing a personal story, are manifestations of a deeply rooted belief in the self's 'harmonious integration into the social fabric' (Yau, 1988: 44). In contrast, the German participants' inclination to use the specific referential 'wir' reflects Western notions of individuality and the freedom 'to express one's genuine self' (Yau, 1988).

On the other hand, referential choice has also been shown to be influenced by the speaker's judgement of the interactional moment as well as their perception of their own and their interlocutor's group membership that is negotiated in context. A sense of situatedness of referring is at play in our data of both languages, providing more evidence for the emergent and context-dependent nature of the speaker's identity in talk-in-interaction. The alignment with any in-group either for the purpose of boundary creation, institutional engagement or prescribing an (a)symmetrical relationship, however, is not mutually exclusive, but is context-dependent and is influenced by the speaker's communicative purpose in the moment.

Note

(1) All participants' names have been changed.

References

Baumgarten, N. (2008) Writer construction in English and German popularized academic discourse: The uses of 'we' and 'wir'. *Multilingua* 27, 409–438.

Biq, Y.O. (1991) The multiple uses of the second person singular pronoun 'ni' in conversational Mandarin. *Journal of Pragmatics* 16 (4), 307–321.

Bourdieu, P. (1991) *Language and Symbolic Power*. Cambridge, MA: Harvard University Press.

Brewer, M.B. and Gardner, W. (1996) Who is this 'we'? Levels of collective identity and self representations. *Journal of Personality and Social Psychology* 71 (1), 83–93.

Brown, R. and Gilman, A. (1960) The pronouns of power and solidarity. In T.A. Sebeok (ed.) *Style in Language* 253–276. Cambridge, MA: MIT Press.

Bucholtz, M. and Hall, K. (2005) Identity and interaction: A sociocultural linguistic approach. *Discourse Studies* 7 (4–5), 585–614.

Budwig, N. (2000) Language and the construction of self. In N. Budwig, I. Užgiris, and J.V. Wertsch (eds) *Communication: An Arena of Development* (pp. 195–214). Stamford, CT: Ablex Publishing Corporation.

Chao, Y.R. (1956) Chinese terms of address. *Language* 32, 217–241.

Coppieters, R. (1982) Description and attitudes: The problem of reference to individuals. *Studies in Language* 6 (1), 1–22.

Holland, D. and Quinn, N. (1987) *Cultural Models in Language and Thought*. Cambridge: Cambridge University Press.

Hsiao, C-H. (2011) Personal pronoun interchanges in Mandarin Chinese conversation. *Language Sciences* 33, 799–821.

Huang, H. and Lu, Y. (2013) Interactions of cultural identity and turn-taking organisation: A case study of a senior Chinese immigrant in Australia. *Chinese Language and Discourse* 4 (2), 229–252.

Kitagawa, C. and Lehrer, A. (1990) Impersonal uses of personal pronouns. *Journal of Pragmatics* 14, 739–759.

Kuo, C.H. (1999) The use of personal pronouns: Role relationships in scientific journal articles. *English for Specific Purposes* 18 (2), 121–138.

Lai, V.T. and Frajzyngier, Z. (2009) Change of functions of the first person pronouns in Chinese. In M. Dufresne, F. Dupuis, and E. Vocaj (eds) *Historical Linguistics 2007: Selected Papers from the 18th International Conference on Historical Linguistics, Montreal, 6–11 August 2007* (pp. 223–231). Amsterdam: John Benjamins.

Lee, C.L. (1999) The implications of mismatched personal pronouns in Chinese. *Text* 19 (3), 345–370.

Lee, C.L. (2012) Self-presentation, face and first-person pronouns in the Analects. *Journal of Politeness Research* 8, 75–92.

Lerner, G.H. and Kitzinger, C. (2007) Extraction and aggregation in the repair of individual and collective self-reference. *Discourse Studies* 9 (4), 526–557.

Mao, L.M.R. (1996) Chinese first person pronoun and social implicature. *Journal of Asian Pacific Communication* 7 (3–4), 106–128.
Markus, H.R. and Kitayama, S. (1991) Culture and the self: Implications for cognition, emotion, and motivation. *Psychological Review* 98 (2), 224–253.
Mühlhäusler, P., Harré, R., Holiday, A. and Freyne, M. (1990) *Pronouns and People: The Linguistic Construction of Social and Personal Identity*. Oxford: Blackwell.
Ochs, E. (1992) Indexing gender. In A. Duranti and C. Goodwin (eds) *Rethinking Context: Language as an Interactive Phenomenon* (pp. 335–358). Cambridge: Cambridge University Press.
Postoutenko, K. (2009) Between 'I' and 'we': Studying the grammar of social identity in Europe (1900–1950). *Journal of Language and Politics* 8 (2), 195–222.
Schegloff, E.A. (2007) Categories in action: Person-reference and membership categorization. *Discourse Studies* 9 (4), 433–461.
Scheibmann, J. (2004) 'Inclusive and exclusive patterning of the English first person plural: Evidence from conversation'. In M. Achard and S. Kemmer (eds) *Language, Culture and Mind* (pp. 377–396). Stanford, CA: CSLI Publications.
Smith, E.R. (1993) Social identity and social emotions: Toward new conceptualizations of prejudice. In D.M. Mackie and D.L. Hamilton (eds) *Affect, Cognition, and Stereotyping: Interactive Processes in Group Perception* (pp. 297–315). San Diego, CA: Academic Press.
Ting-Toomey, S. (1999) *Communicating across Cultures*. New York: The Guilford Press.
Vassileva, I. (1998) Who am I / Who are we in academic writing? A contrastive analysis of authorial presence in English, German, French, Russian and Bulgarian. *International Journal of Applied Linguistics* 8 (2), 163–190.
von Wiese, L. (1965) *Die Philosophie der persönlichen Fürwörter*. Tübingen: J.C.B. Mohr (P. Siebeck).
Whitt, R.J. (2014) Singular perception, multiple perspectives through 'we'. In T.-S. Pavlidou (ed.) *Constructing Collectivity: 'We' across Languages and Contexts* (pp. 45–64). Amsterdam: John Benjamins.
Xiang, X. (2003) Multiplicity of self in public discourse: The use of personal references in two radio sports shows. *Language Sciences* 25 (5), 489–514.
Yau, O.H. (1988) Chinese cultural values: Their dimensions and marketing implications. *European Journal of Marketing* 22 (5), 44–57.

7 Creating, Maintaining and Challenging Rapport Across Languages and Age Groups

Marisa Cordella and Cecilia Kokubu

Introduction

People naturally form social bonds that involve the display of both cognitive and emotional attachment. These social bonds can be general and transient, as in the case of strangers who act in a courteous fashion towards each other during a casual encounter, or they may be far more specific and enduring, their evolution sustained by what Baumeister and Leary (1995: 497) call a sense of *belongingness*: 'a pervasive drive to form and maintain at least a minimum quantity of lasting, positive, and significant interpersonal relationships'. In order to develop this sense of belongingness, individuals must usually submit their behaviour to a process of fine-tuning that is affected by both personality factors and external circumstances. Having done so, however, they have laid the groundwork for relationships based on mutual understanding and a sense of rapport that enhances shared pleasures, facilitates cooperation and enables better resolution of conflicts (Drolet & Morris, 2000).

When interactions run smoothly, feelings of rapport are taken for granted. But when relationships become distant or cold it is the *absence* of rapport that becomes the salient feature of the interaction. This chapter will address how rapport can be established, maintained and repaired, and analyses the linguistic acts that encouraged or discouraged rapport during some of the verbal intergenerational and intercultural exchanges recorded for our project.

Identifying Rapport

Human beings develop rapport through particular verbal and non-verbal cues that are selected during the course of an interaction: the manifestation of rapport is often described as 'clicking' or 'having chemistry' with another person (Tickle-Degnen & Rosenthal, 1990: 286). This experience is vital for the success of any communicative event, since the establishment and maintenance of rapport, while affected by variables of the specific interaction, invariably modifies the quality and outcomes of the communication (Tickle-Degnen & Rosenthal, 1990).

The significant role that rapport plays in social interactions has been studied across different settings, ranging from corner-shop transactions in Ecuador (Placencia, 2004) to the prescribed, customer-service speech styles of call centres on the world (Hultgren, 2011). Other studies have focused on rapport in the analysis of communication difficulties during qualitative interviews (Roulston, 2011), in understanding non-native speakers expressing disagreement in English during business negotiations (Bjørge, 2012), in the realisation of empathy in medical discourse (Cordella, 2004; Cordella & Musgrave, 2009), and, of particular relevance to our study, in the communication strategies used by education professionals (Jiang & Ramsay, 2005; Nguyen, 2007) with diverse language and cultural groups.

Studies carried out on instructor–student relationships have identified rapport as an essential component that facilitates learning, as part of the interactive process of teaching that involves constructing social relationships in the classroom (Jiang & Ramsay, 2005; Nguyen, 2007). The act of building rapport within a learning environment enhances second language learning in particular: through rapport teachers make the practice more pleasurable and reduce the social distance between themselves and their students, thus minimising learners' anxiety and increasing their commitment to the task (Jiang & Ramsay, 2005).

Rapport can help to attenuate some of the challenges associated with intergenerational communication. The Communication Predicament of Aging Model (Ryan et al., 1986) describes how stereotyping of older people by young adults influences their expectations and negatively impacts the possibilities for rewarding relationships between the generations.

One particularly problematic feature of intergenerational communication is *overaccommodation* (Ryan et al., 1986; Coupland et al., 1988; Williams, 1996; Harwood et al., 2000; Yue & Ng, 2000), 'a category of miscommunication wherein a participant perceives a speaker to transcend those sociolinguistic behaviours the participant judges necessary for attuned talk on a particular occasion' (Coupland et al., 1988: 32). Instances of overaccommodation include the use of basic vocabulary and grammar, overstated intonation, and inappropriate terms of endearment (Harwood et al., 2000). Although the speech style resulting from overaccommodation is most likely well intended, it is usually evaluated negatively by the hearer and described as '"patronizing," "demeaning," and "talking down"' (Harwood et al., 2000). Studies conducted in nursing homes also reveal instances of baby talk or 'elderspeak' with older people (Ryan et al., 1994; Kemper et al., 1998).

The other side of the coin is *underaccommodation* (Williams, 1996). This describes a speaker's disregard for the sociolinguistic behaviours required for attuned talk, such as interruptions, inattentiveness and lack of interest (Coupland *et al.*, 1988; Williams, 1996; Yue & Ng, 2000). It originates from both positive and negative speaker intent, but is invariably perceived negatively by the hearer (Coupland *et al.*, 1988).

Significant as the by-products of rapport may be, the concept of rapport itself, although familiar in everyday discourse, has not yet been clearly defined or studied in detail in the field of sociolinguistics. Definitions tend to assume an implicit collective understanding and are limited to vague descriptions of positive interactions (Tickle-Degnen & Rosenthal, 1990). In the field of linguistics, rapport is often treated as a derivative or sub-component of Brown and Levinson's politeness theory (1978) and is not always accompanied by a working definition (Campbell, 2005; Spencer-Oatey, 2002; Nguyen, 2007; Hultgren, 2011; Johnson, 1992; Bjørge, 2012). For instance, Spencer-Oatey terms 'rapport sensitive incidents' (2002: 534) those social interactions in which certain elements of a relationship between interlocutors become noticeable either positively or negatively. This clearly recognises a relationship between rapport and interaction but does not adequately describe rapport *per se*.

Drawing from politeness theory, Spencer-Oatey also proposes a 'rapport management model' (2002: 540) based on the management of a speaker's 'face', i.e. personal and social rights and entitlements. Similarly, Johnson (1992) observes the use of compliments by academics with the intention of moderating potential face-threatening acts (Brown & Levinson, 1987) and establishing rapport during the process of reviewing the work of their peers. Although Johnson's study focuses on compliments, rapport is alluded to as a direct consequence and/or motivation for this form of praise/approval; however no definition is offered for the term and it is not distinctly differentiated from politeness.

While Deborah Tannen does not directly address the concept of rapport, and while rapport is not plainly distinguished from politeness in her writing, the nexus between them is evident nonetheless. In a discussion that relates face and rapport, she describes two types of conversational styles based on the observation of North American subjects of different cultural backgrounds that are directly derived from Lakoff's rules of rapport: 'Rule 1, Don't impose; Rule 2, Give options; and Rule 3, Maintain camaraderie' (cited in Tannen, 2009: 302). According to Tannen, an interlocutor employing a 'high-involvement' conversational style makes the connection with the speaker evident through the use of conspicuous signals such as frequent backchannelling and 'short interturn pauses'. In contrast, conversational partners who favour a 'high-considerateness' style tend to deliberately refrain from imposing, by avoiding overlapping talk and allowing longer interturn pauses. Accordingly, Tannen classifies high-involvement style interlocutors as abiding by Lakoff's Rule 3, 'Maintain camaraderie', and high-considerateness style interlocutors as complying with Rules 1 and 2, 'Don't impose' and 'Give options'.

Another noteworthy, albeit controversial, study involving rapport is that in which Goldberg (1990) traces interruptions, proposing the latter as a potential manifestation of an interlocutor's interest and involvement during the conversation. Based on the extent to which the interrupted speaker's positive and/or negative 'face wants' (887) are attended to, interferences can be evaluated as 'rapport-oriented interruptions' (890); interlocutors who invade a speaker's turn, provided they supply appropriate and relevant remarks, may well tend to their partner's positive face, who in turn may interpret the intrusion as an '[expression] of open empathy, affection, solidarity, interest, concern, etc.' (890). However, the associating of interruptions with rapport-building needs to be treated with caution, as certain speakers may not favour this practice, or the actual motivation behind the interruption may be ambiguous.

Identification of the forms of rapport can advance our understanding of what rapport actually is. Such is the case with Cordella and Musgrave's (2009) linguistic study on the attainment of empathy in medical discourse. Interestingly, and akin to the elusiveness of rapport, the authors make reference to the lack of a 'consistent construct' (2009: 130) in the literature that outlines the notion of empathy. They do, however, mention Frankel's observation regarding the common element in all definitions – 'a response to another's emotion' (Frankel, 2000: 89) – and expand this notion citing Bennett, who describes empathy as the process by which a person identifies with another person's feelings, facilitating a 'shift of perspective away from [their] own to an acknowledgement of the other person's different experience' (1979: 417) – a behaviour that is vital for good interactions. The relationship between empathy and rapport can also be appreciated in Cordella's (2004) work on doctor–patient communication, in which she identifies three types of 'voices' medical practitioners employ during their consultations: the 'Doctor voice', the 'Educator voice' and the 'Fellow Human voice'. This last voice is markedly relevant to the construct of rapport as it is accomplished through the enactment of empathy, inviting patients 'to open up about their personal situations and feelings, and [conveying] affiliation, interest and involvement' (2004: 121). This voice describes conduct that, coupled with a regard for the interlocutor's face needs, should be considered in the shaping of a suitable model of rapport.

Other authors describe rapport as 'friendly relations' (Placencia, 2004: 217), 'the abstract equivalent of small talk' (Hultgren, 2011: 49), 'enjoyable interactions and personal connection' (Campbell, 2005: 424) and 'a positive social relationship characterised by mutual trust and emotional affinity' (Nguyen, 2007: 286); but while presenting a more concrete notion of rapport, these phrases hardly describe its complexity, nor do they account for the linguistic acts that construe rapport or illustrate the dynamic nature of rapport's interpersonal frame (e.g. aspects of non-verbal communication, Tickle-Degnen, 2006).

Additionally, whereas politeness theory certainly highlights elements or strategies that are essential for the establishment and maintenance of rapport, such as consideration of the interlocutor's face needs, we suggest that rapport cannot be solely understood on the basis of the prevention of face-threatening acts.

Considering that the sociolinguistic aspects of rapport have not yet been fully described, this study proposes a preliminary model of verbal rapport and a taxonomy of rapport enactment drawn from Tickle-Degnen and Rosenthal's model of non-verbal rapport (1990) and also from stance theory (Englebretson, 2007; Du Bois, 2007; Jaffe, 2009). The aims of the study are to examine verbal rapport-building practices among individuals – in this case between older native Spanish speakers and young students of Spanish – and to offer a model and a taxonomy for testing, development and use in future research.

A Model of Rapport

We start by providing a brief definition of rapport from a social psychology perspective. We then explain the notion of stance from a sociolinguistic perspective, and list three theoretical approaches that are fundamental to our work: (1) a description of the three components that Tickle-Degnen and Rosenthal identify as essential to the establishment of rapport; (2) the dynamic elements that directly impact the generation of these components; and (3) the five principles Englebretson identifies as inherent to stance that account for the positioning adopted by individuals during the verbal exchange.

Secondly, we discuss how both social psychology and sociolinguistic approaches to human interaction are pivotal to our model. At a macro level, Tickle-Degnen and Rosenthal provide our model's core structure and dynamics, while stance theory supplies the sociocultural matrix that connects rapport-building performance with the social meaning attached to it (Jaffe, 2009). At a micro level, stance theory contributes the notion of stance-taking acts: individual actions serving simultaneously as the building blocks of rapport and as discrete units with which the presence of rapport can be observed, described and measured.

We then continue by presenting an exploratory model of verbal rapport that incorporates the aforementioned elements and illustrates its dynamic nature, and an analytical taxonomy of rapport enactment in which we list, define, exemplify and quantify the stance-taking acts of native-language older participants and young language learners as they establish, maintain, restore and/or undo rapport.

Finally, we consider the limitations of our data and offer suggestions for improved procedures and data collection in future rapport-related studies.

Rapport and Stance

Tickle-Degnen and Rosenthal's (1990) model of non-verbal rapport is particularly suitable for our study as its multi-dimensional conceptualisation (1) positions rapport as an interpersonal phenomenon, (2) emphasises that rapport exists exclusively in interactions and (3) covers numerous aspects of communication. The manifestation of rapport, according to this model, besides needing two or more participants, depends on the presence of three essential components. The first of these is *mutual attentiveness*, which serves to 'focus the attention of the group inwards' and to create a 'boundary to the interaction' (Tickle-Degnen & Rosenthal, 1987: 121). Linguistically, this refers exclusively to facilitating the sensorial perception of a speaker's utterances. That is, employing the appropriate volume, word articulation and speech rate so that the hearer can follow what is being said easily, and avoiding external factors which could intrude into the sound field of the interaction. The second component is the degree of *positivity* between interactants, i.e. feelings of 'mutual friendliness and caring' (Tickle-Degnen & Rosenthal, 1987: 286), while the third is *coordination*, 'the existence of a mutual responsiveness, such that every member of the group reacts immediately, spontaneously and sympathetically to the sentiments and attitudes of every other member' (Park & Burgess cited in Tickle-Degnen & Rosenthal, 1987).

Although these components may seem to be closely related – or indeed even equivalent – they index different attitudes. Two political adversaries engaged in a heated debate reflect a high degree of *mutual attentiveness* but a low degree of *positivity*, or even *coordination*, should they constantly attempt to take over each other's turn. Similarly, friends excitedly talking over each other display high degrees of *positivity* with low degrees of *coordination*. It is also necessary to keep in mind that these components are subordinated to the dynamic and interactive nature of rapport, and that their presence does not always translate into instant or reciprocal affinity. Tickle-Degnen and Rosenthal (1990) propose that rapport is not necessarily openly expressed, but that an individual's feelings go through what they refer to as an *expressiveness filter*, emerging as utterances that may or may not correspond with the original speaker's intention. Once the utterance is produced it undergoes an *accuracy filter* through which the interlocutor interprets the speaker's meaning with varying degrees of accuracy. In brief, a speaker's intention regarding an utterance and a recipient's interpretation of it may not necessarily accord, as different interpretative schemas may cause individuals to perceive and evaluate utterances differently.

Additionally, manifestations of rapport are subject to variability during the course of an exchange: the three essential components of rapport exist in interspersed states of balance and fluctuation. According to Tronick (1990), this is by no means an indication of failure to generate rapport. *Interactive errors*, such as glitches in *mutual attentiveness, positivity* and *coordination* are bound to occur, but one of the features that distinguishes 'good' interactions from 'bad' is the use of *interactive repairs*: the ability to return to a smooth exchange.

Although Tickle-Degnen and Rosenthal's work was conceived for the study of body language from a social psychology perspective, the structure and dynamics of its three components of rapport provide a blueprint for an analysis of verbal exchanges. However, this still leaves us with the need to identify a *verbal* component through which rapport can be observed and measured. Stances, consisting of linguistic and social acts (Jaffe, 2009), provide the missing element that completes the model.

Englebretson (2007) unpacks five principles of stance-taking in naturally occurring exchanges that are applicable to the practice of rapport-building. The first principle identifies stance as a tangible action that is coupled with 'personal belief, attitude and evaluation' (2007: 14). Secondly, stance is characterised as a public act, meaning it is readily recognisable and subject to both interpretation and evaluation. Thirdly, the interactional nature of stance requires a collaborative effort in order to emerge. The fourth principle highlights the notion that stances reflect a 'wider physical context or socio-cultural field' (2007: 15), and the fifth principle posits that stance-taking generates consequences.

These principles are in fact inextricably linked to rapport-building practices. To take the first of these, the process of constructing rapport is indeed influenced by the participants' beliefs, attitudes and evaluations. For example, our older Spanish-speaking immigrants established rapport with the language students in ways that were affected by their beliefs about and attitudes to the younger generation and about the value of the project. Second principle: rapport is dialogically achieved; that is, it only exists if the target of the rapport can readily recognise the rapport-oriented linguistic act, which must be public and readily available for recognition, interpretation and evaluation. Third, rapport, like stance, can only be achieved interactively and consequently requires the collaborative input of all participants involved. Fourth, the development of rapport is also subject to broader social and environmental forces. In our study, the context is multi-faceted: it is at once intergenerational, intercultural and task-oriented. As experts in the target language and as authority figures on account of their seniority (Cordella & Huang, 2012, 2014), the older Spanish speakers had a potentially larger share of control over the manifestation and development of rapport. Lastly, actions taken to develop rapport generate consequences: specifically, the presence or absence of feelings of rapport in all, some or none of the participants.

A Model of Verbal Rapport

Establishing rapport is therefore a stance: it is an action, it is public, it is collaborative, it is dialogical, it is indicative of a wider physical and socio-cultural context, and it generates consequences. Furthermore, rapport stance-taking acts (RSAs) are determined by the position individuals take and assign to others. Through positioning, individuals 'project, assign, propose, constrain, define, or otherwise shape the subject positions of their interlocutors' (Jaffe, 2009: 8). It is thus by virtue of individual RSAs that speakers avail themselves of the building blocks that construct *mutual attentiveness, positivity* and *coordination*, and that observers are provided with discrete verbal units for the gauging of rapport.

We therefore propose a cyclical model in which participants experience *mutual attentiveness, positivity* and *coordination* positively, neutrally or negatively as the result of their interpretation of their interlocutor's RSAs, received in the form of utterances, which in turn undergo two non-verbal stages that can either modify, enhance or reverse their original intention. The outcome of each RSA naturally affects the recipient's ensuing input, resulting in a highly dynamic exchange wherein participants regularly feed each other's responses. Figure 7.1 illustrates each stage of the process.

Participant A's input or intended message passes through a non-verbal *expressiveness filter* (Tickle-Degnen & Rosenthal, 1990) and is transmitted via an utterance that can be neutral, an RSA, an interactive error or an interactive repair (Tronick, 1990). It then reaches B's non-verbal *accuracy filter* (Tickle-Degnen & Rosenthal, 1990) where it is translated into positive, neutral or negative values of *mutual attentiveness, positivity* and/or

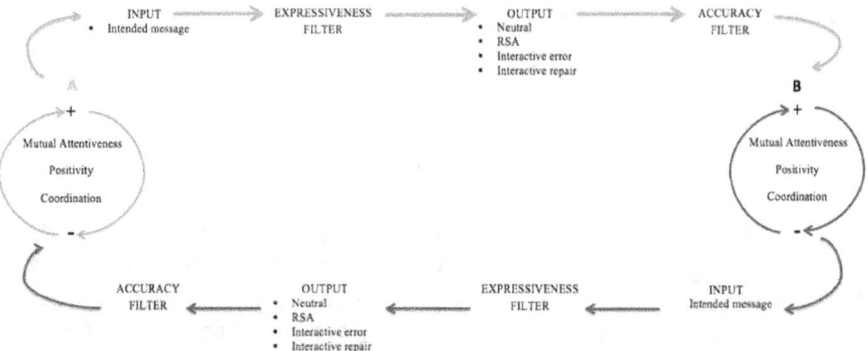

Figure 7.1 A cyclical model of rapport in verbal communication

coordination. B's interpretation of A's message then determines the input of his/her next turn, and so on, re-activating the cycle. As the interaction proceeds, the sum of filters and utterances facilitates the emergence of one of three rapport outcomes that will likely outlast the contact situation: *reciprocal rapport,* in which both participants experience rapport; *unilateral rapport,* in which only one participant experiences rapport; and *no rapport,* where neither participant experiences rapport.

Data Collection and Analysis

Transcriptions of 12 Spanish conversations conducted as part of our project provided the data for this study. The speakers were six student–older participant dyads, recorded on three separate occasions: the first at the beginning of the year (the start of the school year in the southern hemisphere), the second in the middle of the year, and the third at the end of the year. The data analysed in this chapter compared the exchanges held in the first and third recordings (C1) and (C3).

In this part we focus on identifying the verbal RSAs that were employed to establish, maintain, restore or undo each of the three essential components of rapport, and compare their frequency and distribution between participant groups. Each of the three components is discussed separately.

Mutual attentiveness

Mutual attentiveness is achieved by delineating the confines of the interaction and by enabling the effortless sensorial capture of the speakers' utterances. In fact, mutual attentiveness is a pre-requisite for *any* type of successful verbal exchange, irrespective of rapport. Table 7.1 presents a description of the RSAs included in this category.

Table 7.1 RSAs that shape *mutual attentiveness*

RSA	Description
Uses adequate voice volume, word articulation and speech rate	Interlocutor is able to hear and identify speaker's utterance
Minimises external interruptions	Manages background noise and third-party intrusions
Is unintelligible	Voice is inaudible, speaker does not articulate words properly, speech rate is too fast
Is distracted by external factors	The verbal exchange is interrupted or terminated by background noise and/or third-party intrusions

Measuring these RSAs is not straightforward. On the one hand, the requisite of speaker intelligibility is not negotiable; an audible speaking volume, a rate of speech that can be easily followed, and proper word articulation are conditions that must be met for any oral communication to be effective, and these conditions can only be gauged in terms of a continuum of variability of RSAs that accounts for the listener's sensitivity, as shown in Tickle-Degnen's research on Parkinson's disease (Tickle-Degnen, pers. comm.). On the other hand, it is possible to count individual occasions in which participants are momentarily unintelligible or in which they manage or are distracted by external factors. So while the first RSA in Table 7.1 cannot be quantified, the remaining three can be. Consequently, as RSAs were present in the recorded conversations that both could and could not be measured in numbers, and as only one quantifiable RSA of mutual attentiveness was observed in all twelve conversations (see Example 7.1), frequencies for this category are not included.

The limited range of RSAs found in our student–adult exchanges does not mean that this component will fail to deliver information on rapport in future research. It is necessary to consider our data's linguistic context here: older adults were quite thoughtful when changing their voice volume, rate of speech and word articulation for the students. At the same time, the students' language limitations resulted in short and simple utterances that could be easily captured. Additionally, these meetings were classed as a school activity, a setting that is apt to constrain distractions or interruptions. Other types of interactions may provide better material on mutual attentiveness, such as the following extract, in which the older participant seeks to minimise background noise by calling the attention of another participant who is speaking rather loudly and intruding into the boundaries of her conversation with the student.

Example 7.1 'What's the name of that man?'
Spanish conversation: Mrs Fernandez, Rachel*

117	Mrs Fernandez	bueno acá me contestaste ya tú piensa- que cuando (.) cuando termine finalice
		ok here you have already answered do you think that when (.) you finish
118	Rachel	sí
		yes
119	Mrs Fernandez	tu estudio (.) podrás seguir siendo amigos tuyos (.)
		your studies (.) will they still be your friends (.)
120	Rachel	<E some E>
		<E some E>

Example 7.1 (Continued)

121	Mrs Fernandez	cómo/ se llama ese hombre <E the name the man E> [ah oscar]
		what's/ the name of that man <E the name the man E> [ah oscar]
		((older man speaking loudly))
122	Rachel	ahh [oscar]
		ahh [oscar]
123	Mrs Fernandez	OSCAR
		OSCAR
124	Rachel	<@@>
		<@@>
125	Mrs Fernandez	(.) bue- bueno (.) bueno dónde estabas:::: (.) bueno (.) qué es para ti bueno sí se lo dije QUÉ para ti un buen amigo (.) qué pasea contigo (..) qué conversa contigo qué salen a caminar
		(.) ok ok (.) where were you:::: (.) ok (.) what is yes I told him WHAT is a good friend (.) to you someone who goes out with you (..) talks with you goes for a walk with you

* All participants' names have been changed.

The utterance 'Where were you' in line 125 resumes the conversation while the loud calling of the participant's name 'OSCAR' (line 123) and the student's laugh in line 124 index the intrusive nature of Oscar's loud voice into their conversation. This example highlights the degree of attentiveness being maintained by the pair.

Positivity

Positivity operates within a spectrum that ranges from more positive to less positive language behaviours. Table 7.2 illustrates the diverse RSAs that model this particular component of rapport.

As our taxonomy suggests, RSAs of positivity can be enacted by shifting the positions of participants at different points throughout the interaction. The two extracts below illustrate the diversity of such positions; in the first, the older participant closes the age gap between herself and the student by portraying herself as the latter's peer, and in the second the older participant adopts the role of language instructor, enthusiastically commenting on her student's progress.

Table 7.2 RSAs that shape *positivity*

RSA	Description
Gives positive feedback	• Expresses approval regarding interlocutor's utterances and answers through explicit comments, e.g. *that is a good answer; well done*. • Acknowledges progress

Positions her/himself as interlocutor's peer	• Steps out of role generated by activity, i.e. language instructor/student, and/or closes generational gap by:
	  • lowering voice in order to circumvent recording (see Example 7.2)
	  • challenging/deviating from the activity
	  • addressing/treating interlocutor as equal/fellow/friend

Shows personal interest in interlocutor	• Asks (non-scripted) questions about:
	  • personal history
	  • life story
	  • family composition
	  • likes/dislikes, interests, hobbies
	  • opinions/ideology
	• Comments on information previously provided by interlocutor

Makes positive comments about interlocutor	• Welcomes/expresses warm feelings towards partner
	• Compliments interlocutor/interlocutor's family members
	• Is supportive/encouraging of interlocutor's/interlocutor's family members' actions, activities, personal history, future plans and/or ideology
	• Expresses good wishes regarding:
	  • the well-being of interlocutor and their family
	  • interlocutor's plans and future

Expresses approval regarding interlocutor's personal history, ideology, and/or actions	• Qualifies interlocutor's/interlocutor's family members' actions, activities, personal history, future plans, and/or ideology as good, valuable and/or important • Expresses agreement with interlocutor through explicit comments, e.g. *I agree; that's right; you're right*.
Intrudes into interlocutor's talk to articulate utterance for them	• Interrupts turn to speak an utterance that will then be attributed to interlocutor
Is insensitive to interlocutor's feelings	• Makes inappropriate comments • Asks inappropriate questions • Does not consider interlocutor's face

Example 7.2 'I'll repeat the word for you'
Spanish conversation: Mrs Agosto, Lily

199	Lily	<E sorry can you say that again/ E>
		<E sorry can you say that again/ E>
200	Mrs Agosto	buscar trabajo
		to look for a job
201	Lily	<E okay E>
		<E okay E>
202	Mrs Agosto	si TÚ no sabes el <E espelling E> de una palabra [dímelo]
		if YOU don't know the <E espelling E> of a word [tell me]
203	Lily	[hm:::]
		[hm:::]
204	Mrs Agosto	okay/ y yo te la te la repito
		okay/ and I'll repeat it for you
205		((inaudible whispering))
206	Mrs Agosto	<@@> [<@@>]
		<@@> [<@@>]
207	Lily	uhm
		uhm
208		<E [okay] <@@> yeah E> sí
		<E [okay] <@@> yeah E> yes

By lowering her voice and whispering in line 205, Mrs Agosto bypasses the recording, making the exchange private and flouting the activity's acknowledged, albeit unspoken rules. In doing so, she leaves her role of language instructor and authority figure to adopt a stance of complicity with the student as indexed by their laughter in line 208.

Example 7.3 'Your Spanish has improved so much!'
Spanish conversation: Mrs Valdez, Alice

438	Mrs Valdez	nos quedó faltando solamente una pregunta (.) <E okay E>
		this is the only question we're missing (.) <E okay E>
439		ALICE te felicito tu español ha mejorado MUCHÍSIMO desde la última vez que nos vimos
		congratulations ALICE your spanish has improved SO MUCH since we saw each other
440	Alice	(.) *hm* (.) gracias=
		(.) *hm* (.) thank you=
441	Mrs Valdez	=MUCHO MUCHO (.) realmente (.) MUCHO (.) MUCHO que ha mejorado su (..) quieres conservar ésto para [que]

(Continued)

Example 7.3 (Continued)

		=SO MUCH SO MUCH (.) really (.) SO MUCH (.) SO MUCH it's improved (..) would you like to keep this [so that]
442	Alice	[sí]
		[yes]
443	Mrs Valdez	(..) revisa las preguntas/ (..) y trata de pensar en otras respuestas es una buena práctica
		(..) you can review the questions/ (..) and try to think about other answers it's good practice
444		(..) AY te felicito alice=
		(..) OH congratulations alice=
445	Alice	=sí=
		=yes=
446	Mrs Valdez	=has mejorado MUCHÍSIMO tu español
		=your spanish has improved SO MUCH
447	Alice	(..) gracias
		(..) thank you

In this exchange, Mrs Valdez comments effusively on Alice's performance and efforts. Providing feedback is not specifically required by the activity; the fact that the older adult goes beyond her function in order to praise her student's progress could be indicative of her warm feelings towards her, while the nature of the feedback will likely have an encouraging effect on the student. Compliments made too profusely can be interpreted as 'overdoing it', of course, leaving the recipient feeling patronised, but this was not the case in the conversation here or in the many other examples we collected. Older participants spoke regularly of their pride in the language development and interest of their student partners.

Another way in which positivity can be stimulated is through the favourable evaluation and approval of the actions or ideology of the interactant. Example 7.4 illustrates how a student's actions – which are not related to the task – elicit the older participant's interest and encouragement.

Example 7.4 'My holidays in South Africa'
Spanish conversation: Mrs Agosto, Caitlin

1266	Mrs Agosto	(H) bueno (.) cuéntame tu esperas que/
		(H) okay (.) tell me do you hope/
1267	Caitlin	(.) uh:::m::: (.) yo (.) espero:::
		(.) uh:::m::: (.) I (.) hope:::
1268		(.) en el futuro (.) uh:::m (.) la vacació:::n/
		(.) in the future (.) uh:::m (.) holida:::y/

Example 7.4 (Continued)

1269	Mrs Agosto	(.) e:::n las próximas [vacaciones\]
		(.) du:::ring the next [holidays\]
1270	Caitlin	[en la pró]xima vacacione:::s
		[during the ne]xt holiday:::s
1271	Mrs Agosto	=<E the next (.) holidays\ (.) yeah E> (.) [las próximas] vacaciones\
		=<E the next (.) holidays\ (.) yeah E> (.) [the next] holidays
1272	Caitlin	[e:::n:::]
		[i:::n:::]
1273		(.) en sudáfrica/
		(.) in south africa/
1274	Mrs Agosto	(.) (H) ah en sudáfrica\ (.) ah:::=
		(.) (H) ah in south africa\ (.) ah:::=
1275		((a long exchange follows about South Africa followed by the student telling Mrs Agosto that she is working to pay for her ticket))
1276	Caitlin	(.) yo trabaj:::o:::/
		(.) I wor:::k/
1277	Mrs Agosto	(.) <E yeah E>
		(.) <E yeah E>
1278	Caitlin	(.) uh:::m::: ( ) uh:::
		(.) uh:::m::: ( ) uh:::
1279	Mrs Agosto	(.) para pagar/
		(.) to pay/
1280	Caitlin	(.) para (.) para::: (Hx) (H) (.) paga:::/
		(.) to (.) to::: (Hx) (H) (.) pay:::/
1281	Mrs Agosto	(.) tu pasaje/
		(.) your ticket/
1282	Caitlin	(.) por mi vacaciones (.) en sudáfrica\
		(.) for my holidays (.) in south africa
1283	Mrs Agosto	(.) ah:::
		(.) ah:::
1284	Caitlin	[<@ @>]
		[<@ @>]
1285	Mrs Agosto	(.) realmente estás haciendo eso
		(.) are you really doing that
1286	Caitlin	(.) hm/
		(.) hm/
1287	Mrs Agosto	(.) es- (.) realmente estás haciendo eso/
		(.) are (.) you really doing that/

(Continued)

Example 7.4 (Continued)

1288	Caitlin	<E yeah E>
		<E yeah E>
1289	Mrs Agosto	(.) fa:::nTÁ:::Stico
		(.) fanTA:::Stic
1290	Caitlin	<E yeah E>
		<E yeah E>
1291	Mrs Agosto	(.) (H) ah (.) que bueno (.) y dónde trabajas/
		(.) (H) ah (.) that's good (.) and where do you work/

This exchange promotes bi-directional positivity. Firstly, the student receives recognition and approval for her efforts to earn the money for her holiday in South Africa. Secondly, her confident behaviour counteracts any negative 'stereotyped expectations' (Harwood *et al.*, 2000: 37) that may have been held by the older adult concerning young people, and potentially contributes to the older participant's high regard for the student. Lines 1285 and 1287 index Mrs Agosto showing a degree of disbelief about Caitlin working to pay for her airfare: *Are you really doing that?* The student's affirmations in lines 1286 and 1288 prompt an enthusiastic 'fanTÁ:::Stico' from Mrs Agosto in line 1289, followed by a further token of appreciation (*that's good*) in line 1291. The positivity established by Mrs Agosto's warm response to Caitlin's travel plans facilitates a smooth topic transition as she then goes on to ask *And where do you work?*

We expand on this feature with the following example that illustrates the use of mutual compliments.

Example 7.5 'I'm comfortable with you'
Spanish conversation: Mrs Valdez, Alice

581	Mrs Valdez	(.) cuantos años tenías cuando llegaste a australia
		(.) how old were you when you arrived in australia
582	Alice	(.) en australia um (..) ocho años
		(.) in australia um (..) eight years old
583	Mrs Valdez	(.) ocho años
		(.) eight years old
584	Alice	(.) sí (.) u:::m
		(.) yes (.) u:::m
585	Mrs Valdez	(.) fue difícil para ti/ llegar aquí sin amigos:::=
		(.) was it hard for you/ to come here without any friends:::=
586	Alice	=um (..) es poco difícil (..) porque (.) cuando (..) fue en la escuela/
		=um (..) it is a bit hard (..) because (.) when (..) i went to school/

Example 7.5 (Continued)

587	Mrs Valdez	fui a la escuela=
		went to school=
588	Alice	=fui a la escuela (.) no (.) no tengo amigas=
		=went to school (.) i have (.) no friends=
589	Mrs Valdez	=(.) no tenías amigos
		=(.) had no friends
590	Alice	=no tengo amigos::: (..) y:::
		=i have no friends::: (..) a:::nd
591	Mrs Valdez	(..) fue difícil/ (.) tener amigos/ (.) fue difícil tener amigos/ o no
		(..) was it hard/ (.) to make friends/ (.) was it hard to make friends/ or not
592	Alice	(.) um (..) si (.) [um] en la pasada es muy difícil
		(.) um (..) yes (.) [um] in the past it is very hard
593	Mrs Valdez	[sí]
		[yes]
594		(.) porque
		(.) because
595	Alice	(.) porque (.) <E how do you say i was shy/ E>
		(.) because (.) <E how do you say i was shy/ E>
596	Mrs Valdez	(.) ah eres tímida/
		(.) oh you are shy/
597	Alice	(.) sí (.) soy es muy tímida=
		(.) yeah (.) i'm very shy=
598	Mrs Valdez	=eres tímida/ [no] parece
		=you're shy/ [it doesn't] look like it
599	Alice	[sí]
		[yes]
600		(.) muy tímida y::: (.) yo::: no se hablar (..) con (..) otras personas:::
		(.) very shy a:::nd (.) I::: don't know how to talk (..) with (..) other people:::
601	Mrs Valdez	(.) pero conmigo sí
		(.) but you can talk to me
602	Alice	(.) sí
		(.) yes
603	Mrs Valdez	(..) por qué conmigo no eres tímida/
		(..) why aren't you shy with me/
604	Alice	(.) porque::: um (..) ah (.) um (..) soy (..) conforbo
		(.) becau:::se um (..) ah (.) um (..) I'm (..) comfor

(Continued)

Example 7.5 (Continued)

605	Mrs Valdez	(..) hm=
		(..) hm=
606	Alice	=confor- (.) confortable confortable=
		=comfor- (.) comfortable comfortable=
607	Mrs Valdez	=confortable/
		=comfortable/
608	Alice	(.) con- sí
		(.) com- yes
609		(.) so um (..) <E I know so E> (.) sé/
		(.) so um (..) <E I know so E> (.) know/
610	Mrs Valdez	(..) hm
		(..) hm
611	Alice	(.) <E cause E> en la pasada yo no sé hablar con [person]as:::
		(.) <E cause E> in the past I don't know how to speak to [peo]ple:::
612	Mrs Valdez	[ah]
		[ah]

Here Mrs Valdez compliments young Alice by expressing surprise at the latter's description of herself as shy in lines 595, 597, 599, 600 and 611 (presented in the extract as an undesirable trait) and Alice promptly reciprocates by telling her that she makes her feel at ease (lines 603–610). This makes the exchange a particularly fruitful one in terms of positivity as both participants simultaneously express their emotional engagement with the other.

But positivity can also be hindered by certain RSAs. Our data uncovered two specific practices that were detrimental to rapport: the first when a participant took over her partner's turn and articulated an answer for her (Example 7.6); and the second when the speaker's utterances demonstrated a disregard for her interlocutor's feelings (Example 7.7).

Example 7.6 'Can you slow down a bit?'
Spanish conversation: Mrs Agosto, Lily

84	Mrs Agosto	(.) qué es un buen amigo para ti/
		(.) what is a good friend to you/
85	Lily	(.) <E yeah E> (..) u:::hm (.) a mi (.) ah un buen amiga
		(.) <E yeah E> (..) u:::m (.) for me (.) ah a good friend
86		(..) es amiga::: (.) u:::hm (..) hay (..) siem- ah no
		(..) is a friend (.) u:::m (..) there's (..) alway- um no

Example 7.6 (Continued)

87		(.) sí ah no (.) siempre <E how do I say um (.) always there (.) whenever [you need] her E>
		(.) yes ah no (.) always <E how do I say um (.) always there (.) whenever [you need] her E>
88	Mrs Agosto	<E [yeah] E>
		<E [yeah] E>
89		(..) quieres decir que [el amigo e]stá a- a- está allí para ti (.) <E every time E> que eh que tú necesitas (.) e- e- esa persona está siempre dispuesta
		(..) you mean that [this friend i]s a- a- always there for you (.) <E every time E> eh that you need (.) th- th- that person they are always willing
90	Lily	[siempre]
		[always]
91	Mrs Agosto	ayudarte está siempre a tu servicio cuando tú la necesitas
		to help you they're always at your service when you need them
92	Lily	(..) <E can you slow down a bit E> <@@>=
		(..) <E can you slow down a bit E> <@@>=
93	Mrs Agosto	=ah ya=
		=oh okay=
94	Lily	=<E sorry E> <@@>
		=<E sorry E> <@@>
95	Mrs Agosto	(.) quieres decir que (..) <E is there for you:::) E> (.) quieres decir que (.) esa persona
		(.) this means (..) <E is there for you:::) E> (.) it means (.) that person
96	Lily	(.) <E yeah E>
		(.) <E yeah E>
97	Mrs Agosto	(.) está ahí (.) para ti
		(.) is there (.) for you
98	Lily	(.) uh:::m
		(.) uh:::m
99	Mrs Agosto	(.) tú puedes contar con ella (..) tú tienes un problema/ (.) y se lo cuentas
		(.) you can count on her (..) if you have a problem/ (.) you tell her
100	Lily	(.) <E yeah E>=
		(.) <E yeah E>=
101	Mrs Agosto	=o tienes un problema y le dices ese problema ella (.) te ayuda solo- o a (.) resolverlo o (..) simplemente te escucha

(Continued)

Example 7.6 (Continued)

		=or you have a problem and you tell her about this problem (.) she helps you only or to (.) to solve it or (..) she just listens to you
102	Lily	(.) hm
		(.) hm
103	Mrs Agosto	(..) te da el cómo se 'dice' el soporte
		(..) she gives you how do 'you say it' support
104	Lily	(.) <E yea:::h E>=
		(.) <E yea:::h E>=
105	Mrs Agosto	=que necesitas (..) [eso] es lo que tú dices no (..) <E [this] is what you mean E>
		=that you need (..) [that's] what you are saying right (..) <E [this] is what you mean E>
106	Lily	[<E yeah E>]
		[<E yeah E>]

In this extract, Mrs Agosto warms to her topic (friendships) at the expense of her partner's comprehension of her talk – a failure of mutual attentiveness (Table 7.1). She ignores Lily's request for her to *slow down a bit* in line 92 and continues to speak at the same pace. The student's contribution is therefore confined to backchannelling (lines 96, 98, 100, 102, 104 and 106) and laughter (lines 92 and 94). Rather than helping Lily to produce an answer in Spanish, Mrs Agosto speaks for her. Positivity is threatened in this case not only because the speaker's turn is intruded upon, but also because the older interactant is unwilling to modify her talk to enable the other to follow what she is saying even after she has been politely requested to do so.

Example 7.7 'Let's not waste any more time'
Spanish conversation: Mrs Fernandez, Rachel

224	Rachel	mi madre (.) traba:::-
		my mother (.) wor:::-
225	Mrs Fernandez	trabaja
		works
226	Rachel	tra-baja (.) con (.) los (.) ahh (..) <E disability E>
		works (.) with (.) the (.) um (..) <E disability E>
227	Mrs Fernandez	cómo/
		pardon/
228	Rachel	ah::: dis::: (..) umm (.)
		ah::: dis::: (..) umm (.)

Example 7.7 (Continued)

229	Mrs Fernandez	tu mamá trabaja con=
		your mum works with=
230	Rachel	=con (.) umm
		=with (.) um
231	Mrs Fernandez	en una empresa/
		in a company/
232	Rachel	(.) no=
		(.) no=
233	Mrs Fernandez	=negocio/
		=shop/
234	Rachel	(.) umm <E with disability (.) m- (.) E> umm personas (.) mi madre (.) trabajar con los personas (.) umm (.) <E dis:::- E>
		(.) um <E with disability (.) m- (.) E> um people (.) my mother (.) works with people (.) um (.) <E dis:::- E>
235	Mrs Fernandez	<E disability E>
		<E disability E>
236	Rachel	sí
		yes
237	Mrs Fernandez	ahh con personas enfermas
		oh with sick people
238	Rachel	(.) sí
		(.) yes
239	Mrs Fernandez	a:::h tu mamá e- no es es enfermera/
		o:::h your mum is- is she a nurse/
240	Rachel	(.) no
		(.) no
241	Mrs Fernandez	*no* (..) es es solamente colaboradora (.) [trabaja] (.) eh::: como::: (..) tu mamá trabaja como (.) este <E social work E>/
		**no* (..) she is just a helper (.) she [works] (.) eh::: a:::s (..) your mum works as (.) is <E social work E>/*
242	Rachel	[*umm*] (.) ah no
		*[*umm*] (.) ah no*
243	Mrs Fernandez	no
		no
244	Rachel	(.) <E ca- (..) carer li- (..) [umm] (..) *i don't know how to say it* E> (..) es [<@@>]
		*(.) <E ca- (..) carer li- (..) [um] (..) *i don't know how to say it* E> (..) she is [<@@>]*

(Continued)

Example 7.7 (Continued)

245	Mrs Fernandez	bueno no importa no perdamos más tiempo y tu papá/
		okay never mind let's not waste any more time and your dad/
246	Rachel	(.) no no tengo una (.)
		(.) no i don't have one (.)
247	Mrs Fernandez	no tenés papá/
		you don't have a dad/
248	Rachel	oh no tengo papá=
		oh no i do have a dad=
249	Mrs Fernandez	=<@@> [<@@>]
		=<@@> [<@@>]
250	Rachel	[<@@>] (.) mi mi papá no tengo=
		[<@@>] (.) my my dad don't have=
251	Mrs Fernandez	=no [tiene] trabajo
		=[doesn't] have a job
252	Rachel	[no] no
		[no] no
253	Mrs Fernandez	por qué no trabaja/
		why doesn't he work/
254	Rachel	umm (.) <E i don't know E> <@@>=
		umm (.) <E i don't know E> <@@>=
255	Mrs Fernandez	=tiene negocio/
		=does he own a shop/
256	Rachel	no no no traba::jar
		no no no doesn't wor::k
257	Mrs Fernandez	no trabaja (..) [eh:::] digamo- (.) no trabaja porque no hay trabajo
		he doesn't work (..) [eh:::] let's say (.) he doesn't work because there are no jobs
258	Rachel	[umm] (..) sí
		[uhm] (..) yes

There are two instances in this exchange in which the older participant does not appear to be sufficiently sensitive to the student's feelings. First, due to Rachel's difficulties with the language, Mrs Fernandez dismisses her attempts to explain her mother's job with the statement *Okay, never mind, let's not waste any more time. And your Dad?* (line 245). This comment may have been meant as a positive topic shift to allow the student to talk about something she would find easier to explain in Spanish, but the disjunctive move slights the student's efforts and also suggests that the issue of Rachel's mother's employment is of no interest to her. Second, Mrs Fernandez asks

Rachel why her father is unemployed (line 253), a question which may be considered inappropriate due to its personal nature and because of the potential discomfort for the student in disclosing family matters.

This exchange highlights the need for interactants to find common ground in their talk as a foundation for building rapport. Here it seems likely that Mrs Fernandez is unfamiliar with the career of disability worker, and tries to reframe the student's explanation of what her mother does in terms of a job she understands: *shop* (line 233), *sick people* (line 237), *just a helper* (241). Similarly, she asks about Rachel's father, *Does he own a shop?* (line 255) because this would be work that has meaning for her. When Rachel replies *no no* Mrs Fernandez finds it easier to explain this situation away as *There are no jobs* (line 257). The older interactant's dismissive remarks about Rachel's parents could be read as face-saving acts in order to avoid further discussion about a subject that is outside her realm of experience. The abrupt change of topic in line 245 *And your Dad?* could also have been intended as an interactive repair in order to move on from the difficult conversation about Rachel's mother, but unfortunately the topic of Rachel's father proves to be just as difficult. However one interprets the passage, this particular exchange is obviously quite a frustrating one for both participants.

Positivity frequencies

The RSAs employed to enact or discourage positivity are numerous and, more significantly, vary from one individual and one communicative event to another. The diversity of personal approaches concerning this component of rapport is particularly salient after observing the frequency and distribution of RSAs for every participant (Table 7.3).

As one would expect, the number of individual RSAs performed to both foster and discourage positivity was radically larger for L1 speakers than for L2 learners. This behaviour is hardly surprising and is most likely attributable to the fact that age, experience, self-assigned role in the task and knowledge of the target language positioned older citizens as authority figures who not only possessed the linguistic resources to enact these stances, but were also in command of the communicative event as a whole.

Another result worth mentioning is the high frequency of the RSA 'Shows personal interest in interlocutor' for both age groups. Considering the interaction's purpose and context it was expected that the conversation partners would turn to this strategy, as they did not know each other well or may not have had much in common. Additionally, asking questions about the other is a device that is easily available to students and is frequently utilised in language teaching to obtain information. On the other hand, the older participants paid many more compliments to the students than the other way round. In part this was due no doubt to the older participants' encouragement and praise of the students' efforts with the target language

Table 7.3 Dyadic RSA frequencies for positivity

Conversation / Dyad	Gives positive feedback		Positions her/himself as interlocutor's peer		Shows personal interest in interlocutor		Makes positive comments about interlocutor		Expresses approval regarding interlocutor's personal history, ideology and/or actions		Intrudes into interlocutor's talk to articulate utterance for them		Is insensitive to interlocutor's feelings		Conversation totals	
	Older participant	Student	Older participant	Student	Older participant	Student	Older participant	Student	Older participant	Student	Older participant	Student	Older participant	Student	Older participant	Student
C1 Mrs Agosto, Lily	0	0	4	0	1	9	0	0	1	1	0	0	0	0	6	10
C1 Mrs Agosto, Caitlin	0	0	0	0	22	1	2	0	4	0	0	0	1	0	29	1
C1 Mrs Fernandez, Rachel	0	0	0	0	2	3	0	0	4	1	0	0	0	0	6	4
C1 Mrs Ramos, Sarah	1	5	1	2	4	8	2	0	0	2	1	0	0	0	9	17
C1 Mr Diaz, Maddy	0	0	0	0	1	6	0	0	0	0	0	0	0	0	1	6
C1 Mrs Valdez, Alice	0	0	2	0	29	11	6	1	7	1	0	0	0	0	44	13
C3 Mrs Agosto, Lily	0	0	2	1	8	0	2	1	3	0	4	0	0	0	19	2
C3 Mrs Agosto, Caitlin	1	0	1	0	4	2	3	1	2	8	0	0	0	0	11	11
C3 Mrs Fernandez, Rachel	0	0	1	0	5	0	0	0	0	0	3	0	6	0	15	0
C3 Mrs Ramos, Sarah	16	0	11	2	3	0	4	2	2	0	1	0	0	0	37	4
C3 Mr Diaz, Maddy	2	0	2	0	13	0	3	0	2	0	0	0	0	0	22	0
C3 Mrs Valdez, Alice	5	0	0	0	13	0	7	0	3	0	0	0	0	0	28	0
RSA Totals	25	5	24	5	105	40	29	5	28	13	9	0	7	0		

(e.g. Example 7.3), but in addition the students may have felt uncomfortable making personal comments about a significantly older person, particularly when their language skills were limited.

Our data did offer some unanticipated results. The utilising of RSAs that shape positivity varied not only from one individual to another but throughout the communicative event and between conversations. The highest number of RSAs performed by an L1 speaker in a single conversation was 44 (C1, Mrs Valdez); the lowest only 1 (C1, Mr Diaz). The same older man then increased his RSAs to 22 during the third conversation, while Mrs Valdez's RSAs dropped by almost 50% (28 instances). Similarly, the students' RSAs also varied. The highest number of RSAs performed by a student in a single conversation was 17 (C1, Sarah), but in her third conversation with Mrs Ramos this dropped to 4. Our data is insufficient to determine the causes for this variability that seems to lack a consistent pattern. It may be due to features of the activity itself, such as the pre-set topics and questions for each interaction, or to other factors such as personal events or feelings that were external to the activity and not related to how the participants felt towards each other.

One interesting and unexpected pattern did emerge from our data. The total number of RSAs employed by the older participants to elicit positivity remained more or less stable in both conversations. However, the RSAs that *discourage* positivity increased in number during the second conversation, a statistic that could signal a change in disposition. Moreover, the total number of RSAs employed by students to elicit positivity dropped dramatically in the second conversation (see Table 7.4).

A negative reading of these results would be that the relationships between the older participants and students deteriorated a little over time. A more positive reading, on the other hand, would suggest that the participants (particularly the young students) felt more at ease by the end of the year and intuitively considered rapport to be already established, a reading in keeping with the finding that the speech act of complimenting occurs with greater frequency in relationships that are still finding their feet (e.g. Payne, 2013; Othman, 2011). A lengthier study and an increased sample size would allow this possibility to be more fully explored.

Table 7.4 Summary of RSA frequencies for *positivity*

Conversation	L1 RSAs that potentially increase positivity	L2 RSAs that potentially increase positivity	L1 RSAs that potentially decrease positivity	L2 RSAs that potentially decrease positivity
C1	93	51	2	0
C3	118	17	14	0

Coordination

The third essential component of rapport describes a conversation in which participants show high levels of responsiveness towards each other. Table 7.5 provides a list of stance-taking acts that contribute to either achieving or disrupting coordination.

Table 7.5 RSAs that shape *coordination*

RSA	Description

Contributes to developing the conversation	• Guides conversation by:
	  • negotiating topic with interlocutor
	  • asking questions (scripted, spontaneous, follow-up) changing topic
	• Provides relevant comment/narrative/personal information in response to interlocutor's discourse

Provides 'helpful utterance completions' (Ferrara, 1992)	• consisting of 'minimal additions offered by a listener who detects some difficulty on the part of a speaker in accessing an item in the mental lexicon' (Ferrara, 1992: 220)
Builds discourse with interlocutor	• Discourse/narrative is co-constructed by both participants: 'utterance extensions' and 'predictable utterance completions' (Ferrara, 1992: 217ff)
Mirrors interlocutor's utterance/response	• Reproduces utterance or fragments of utterance identically • Reproduces paralinguistic elements: laughter, gasps, etc.
Responds according to emotional tone/cues of discourse	• through explicit comments, e.g. 'sorry to hear that' • through paralinguistic elements: laughter, gasps, etc.
Interrupts	• Intrudes into interlocutor's talk 'without regard to the syntactic or semantic output of the first speaker' (Ferrara, 1992: 216; Zimmerman & West, 1975)
Changes topic in an untimely manner	• before interlocutor has finished addressing it
Disregards content of interlocutor's discourse	• Is not attentive to interlocutor's discourse • Asks questions that have previously been answered • Asks same question more than once • Restates content of interlocutor's previous utterances inaccurately
Ignores or misinterprets emotional tone/cues of interlocutor's discourse	• Does not express sympathy when/if appropriate/expected • Is oblivious to/misunderstands interlocutor's intended affective reactions (laughter, surprise, regret, etc.)

A fundamental way in which conversational partners show coordination is by actively driving the interaction forward. This can be accomplished by negotiating the topic, accurately gauging the right time to change the subject, and asking relevant follow-up questions or responding with comments or anecdotes that are pertinent to what is being said.

A well-established sense of coordination can also be marked by participants working together to develop a shared idea. In the following example Mrs Agosto and Caitlin collaboratively list the health hazards of using headphones (lines 1000–1003) and the effect that being regularly connected to a headphone (line 1004) has on the communication skills developed with others (lines 1006–1010). They are jointly constructing the discourse, despite the student's poorer language proficiency. For example, in the interests of elaborating on the topic, Caitlin wants to introduce a new idea, which she states in English: *if they listen too much, and also*. Mrs Agosto picks up on the conjunction *also* and repeats it in Spanish, 'y también', which is immediately modelled by the student in line 1005.

Example 7.8 'If they use it a lot they will go deaf'
Spanish conversation: Mrs Agosto, Caitlin

1000	Mrs Agosto	está (.) qu- e- con esto acá/ (.) con los oídos (.) qu- qué es lo qué qué es lo qué te parece que va a pasar (.) en el fondo (.) después si e- si lo- si lo usan mucho van a quedar sordos (.) <E you know what E> sordo es/
		this (.) with this here/ (.) with the ears (.) wh- what do you what do you think will happen (.) in the end (.) then if they if they if they use it a lot they will go deaf (.) <E you know what E> sordo means/
1001	Caitlin	(.) em:::
		(.) em:::
1002	Mrs Agosto	(.) <E deaf E>
		(.) <E deaf E>
1003	Caitlin	(.) <E yeah (.) if they listen too much/ (.) and also a:mh E>=
		(.) <E yeah (.) if they listen too much/ (.) and also a:mh E>=
1004	Mrs Agosto	=y también/=
		=and also/=
1005	Caitlin	=y también/ (.) am: (.) los:: niños (.) comuni- <E -cation skills E>/
		=and also/ (.) um: (.) the:: kids (.) communi <E cation skills E>/
1006	Mrs Agosto	(.) ah sí (.) sí el la::: (.) e::::: (H) (.) la comunicación
		(.) oh yes (.) yes the::: (.) um::::: (H) (.) communication
1007	Caitlin	(.) la comunica[shon]

(Continued)

Example 7.8 (Continued)

		(.) communica[tion]
1008	Mrs Agosto	la comunicación [sí]
		communication [yes]
1009	Caitlin	[<E yeah E>] (.) <E skills is less::: E>
		[<E yeah E>] (.) <E skills is less::: E>
1010	Mrs Agosto	(.) (H) ah:=
		(.) (H) ah:=
1011	Caitlin	=<E if they [always E>]
		=<E if they [always E>]
1012	Mrs Agosto	[AH] SÍ SÍ=
		[OH] YES YES=
1013	Caitlin	=<E so then less E>=
		=<E so then less E>=
1014	Mrs Agosto	=si es n- no es no comunicación entre las dos generaciones o entre ellos mismos=
		=yes there's n- no there's no communication between the two generations or among themselves=
1015	Caitlin	=mh/
		=mh/

Further RSAs that suggest coordination include the spontaneous emulation or mirroring of utterances (lines 1004–1008): see the seminal work of Duranti and Brenneis (1986), Ferrara (1992) and Tannen (1984, 1989), to mention a few. Another is the articulation of quick successions of participatory tokens: the emotional cue initiated by Mrs Agosto's inhalation in line 1010 latches Caitlin's talk and is followed by a forceful positive remark (line 1012) which is then latched by the student and immediately latched again by the older person's contribution in line 1014: *Yes there's no communication between the two generations or among themselves*. The student closes with an acknowledgement token in line 1015.

Example 7.9 'I've lived here for twenty years'
Spanish conversation: Mrs Ramos, Sarah

1	Sarah	(..) cómo estás/
		(..) how are you/
2	Mrs Ramos	muy bien [y tú]
		very well [and you]
3	Sarah	[ah] muy bien muy bien (.) u:::m (.) por qué inmigración (.) a la australia/
		[ah] very well very well (.) u:::m (.) why immigration (.) to australia/

Example 7.9 (Continued)

4	Mrs Ramos	(.) a:::h emigré a Australia (.) por problemas de gobierno
		(.) a:::h i emigrated to australia (.) because of government problems
5		(.) porque había um (.) guerra (.) en mi país
		(.) because there was a (.) war (.) in my country
6	Sarah	(.) guerra
		(.) war
7	Mrs Ramos	(.) sí
		(.) yes
8	Sarah	(.) su país
		(.) in your country
9	Mrs Ramos	sí
		yes
10	Sarah	(.) cuántos años hace (.) que vive en (..) australia/
		(.) how many years have (.) you lived in (..) australia/
11	Mrs Ramos	(..) (H) ah (.) vivo hace (..) (H) acabo de cumplir veinte años:::
		(..) (H) ah (.) i've been here since (..) (H) it's recently been twenty years:::
12	Sarah	(..) veinte años
		(..) twenty years
13	Mrs Ramos	sí
		yes
14	Sarah	(.) ah sí (..) muy buena (..) ah qué pasatiempo (.) tiene/
		(.) ah yes (.) very good (..) ah what hobbies (.) to you have/

Although this extract consists of a succession of scripted questions rather than a natural, free-flowing conversation, the student, despite her language limitations, is able to express a certain degree of involvement through her echoing of the last few keywords produced by her partner. By repeating 'guerra' (line 6), 'su país' (line 8) and 'veinte años' (line 12), she shows that she is following what Mrs Ramos is saying and using modelling to reinforce her acquisition of the vocabulary. She also shows her appreciation of the number of years Mrs Ramos has been living in Australia with *Ah yes, very good* (line 14).

Example 7.10 'I will always feel grateful'
Spanish conversation: Mrs Agosto, Lily

707	Mrs Agosto	(.) eh (..) yo siempre le voy a estar agradecida
		(.) eh (..) i will always feel grateful

Example 7.10 (Continued)

708		(.) con toda mi alma (..) a australia (..) porque cuando yo llegué a australia
		(.) from the bottom of my heart (..) towards australia (..) because when I arrived in australia
709		(..) llegué como inmigrante (.) con dos años de contrato (.) como todo el mundo
		(..) i arrived as an immigrant (.) with a two year contract (.) like everyone else
710		(.) pero cuando yo llegué (..) mis hijos tenían (..) nosotros en español decimos el
		(.) but when i arrived (..) my children had (..) in spanish we say
711		techo y teníamos comida (.) entiendes (..) quiere decir que yo no llegué y me abandonaron
		a roof and we had food (.) do you understand (..) it means that i got here and they didn't leave me to my own devices
712	Lily	(.) hm=
		(.) hm=
713	Mrs Agosto	=no (.) el gobierno me dio el techo para mis hijos/ (.) me dio la comida y me dio la asistencia
		=no (.) the government gave me a roof for my children/ (.) it gave me food and it gave me assistance
714	Lily	(..) está muy difícil la vida (..) la vida es muy difícil
		(..) it's very hard life (..) life is very hard
715	Mrs Agosto	(H) (..) es sí (.) es difícil (.) es difícil pero
		(H) (..) yes it's (.) it's hard (.) it's hard but
716		(..) que se va a hacer (.) eh es difícil
		(..) what can you do (.) eh it's hard

In this rather poignant extract the student accurately decodes her partner's underlying message, 'está muy difícil la vida' (line 714). Mrs Agosto does not explicitly speak negatively of her first experiences in Australia; nevertheless Lily swiftly empathises with the immigrant as she refers to what was clearly a difficult period of adjustment. In stating for her that life is hard, she displays sensitivity to the older participant's sharing of past experiences and acknowledges (and perhaps for the first time is made aware of) the hardships of immigration. The student's stance is likely to be received favourably – as is hinted by Mrs Agosto instantly agreeing – and this expression of coordination will likely enhance feelings of rapport.

It is interesting to compare this exchange with the one between the same dyad in Example 7.6. In both extracts the older participant holds the floor to give an extended account of the topic (friendship, the migration experience) in spite of the student's verbal cues that indicate her difficulty following the Spanish. In Example 7.10, however, Lily is able to understand that Mrs Agosto is describing a painful life experience, and offers an empathic response. In this exchange, therefore, rapport is established through the student's use of *coordination* even though *mutual attentiveness* on the part of the older participant may have been compromised.

Failure to read a partner's emotional cues, however, can result in RSAs that are detrimental to the relationship. Example 7.11 shows how the older participant does not offer an emotionally attuned response to a piece of sensitive information shared by the student.

Example 7.11 'OK ... and your Mum?'
Spanish conversation: Mr Diaz, Maddy

131	Mr Diaz	(.) tu ma- tu papá que trabaja
		(.) your mu- your dad what does he do
132	Maddy	(.) um (.) <e> el (.) trabaja en el casa/ en la casa/=
		(.) um (.) <e> he (.) works at home/ at home/=
133	Mr Diaz	=en la casa/=
		=at home/=
134	Maddy	=pero antes (.) um (.) fue (.) un (.) <E like a medical representative E>
		=but before that (.) um (.) he was (.) a (.) <E like a medical representative E>
135	Mr Diaz	(.) mmmm:: [médico]
		(.) mmmm:: [doctor]
136	Maddy	[<E but now E>] (.) <E but he (.) he got hurt so now he is (.) working E>=
137	Mr Diaz	=m ya=
		=hm okay=
138	Maddy	=en (.) la casa
		=at (.) home
139	Mr Diaz	(.) y tu mama/=
		(.) and your mum/=

When a speaker mentions an unfortunate event, such as the student here trying to explain about her father's injury, it is usual to follow with a suitable response – a sympathetic remark or a query related to the incident/situation. In this extract, however, Mr Diaz barely reacts. It is possible that he did not understand the information, as the student spoke in English, so the lack of an appropriate comment may be due to language difficulties rather than inattentiveness. Nevertheless, there is a momentary breakdown in coordination since the older participant does not respond as would be expected (cf. Example 7.7 above).

Another quite straightforward way of harming the synchronisation of the exchange is through untimely or unwelcome interruptions. In the following extract (Example 7.12) the student reads one of the questions she has prepared for the class. She initiates her turn with 'Who is the most important person in your life and why?'. The older participant does not answer the question but instead uses overlap ('-portant in your life', line 675) and hesitation (line 677), prompting the student to respond instead.

Lily is clearly struggling with the Spanish as she asks the question. She initiates her turn in line 678 by using the particle 'ah' and raising her tone at the end of the utterance 'una persona más importante en mi vida' as a way of playing for time. Mrs Agosto, instead of giving her a moment to reflect on and construct her answer, cuts in with the overlapping phrase in line 679, and then rather peremptorily poses the question 'Who is it?'.

This lack of coordination has a potentially negative impact on the interaction. The older participant has interrupted the student's turn, causing her to lose confidence in asking the question, and has then misinterpreted the student's recapping of the question as an inability to understand what is being asked of her.

Example 7.12 'Who is the most important person in your life?'
Spanish conversation: Mrs Agosto, Lily

671	Lily	(.) okay (.) u:::m (..) una persona importante (.) quien es la persona más
		(.) okay (.) u:::m (..) an important person (.) who is the person the most
672	Mrs Agosto	(..) <E yeah E>
		(..) <E yeah E>
673		((off topic due to sudden interruption))
674	Lily	impor[tante en tu vida] (..) por qué/ (..) u:::m
		impor[tant in your life] (..) and why/ (..) u:::m
675	Mrs Agosto	[-tante en tu vida]
		[-portant in your life]
676	Lily	(.) más importante/
		(.) most important/
677	Mrs Agosto	(.) hm
		(.) hm
678	Lily	(.) ah una persona (.) una persona importa- más impor[tante en mi vida/]
		(.) ah a person (.) a person importa- most impor[tant in my life/]
679	Mrs Agosto	[la persona que es más im]portante en tu vida quien es =
		[the person who is the most im]portant in your life who is it=

Example 7.12 (Continued)

680	Lily	<E=yeah E> (.) una persona (.) más importante en mi vida (.) es::: (..) no son mi padre (.) mi padre (.) mi hermana
		<E=yeah E> (.) the person (.) most important in my life (.) i:::s (..) not my father (.) my father (.) my sister

Coordination frequencies

As we saw with positivity, the RSAs that shaped coordination were varied and presented some similarities with the former in terms of frequencies and distribution. Our findings are given in Table 7.6. The total number of coordination RSAs performed by the L1 speakers was appreciably higher than those performed by the students (769 vs. 370), but their presence fluctuated across participants and conversations. Mrs Agosto had the highest single conversation total (120) in her third conversation with Lily, but scored only 19 in her first conversation with the same student. She also scored the highest number of interruptions (7).

The opposite occurred in her two conversations with Caitlin, with a total of 119 in the first conversation and only 18 in the third. Mrs Valdez also achieved 119 in her first conversation with Alice, but a reduced 73 in their third conversation together. The lowest numbers went to Mr Diaz (10 and 59). As for the students, Sarah was responsible for both the greatest and the smallest number of RSAs, with 77 and 5 instances respectively. The RSAs were however overwhelmingly positive. Mrs Fernandez was the older participant most inclined to disregard the content of the student's talk (3 and 8), as we saw in Example 7.7.

Although the older participants more than doubled the contributions of the students to developing the conversation, with frequencies of 356 and 152 respectively, the students were the clear winners in the number of empathic responses they provided (86 as against 53). Again these results are perhaps not surprising. The immigrants' facility in the target language and their self-positioning as persons of authority to young people (see Chapter 4) allowed them to do most of the talking during the recorded sessions. In addition, large portions of the first conversation consisted of detailed accounts of the immigrants' early experiences in Australia, and these sometimes difficult personal stories naturally elicited empathic responses from the students.

An interesting aspect of coordination was its wider range of RSAs and higher rate of occurrence in both groups compared to positivity. The RSAs of the L1 older speakers totalled 769 instances as opposed to the 227 cases recorded for positivity, while for the students the totals were 370 as against 68. Further research will be required to investigate the reasons for this, but our preliminary findings may indicate that such stances, being perhaps less

Table 7.6 Dyadic RSA frequencies for coordination

Conversation / Dyad	Contributes to develop the conversation		Provides 'helpful utterance completion'		Builds discourse with interlocutor		Mirrors speaker's utterance/response		Responds according to emotional tone/cues of discourse		Interrupts		Changes topic in an untimely manner		Disregards content of interlocutor's discourse		Ignores or misinterprets emotional tone/cues of interlocutor's discourse		Conversation totals	
	L1	L2	L1	L2	L1	L2	L1	L2	L1	L2	L1	L2	L1	L2	L1	L2	L1	L2	L1	L2
C1 Mrs Agosto, Lily	13	18	3	1	0	0	2	7	1	9	0	0	0	0	0	0	0	0	19	35
C1 Mrs Agosto, Caitlin	52	9	6	1	10	0	44	23	5	8	0	0	2	0	0	1	0	1	119	43
C1 Mrs Fernandez, Rachel	23	6	7	2	6	0	11	4	1	14	0	0	1	0	3	0	0	0	52	26
C1 Mrs Ramos, Sarah	16	40	2	0	4	2	21	24	7	11	0	0	0	0	0	0	0	0	50	77
C1 Mr Díaz, Maddy	2	31	0	0	0	3	6	6	1	8	0	0	1	0	0	0	0	1	10	49
C1 Mrs Valdez, Alice	60	17	3	0	14	2	32	20	10	5	0	0	0	0	0	0	0	0	119	44
C3 Mrs Agosto, Lily	38	21	11	1	20	0	25	14	16	9	7	0	1	0	2	0	0	0	120	45
C3 Mrs Agosto, Caitlin	16	4	0	1	2	7	0	0	0	9	0	0	0	0	0	0	0	0	18	21
C3 Mrs Fernandez, Rachel	36	3	6	1	6	0	18	1	3	1	3	0	3	0	8	0	0	0	83	6
C3 Mrs Ramos, Sarah	26	0	7	0	7	1	4	2	3	2	0	0	0	0	0	0	0	0	47	5
C3 Mr Díaz, Maddy	34	2	0	1	3	0	18	0	2	8	0	0	0	0	1	0	1	0	59	11
C3 Mrs Valdez, Alice	40	1	6	0	14	0	8	5	4	2	0	0	0	0	1	0	0	0	73	8
RSA Totals	356	152	51	8	86	15	189	106	53	86	10	0	8	0	15	1	1	2		

Table 7.7 Summary of RSA frequencies for *coordination*

	L1 RSAs that potentially increase coordination	L2 RSAs that potentially increase coordination	L1 RSAs that potentially decrease coordination	L2 RSAs that potentially decrease coordination
C1	362	271	7	3
C3	373	96	27	0

personal in nature, are preferred devices among people who do not know each other very well or who may not have much in common.

Lastly and similarly to positivity, the students tended to withdraw from the process of fostering rapport over time, and the older participants seemed to be more cavalier in regards to avoiding negative RSAs during the second conversation (see Table 7.7).

Although these bald frequencies suggest a decline in rapport, such an assumption seems counterintuitive. One would expect (or at least hope) that there would be an *increase* in rapport between each older participant–student pair over the course of their acquaintance, if not a degree of fondness and affection, and certainly an attenuation in any preconceived, negative ideas about the other generation. We can only suggest that the numbers do not give the full picture and that other variables must be identified and considered. Moreover, since the decrease in student RSAs that stimulate positivity and coordination is not paired with an increase in RSAs that inhibit them, it is not safe to conclude that these components on their own are accurate measurements of rapport.

Discussion and Further Development

We have been concerned in this chapter with the development of a verbal rapport model and a taxonomy of rapport enactment as a means to better understand rapport-building practices between conversational partners. The analysis was based on Tickle-Degnen and Rosenthal's psychological model (1990) and took a sociolinguistic and discourse analysis approach to produce a taxonomy that may be used to shed light on participants' interactions.

The topic offers an opportunity in the field of sociolinguistics, given that previous research typically treats rapport as a tacit yet vaguely defined subcomponent of politeness. However, we believe that while politeness plays an important role in the fostering of rapport, it is not its sole contributor.

With respect to our study, two main aspects emerged serving as valuable input on the subject: our model's thorough representation of the dynamics of rapport, and its versatility. In the first place, it considered every stage involved in the performance of rapport, including speakers' utterances, their intent when forming said utterances, and their hearers' ability to accurately interpret what was being said. Attention to each of these factors was necessary as interlocutors may express and understand ideas, feelings and intentions with varying degrees of success. Secondly, the model is functional in numerous contexts. This study is concerned with intercultural and intergenerational communication, but with some adjustments to group-specific RSAs it should be possible to carry out rapport studies amongst other groups in other communicative situations leaving the model's structure intact.

Further, the model facilitates the identification of several possible outcomes for a single interaction rather than the somewhat limited rapport/ no rapport binary. By studying both expressiveness and accuracy filters, we can detect whether rapport is fostered and/or felt by all, some or none of the participants, an advantage that simultaneously renders accurate analyses while providing valuable insight into the exact factors that promote or discourage rapport. The implications are far-reaching: isolating the precise features that regulate the emergence of rapport can help speakers sustain better interactions, and can orientate researchers on how to alleviate issues of ageism by understanding whether unsuccessful interactions fail due to generational incompatibility or to adjustable communicative practices.

A further point of interest can be found in the observation of RSA frequencies in this study. The total number of RSAs performed by the older participants that discouraged positivity and coordination increased significantly during the third conversation. Simultaneously, the total number of student RSAs that elicited these components dropped dramatically. At first glance, it seems that relationships between these individuals deteriorated over time. However, this assumption is questionable. The statistics may indicate rather that once a bond is established participants do not feel the need to express feelings of rapport as explicitly. Needless to say, a longitudinal study is indispensable to explore this idea further (see also Tickle-Degnen, 2006).

On that note, as much as our model proposes a solid foundation as well as a departure point for the study of rapport, additional procedures are necessary to support our findings. Some suggestions follow that may prove useful for future studies.

To further test our model, supplementary data collection methods are necessary. Firstly, we suggest preliminary and closing surveys completed by the participants. Thus far the effects of the interaction's verbal aspect – neutral utterances, RSAs, interactive errors and interactive repairs – have been analysed by observers. Logically this method does not fully confirm or refute the impact of RSAs on the mechanisms of rapport, and cross-examination of our findings with the participant surveys is therefore an important part of the process. The preliminary survey should focus on participants' presuppositions about the project, including general views on the opposite age group, and on what they hope to gain from the experience. This information should be complemented with the responses in the closing surveys, which would ideally examine any changes in the participants' appraisal of each other, verify whether rapport has in fact been established, and seek to learn what specific verbal behaviours or RSAs enhanced or damaged rapport during the conversations. The focus group surveys, telephone interviews and quiz on ageing conducted as a part of our project (see Chapter 3) provided incidental and anecdotal evidence of positive rapport building during the conversation sessions, but it would be beneficial to employ other tools that could more accurately measure rapport.

We also recommend studying how participants' *expressiveness* and *accuracy filters* actually operate. To gauge if speakers are able to produce utterances that agree with the intentions behind them, participants should be asked to choose or formulate what they think are the most effective ways of communicating different types of messages. To evaluate how accurately they apprehend meaning, they would be presented with different scenarios and asked to interpret their intended messages based on the information provided. Additionally, it is to be noted that the design of this exercise should be undertaken with great care in order to produce scenarios that require a certain degree of analytical skill without being overly demanding.

Concerning our taxonomy of rapport enactment, two topics may also benefit from further research. The first one relates to the specific RSAs that surfaced during participant conversations. While this taxonomy's RSAs can be used as a reference in other studies, different types of dyads will render different results. Most likely, conversational partners of a similar age group and cultural background will approach rapport in a different manner from that of our participants. The new styles employed may thus require the addition of new RSAs and/or the elimination of others that become irrelevant. Another question worth considering is the influence individual RSAs exert on rapport: some may carry more weight than others or may vary in significance at different stages of a relationship.

Our data has allowed us to conceive a model of verbal rapport that describes its dynamic nature as well as a taxonomy of rapport enactment that lists a number of distinct and discrete units with which rapport can be measured. That being said, some questions remain: mainly, whether the participants in our study in fact fostered or experienced rapport through the means here described. A larger, more exhaustive study is needed to reach decisive results. Until then, we offer our findings as a departure point for other analyses of this multi-faceted topic in the hope of opening new, fruitful discussions.

References

Baumeister, R.F. and Leary, M.R. (1995) The need to belong: Desire for interpersonal attachments as a fundamental human motivation. *Psychological Bulletin* 117 (3), 497–529.
Bennett, M.J. (1979) Overcoming the golden rule: Sympathy and empathy. In D. Nimmo (ed.) *Communication Yearbook 3. An Annual Review* (pp. 407–433). New Brunswick, NJ: International Communication Association.
Bjørge, A.K. (2012) Expressing disagreement in ELF business negotiations: Theory and practice. *Applied Linguistics* 33 (4), 406–427.
Brown, P. and Levinson, S.C. (1987) *Politeness: Some Universals in Language Usage*. Cambridge: Cambridge University Press.
Campbell, K.S. (2005) The rapport management model: How physicians build relationships with patients. In *Professional Communication Conference, 2005. Proceedings. International* 422–432. [n.p]: IEEE, 2005.
Cordella, M. (2004) *The Dynamic Consultation: A Discourse Analytical Study of Doctor–Patient Communication*. Amsterdam: John Benjamins.
Cordella, M. and Huang, H. (2012) Encuentros intergeneracionales e interculturales en Australia: Los roles participativos del adulto mayor y el estudiante de EL 2. *Signo y Seña* (Buenos Aires) 22, 13–33.
Cordella, M. and Huang, H. (2014) L1 and L2 Chinese, German and Spanish speakers in action: Stancetaking in intergenerational and intercultural encounters. In J. Hajek and Y. Slaughter (eds) *Challenging the Monolingual Mindset* (pp. 97–112). Bristol: Multilingual Matters.
Cordella, M. and Musgrave, S. (2009) Oral communication skills of international medical graduates: Assessing empathy in discourse. *Communication & Medicine* 6 (2), 129–142.
Coupland, N., Coupland, J., Giles, H. and Henwood, K. (1988) Accommodating the elderly: Invoking and extending a theory. *Language in Society* 17, 1–41.
Drolet, A.L. and Morris, M.W. (2000) Rapport in conflict resolution: Accounting for how face-to face contact fosters mutual cooperation in mixed-motive conflicts. *Journal of Experimental Social Psychology* 36 (1), 26–50.
Du Bois, J.W. (2007) The stance triangle. In R. Englebretson (ed.) *Stancetaking in Discourse: Subjectivity, Evaluation, Interaction* (pp. 139–182). Amsterdam: John Benjamins.
Duranti, A. and Brenneis, D. (eds) (1986) *The Audience as Co-Author*. Special Issue: *Text: Interdisciplinary Journal for the Study of Discourse* 6 (3).
Englebretson, R. (2007) *Stancetaking in Discourse: Subjectivity, Evaluation, Interaction*. Amsterdam: John Benjamins.
Ferrara, K. (1992) The interactive achievement of a sentence: Joint productions in therapeutic discourse. *Discourse Processes* 15, 207–228.
Frankel, R.M. (2000) The socio-linguistic turn in physician-patient communication research. In J.E. Alatis, H.E. Hamilton and A.Tan (eds) *Round Table on Languages and Linguistics* (pp. 81–103). Washington: Georgetown University Press.
Goldberg, J.A. (1990) Interrupting the discourse on interruptions: An analysis in terms of relationally neutral, power- and rapport-oriented acts. *Journal of Pragmatics* 14, 883–903.
Harwood, J., McKee, J. and Lin, M. (2000) Younger and older adults' schematic representations of intergenerational communication. *Communication Monographs* 67 (1), 20–41.
Hultgren, A.K. (2011) 'Building rapport' with customers across the world: The global diffusion of a call centre speech style. *Journal of Sociolinguistics* 15 (1), 36–64.
Jaffe, A. (ed.) (2009) *Stance: Sociolinguistic Perspectives*. Oxford: Oxford University Press.

Jiang, W. and Ramsay, G. (2005) Rapport-building through CALL in teaching Chinese as a foreign language: An exploratory study. *Language Learning & Technology* 9 (2), 47–63.

Johnson, D.M. (1992) Compliments and politeness in peer-review texts. *Applied Linguistics* 13 (1), 51–71.

Kempera, S., Finter-Urczykb, A., Ferrellb, P., Hardenc T. and Billingtond C. (1998) Using elderspeak with older adults. *Discourse Processes* 25 (1), 55–73.

Nguyen, H.T. (2007) Rapport building in language instruction: A microanalysis of the multiple resources in teacher talk. *Language and Education* 21 (4), 284–303.

Othman, N. (2011) Pragmatic and cultural considerations of compliment responses among Malaysian-Malay speakers. *Asiatic* 5, 86–103.

Payne, S. (2013) Compliment responses of female German and Italian university students: A contrastive study. *Language Studies Working Papers, University of Reading* 5, 22–31.

Placencia, M.E. (2004) Rapport-building activities in corner shop interactions. *Journal of Sociolinguistics* 8 (2), 215–245.

Roulston, K. (2011) Interview 'problems' as topics for analysis. *Applied Linguistics* 32 (1), 77–94.

Ryan, E.B., Giles, H., Bartolucci, G. and Henwood, K. (1986) Psycholinguistic and social psychological components of communication by and with the elderly. *Language and Communication* 6, 1–24.

Ryan, E.B., Hamilton, J.M. and Kwong See, S. (1994) Patronizing the old: How do younger and older adults respond to baby talk in the nursing home? In E.B. Ryan (ed.) *Intergenerational Communication: Evaluations and Analyses of Talk Exchanged Between Older Adults and Younger Adults*, Amityville, NY: Baywood Publishing Company.

Spencer-Oatey, H. (2002) Managing rapport in talk: Using rapport sensitive incidents to explore the motivational concerns underlying the management of relations. *Journal of Pragmatics* 34, 529–545.

Tannen, D. (1984) *Conversational Style: Analyzing Talk among Friends*. Norwood, NJ: Ablex.

Tannen, D. (1989) *Talking Voices: Repetition, Dialogue, and Imagery in Conversational Discourse*. Cambridge: Cambridge University Press.

Tannen, D. (2009) Framing and face: The relevance of presentation of self in everyday life to linguistic discourse analysis. *Social Psychology Quarterly* 72 (4), 300–305.

Tickle-Degnen, L. (2006) Nonverbal behavior and its functions in the ecosystem of rapport. In V. Manusov and M.L. Patterson (eds) *The SAGE Handbook of Nonverbal Communication* (pp. 381–399). Thousand Oaks, CA: Sage Publications.

Tickle-Degnen, L. and Rosenthal, R. (1987) Group rapport and nonverbal behaviour. In C. Hendrick (ed.) *Review of Personality and Social Psychology: Vol. 9. Group Processes and Intergroup Relations* (pp. 113–136). Newbury Park, CA: Sage.

Tickle-Degnen, L. and Rosenthal, R. (1990) The nature of rapport and its nonverbal correlates. *Psychological Inquiry* 1 (4), 285–293.

Tronick, E.Z. (1990) The development of rapport. *Psychological Inquiry* 1 (4), 322–323.

Williams, A. (1996) Young people's evaluations of intergenerational versus peer under accommodation: Sometimes older is better? *Journal of Language and Social Psychology* 15 (3), 291–311.

Yue, X.D. and Ng, S.H. (2000) Effects of age and relation on intergenerational communication: A survey study in Beijing. *Psychologia* 43, 102–113.

Zimmerman, D.H. and West, C. (1975) Sex roles, interruptions, and silences in conversation. In B. Thome and N. Henley (eds) *Language and Sex: Difference and Dominance* (pp. 105–129). Rowley, MA: Newbury House.

8 'I feel very happy that I can contribute to society': Exploring the Value of the Project for Older People

Harriet Radermacher, Colette Browning and Susan Feldman

Introduction

While the primary aim of our project was to provide opportunities for young language learners to converse with native speakers, an important secondary goal was to engage older people in meaningful and active tasks through formally structured intergenerational encounters. Underpinning this gerontological approach was the intergenerational schools-based study of Feldman *et al.* (2002: 21), which concluded that by utilising the 'talents and skills of older persons for use with students ... the potential exists for a mutuality of benefit – both students and older persons stand to gain from the experience'. In bringing together older and younger people for a specific purpose, it was anticipated that not only would the students' language proficiency be improved but that there would be a whole host of additional benefits on both sides. These potential benefits included, but were not limited to: encouraging the exchange of cultural, linguistic and intergenerational skills, knowledge and values; challenging intergenerational stereotypes; and improving the psychosocial health of both younger and older participants.

Focusing on the outcomes of intergenerational learning programmes, with a view to identifying the benefits, has been a preoccupation of mainstream research. Heydon (2013) argues that while there is plenty of evidence to indicate that intergenerational learning programmes are needed and beneficial, thinking about programmes just in terms of their benefits can be problematic. Heydon's concern is that 'in all of the measurement and evaluation, the view of participants in intergenerational learning as living social actors, as people with feelings, desires, and intentionality may be lost' (2013: 32).

Intergenerational studies have historically employed objective and quantitative psychological measures to evaluate the impact of a programme on participants (Ventura-Merkel et al., 1989; Ward, 1999). While it is acknowledged that objective outcome measures can be useful, their value in demonstrating impact can be limited due to the complexity of such programmes (Heydon, 2013; Sanchez et al., 2007; Ward, 1999). Objective outcome measures are selected based on researcher assumptions about how the programme might influence participants, choice is restricted by the tools available, and there are issues regarding cross-cultural application. Furthermore, Heydon argues that the 'focus on quantifiable benefits is premised on a problematic needs discourse' (2013: 32) and runs the risk of being culturally insensitive because of being framed by social and cultural understandings about what is valuable.

The aim of this chapter therefore is to draw on the *qualitative* data generated in our study to explore the experience of the project from the perspective of the older participants themselves. We hope that this may contribute to a more comprehensive understanding of the meaning and value of such a programme for older people, particularly those from culturally and linguistically diverse communities. In doing so, this chapter raises pertinent issues to consider when undertaking intergenerational work and particularly its evaluation.

In order to provide a context for interpreting and understanding the data, the concept of 'healthy ageing', particularly in a multicultural Australia, will first be described. This will be followed by a review of the role and value of intergenerational programmes in promoting healthy ageing.

Ageing Well and Cultural Diversity

As the proportion of people over the age of 65 grows exponentially in Australia and elsewhere (AIHW, 2007, see also Chapter 2 in this volume), understanding what it means to 'age well', and the need to develop and implement strategies to promote healthy ageing have become increasingly of interest to researchers, policy makers and service providers. One of the most commonly used terms is 'successful ageing', which comprises three distinct domains: avoidance of disease and disability, maintenance of high physical and cognitive function, and sustained engagement in social and productive activities (Rowe & Kahn, 1996). Our project mostly taps into the latter, psychosocial domain, although it is acknowledged that all three domains are relevant, overlap and interrelate.

While sustained engagement in social and productive activities is an important component of ageing well, there is increasing evidence to suggest that it is the meaningfulness of the engagement that is of utmost importance (Browning et al., 2013; Feldman et al., 2012; WHO, 2002). Other psychosocial aspects also known to be important for ageing well, and related to the maintenance of good mental health, include self-esteem, identity, feeling valued, having a sense of purpose, and good relationships with others (Browning et al., 2013; Feldman et al., 2012). Many older people feel that being able to make a contribution to society (e.g. via volunteering) and being adequately acknowledged are good for their mental well-being (ACMHF, 2006).

Concepts of healthy and successful ageing have in the past been based on clinical and researcher objectives. In more recent times there have been developments in recognising the importance of understanding older people's own views on what it means to age well (Bowling & Dieppe, 2005). However, this evidence has been generated predominantly in developed countries, with white middle-class participants, and subsequently there are distinct gaps in our understanding about cross-cultural perspectives on ageing. These gaps are beginning to be addressed by some researchers (Hsu, 2007; Matsubayashi et al., 2006; Ng, 2009; Tohit et al., 2012), but evidence is sparse. With the large proportion (25%) and rapidly increasing rate of older Australians born overseas (faster than the rate of non-overseas born) (AIHW, 2007), there is an even greater rationale for studies such as ours and a need to increase knowledge about the values and opinions of people in a multicultural and multilingual society in relation to ageing well.

The Role and Value of Intergenerational Programmes in Promoting Healthy Ageing

Intergenerational programmes can provide opportunities for older people to continue to engage with their communities, opportunities that might not otherwise be available. Of particular relevance to our discussion here are studies which have shown that the health and well-being of older people benefits from contact with younger people (Aday et al., 1991; MacCallam et al., 2006; Sanchez et al., 2007; Seefeldt, 1989).

Disengagement Theory posited that ageing is associated with becoming less mobile, more withdrawn, and socially isolated (Cumming & Henry, 1961). This controversial theory was widely criticised, and Activity Theory (Havighurst, 1961) and Continuity Theory (Atchley, 1971) soon emerged in response. These theories emphasised active maintenance of relationships as well as ongoing engagement in meaningful pursuits (Achenbaum, 2008). It is of interest that older immigrants have been identified as being at greater risk of becoming disengaged from the wider community (Angel & Angel, 1992; Kritz et al., 2000; Lee & Crittenden, 1996; Litwin, 1995). Not speaking the official language is likely to be a primary reason for this potential disengagement (Radermacher et al., 2008). Any programme or intervention that can assist older immigrants to keep active and engaged may therefore have an important role in promoting health and well-being.

Unfortunately, however, intergenerational programmes can be somewhat contrived, tokenistic and subsequently lacking in meaning (Heydon, 2013; Sanchez *et al.*, 2007). Further, many of these programmes have tended to assume that older people are the sole benefactors, and have overlooked what older people themselves can offer. Older people continue to be perceived as a burden and dependent on others, despite ample evidence which counters such stereotypes (Angus & Reeve, 2006; Feldman *et al.*, 2012; Palmore, 1998, 2005). In response, the concepts of *generativity* and *reciprocity* have emerged as part of a theoretical approach which challenges the notion that older people can only be takers, not givers. Generativity describes the process of older people giving back to younger generations through sharing their knowledge and resources (Erikson, 1963). Reciprocity, which embraces the concept of generativity, emphasises the two-way nature of exchanges between the generations (Hatton Yeo, 2006; Mannion, 2012). These terms (discussed in depth in Chapter 2) are used in the present chapter as conceptual tools for understanding the value of intergenerational programmes for older people as well as for younger L2 learners.

Our project was framed somewhat differently from traditional intergenerational programmes. Firstly, older and younger people came together in dyads for a specific and observable purpose – namely, to improve the students' language proficiency. Secondly, the project was conceptualised on the basis that older people have skills and expertise and are an important resource. Thirdly, the conversation sessions were held regularly over a period of at least a year, allowing each pair to develop feelings of trust and rapport (cf. Chapter 7 on rapport). The uniqueness of the project therefore was that it provided genuine opportunities for older people to utilise their skills in meaningful ways, and in so doing to enhance their own health and well-being.

An important aspect of intergenerational programmes is their ability to challenge age-based stereotypes. While such programmes can be extremely valuable for breaking down young people's negative perceptions of the aged and ageing, in this chapter our focus is the other way round: that is, the potential for the programme to help older people better understand and feel more comfortable around young people. Programmes such as ours that have a specific goal and enable prolonged contact between individuals have been shown to be more effective at changing attitudes of older people towards the younger generation (Zeldin *et al.*, 2000).

Design of the Study

In order to investigate the impact of the project on older participants, a mixed methods design was employed. Quantitative questionnaires were administered both before and after the project was implemented in each year of the study. Qualitative structured telephone interviews and focus groups were conducted after the project's completion. In this chapter, however, we draw specifically on the qualitative data generated by the telephone interviews. Our aim was not to quantify the outcomes for older people but to explore the range of experiences they described, and ultimately to identify the value and meaning of the project for them, particularly in relation to their health and well-being. Furthermore, asking older participants to describe their experiences in their own words was considered to be particularly important with a cohort that was culturally and linguistically diverse.

Structured telephone interviews

The older participants in our study were invited to take part in a structured one-on-one telephone interview in their preferred language. Once they had agreed to this they were telephoned within a few weeks of the final meeting with their students. Questions about demographic background (including gender, age, country of birth, year of arrival in Australia, marital status, number of children, home ownership, income and self-rated health) preceded longer open-ended questions about the project. The immigrants were asked about their experiences of meeting the students, what they found interesting, and what they perceived to be the value and impact of the sessions both for themselves and for the students. The interviews took about 30 minutes and were conducted by bilingual researchers. These were audio-recorded, and the responses were translated by the researcher into English more or less verbatim and written down during the conversation.

Of the total number of German, Spanish and Chinese speakers who took part in the project over its three-year duration (see Chapter 3), qualitative data via the telephone interviews was collected from 62 individuals only (44 Chinese, 12 Germans and 6 from Latin America). Unfortunately it was not possible to contact and invite all the older participants to be interviewed as many were not available or had gone overseas during the period of data collection.

Analytic approach

Demographic data was managed using SPSS Software (version 20) and descriptive statistics were used to generate a participant profile. Qualitative data (the English translations) were analysed by Harriet Radermacher. As a first step, the recorded responses to the interview questions were read in conjunction with the demographic data to gain an understanding of the experience of each individual participant. Secondly, the responses to each question were entered into an Excel spreadsheet in order to review the data question by question. Initial codes were identified throughout this two-stage process, which were then organised into a preliminary set of themes (Braun & Clarke, 2006). In developing the themes, the raw data was revisited multiple times. Preliminary themes were discussed and reviewed by the research team, which included the bilingual interviewers. Qualitative data used to illustrate the themes was de-identified. The language group, gender and age of participants were noted for the purpose of reporting the data.

As we interpreted the data, the aim was not to compare the experiences of people from different language groups. Diversity in the opinions and perspectives of participants could be attributed to many factors beyond that of language spoken, such as age, gender, educational background, country of origin, English proficiency, reason for migration and the amount of time spent in Australia. Comparing and contrasting experiences by language group can contribute to unhelpful and inaccurate stereotyping, and, given the variation in numbers across the groups, was not particularly appropriate. At times, however, participants' feedback elucidated similarities and differences both within and across language groups which will be described where relevant below.

Participant profile

Of the 62 participants, the average age was 67, ranging from 41 to 93 years old (see Table 8.1). The majority were female (63%), married (82%), with children (96%), living in their own home (60%), retired (83%), perceiving themselves to be comfortable financially (66%) and in good health (61%). The median year of arrival in Australia was 1998, ranging from 1954 up to the start of the project in 2010.

It should perhaps be pointed out that this profile of participants by language group was not representative of the whole sample. The majority of the 12 German participants were male (67%), unmarried (58%), and half of them had children. All of the six Spanish speakers were female, half were married, and the majority (83%) had children. The majority of the 44 Chinese participants were female (66%), married (73%) and had children (98%). All the Chinese older participants spoke Mandarin, as this was the language the students were learning. However several Chinese participants also spoke Cantonese and other Chinese dialects.

In general, a greater proportion of the German participants were male, unmarried, without children, and still employed as compared with the two other language groups. The Germans also had a higher mean age, had been in Australia a longer time, and all of them had been involved in the project for more than a year. The Chinese immigrants had not been in Australia as long as the German and Spanish speakers and a smaller proportion owned their own homes. The majority of German and Chinese participants said

Table 8.1 Older participants in the telephone interviews

	German	Spanish	Chinese	All participants
No. of participants	12 (19%)	6 (10%)	44 (71%)	62 (100%)
Mean age in years in 2010	70.6	65.5	66.8	67.4
(Range)	(60–80)	(62–69)	(41–93)	(41–93)
Gender				
Female	4 (33%)	6 (100%)	29 (66%)	39 (63%)
Male	8 (67%)	0	15 (34%)	23 (37%)
No. of years participation				
1	0	2 (33%)	18 (41%)	20 (32%)
2	8 (67%)	4 (67%)	18 (41%)	30 (48%)
3	4 (33%)	0	8 (18%)	12 (19%)
Married	5 (83%)	3 (50%)	32 (87%)	40 (82%) [no data for 13 participants]
No. with children	6 (100%)	5 (83%)	43 (98%)	54 (96%) [no data for 6 participants]
Median year of arrival in Australia (Range)	1962 (1954–2006)	1978 (1975–1999)	1999 (1980–2010)	1998 (1954–2010)
Housing status				
Home owner	5 (83%)	5 (83%)	22 (54%)	32 (60%)
Renting	1 (17%)	1 (17%)	7 (17%)	9 (17%)
Other	0	0	12 (29%)	12 (22%) [no data for 9 participants]
Retirement status				
Completely retired	2 (33%)	6 (100%)	36 (88%)	44 (83%)
Partly retired	2 (33%)	0	3 (7%)	5 (9%)
Not retired	2 (33%)	0	2 (5%)	4 (8%) [no data for 9 participants]
Financial situation				
Can't make ends meet	1 (17%)	3 (50%)	3 (8%)	7 (14%)
Just enough to get by	0	1 (17%)	10 (26%)	11 (22%)
Comfortable	5 (83%)	2 (33%)	26 (67%)	33 (65%) [no data for 11 participants]

(Continued)

Table 8.1 (Continued)

	German	Spanish	Chinese	All participants
Self-rated health status				
Excellent	0	0	1 (4%)	1 (3%)
Very good	0	1 (17%)	2 (7%)	3 (8%)
Good	3 (75%)	2 (33%)	18 (64%)	23 (61%)
Fair	1 (25%)	3 (50%)	6 (21%)	10 (26%)
Poor	0	0	1 (4%)	1 (3%)
				[no data for 24 participants]

that financially they were comfortable, but only a third of those from Latin America supported this statement. While the project targeted older adults over the age of 60, two Chinese women in their 40s who were keen to be involved also participated.[1]

Findings of the Study

Overview

On the whole, the immigrants appreciated the opportunity to share their experiences. They said that the project was interesting and enjoyable and an activity they would recommend to others. They saw it as providing students with real-life opportunities to practise speaking the target language in a more casual and relaxed environment than a more formal classroom.

As regards their own well-being, the older participants generally reported that it was nice to feel useful, good to have an opportunity for social interaction, and that talking with the students was a fulfilling experience that gave them a lift, particularly in terms of their mental health. They also reported improvements in their own English language learning.

There were mixed reports concerning the impact of the programme on their physical health. One participant stated bluntly that 'my health does not relate to this project' (German, male, 71). Another German, Werner,[2] commented similarly that the project had had no impact on his physical health, but it did improve his cognitive capacity: 'I am in the last phase of my life, I have seen a lot. It has not changed my physical health, but my mental health, it has triggered a lot of thinking and mental activity' (age 74).[3] But other participants spoke more positively about the effects on their physical health, as in the case of the following 72-year-old Chinese woman: 'To spend time with young people makes me feel younger. Good communication encourages good sleeping, I feel so dynamic and healthy now.'

Two-thirds of participants returned for a second or even a third year, which strongly suggests their positive endorsement of the project. Indeed, one German older woman (age 68) said of her experience, 'I enjoyed it, otherwise I would not have done it for two years. I really enjoyed that my student improved a lot.' There were also indications that the interactions were not just limited to the classroom: 'I would like to continue with him [the student] and we are also meeting during the holidays' (German, male, 63).

The older people were not asked specifically about their attitudes towards the students, nor whether their participation in the project had changed their views about younger people generally. However, it is clear from some of their comments that many of them had been somewhat surprised by the keenness of the students to learn and by their hardworking approach, as illustrated by the following remark: 'We always believed children have reverse psychology, but from my experience of these meetings, after listening to the students, I was so surprised and touched that they have been really thinking about others. This really impressed me' (Chinese, female, 73). Others noted the different attitudes of the students they observed as compared to young people back in their home countries: '… the students are different from students in China … These students are not very shy and like to answer the questions directly' (Chinese, female, 62). For some older participants, however, the young people did not meet their high expectations: 'The students are not interested in learning about the culture and history of China, which shocked me' (Chinese, female, age not disclosed).

While the majority of older participants spoke voluminously about their positive experiences in being part of the project, it is important to note that this was not always the case. Some, when asked about the potential impact of the programme on their lives, said that they needed more time to appreciate any noticeable benefits. Others were of the general view that the project did not have a significant impact on their well-being and self-esteem beyond being something interesting and enjoyable to do. As one 60-year-old German woman described it, the project had 'no impact because I have a family and I do not feel lonely'. In one instance, however, a participant reported that the project had posed a risk to her self-esteem as she could not see any direct benefits for the student: 'Actually, I don't have a sense of achievement. Because of my poor English, I think I cannot help the students a lot. I am worried that I cannot do anything to help students' (Chinese, female, 78).

This overview illustrates the range of experiences, setting the scene for a more in-depth exploration. While each response was different, three key themes were identified as particularly important and worthy of further examination. The first was the clear value of the programme for the participants' sense of self-worth. The second related to the sense of pride, duty and citizenship experienced as a result of taking part. The third theme concerned the connections and relationships arising out of the student–older participant interactions, which served as a vehicle for cultural and generational exchange. These themes are of course interrelated. Before describing each theme in depth, a short case study will be presented. It has been selected because it effectively encapsulates many aspects of the participants' experiences, in particular the reciprocal nature of being involved in the project.

A case study in reciprocity

Klaus Schmidt was an 80-year-old German who participated in all three years of the study. In 2010 he said that the experience was a 'lift up for me because I lost my partner this year and did not have anything to do and the project helped me to get back into society'. He went on to say, 'It was very good because I went through bad times. I enjoyed talking to everyone (also teachers) and felt good going home.' In 2011 Klaus reported that 'the whole experience led me to teach German at the University of the Third Age and to engage in other activities with kids – it was a gateway for me to expose myself to other experiences'. Not only did participating in the programme enable Klaus to get back on track and start enjoying life again, it opened the door for him to make a further contribution to society. And as well as acknowledging how the programme had impacted on his own life, he could see the benefits for the students: 'It is a great experience because the students learn and for me it is also a learning experience.' Klaus reflected on the potential benefits of creating opportunities for interactions across the generations: 'The project is very interesting, especially if you have not had much contact with young people before. It is very interesting to talk to young people and to get their points of view.' However, he did voice his concern that student attendance was poor, and in his mind success depended on whether the students themselves wanted to learn the language or whether they had been told they had to by their parents.

Improved sense of self-worth

Knowing that their contribution was assisting students to learn made the immigrants feel good about themselves. Werner commented, 'It is great because the project gives students another dimension of life and learning and I enjoy being part of that and being able to contribute to that'. Another German talked of a 'feeling of belonging, you do something for somebody else, it makes you feel good' (male, 75). A 60-year-old Spanish woman remarked that she felt 'more important as a person as I can share [my experiences] with others'. Two of the Chinese women spoke in similar terms about how being involved in the programme made them feel satisfied and more confident: 'I get satisfaction from knowing I can do something for society, even though I am old' (age 65); 'Taking part in this project makes me feel that I can contribute to society even though I am old. I am becoming more confident' (age 78). We note here that these Chinese participants expressed a degree of surprise that they had something to offer despite being 'old', indicative of their own ageist assumptions.

The data also revealed that participation in the project was important for boosting a sense of agency and autonomy: 'I feel like I can still help other people, instead of waiting for other people's help all the time. And it is much better to join in some activities like this than staying at home' (Chinese, female, 60).

Hearing that a student was keen to continue learning the language was of sufficient interest to one participant to share it with the researchers: 'One of the students sent me an email saying that he will continue with German after the meetings with me' (German, male, 62). It is not hard to imagine that the student's decision would be a boost to the older participant's sense of self-worth.

Pride, duty and citizenship

While some participants said they felt the programme had little or no impact on their lives, others, particularly the Chinese who took part in 2011 and 2012, talked at length about the pride they felt in being able to assist young people to learn, about their sense of achievement, and about the associated feelings of happiness. A sentiment that was expressed over and over was their sense of responsibility, which included not only giving back to and feeling a part of Australian society that had been good to them, but also the opportunity it afforded them to continue to spread knowledge about Chinese culture. These sentiments are beautifully and powerfully encapsulated in the following comments:

> I feel very proud that I can do something for my motherland. As Chinese, it is our responsibility. (male, 93)
>
> Since I came to Australia, the government of Australia has taken care of us, and we have to try our best to do something to repay what we have received from the Australia government. (female, 73)
>
> I have a sense of accomplishment from this project. It is a good way to spread Chinese culture. Although I am now in Australia, I am Chinese. I love China. I feel very proud to be taking part in this project. I think is our responsibility. (female, 76)
>
> Yes, I have a sense of achievement. Firstly, when the students who have talked with us achieved good marks we felt very proud. Secondly, I took part in this project as a volunteer. I feel very happy that I can contribute to society. (female, 59)
>
> Firstly, I feel I can help students to some extent. And I also feel that I become younger by taking part in this project. Secondly, everyone is

doing the volunteer in Australia. I was a volunteer and did something to repay the society, so I feel very happy. (female, 70)

Jessie, at 44 years of age, was not an older participant but one of the two middle-aged Chinese women who were keen to participate in the project. She described her experiences in very similar terms to those of the older participants. She arrived in Australia in 2007 and spoke of the importance of the experience for engaging with a new society:

Yes, firstly, because when I was young I dreamed to be a teacher. This project to some extent has made the dream come true. I taught the students for a while. Secondly, to be a volunteer is very common in Australia. This time I was a volunteer, and I feel I have become a member of the whole society. It will help me to engage in the society step by step.

Interestingly, this sense of pride and duty, and the desire to give back to Australian society was not expressed by the German or Spanish participants but was unique to the Chinese immigrants in our study. It would be of value to further research this finding in relation to the discussion in Chapter 6 about construal of the self and the greater degree of connectedness and regard for the collective welfare observed in Asian cultures. This idea of the interdependent self in the social whole is also discussed below.

Connection as a vehicle for cultural and generational exchange

As well as Klaus and his experience of positive reciprocity, described above, other participants acknowledged the value of communication with the students, having interpersonal contact, and the associated opportunity to establish a relationship: 'I feel very happy to have taken part in this project, because I can help other people during the process. And I made friends with the students too, which is a really nice thing' (Chinese, male, 73). Some of the immigrants stated that the project helped them to feel less isolated, especially if relationships with their own family members were not strong.

Werner, the 74-year-old German, said that the feeling of communicating was good, and that the trust that developed between him and the student was important. He said that while his student partner's language proficiency was of quite a low standard, it did improve, and this was likely to have been facilitated by the developing sense of trust and a respectful relationship:

It is another dimension of the project for me. It is a good feeling that people listen to you and respect you and we appreciate that because in every one of us there is a teacher: 'In jedem steckt ein Lehrer drin'.

Establishing a respectful and equal relationship also appeared to be important for facilitating cultural and generational exchange. Like Klaus, 63-year-old Tobias clearly appreciated the interaction and the sharing of different perspectives:

> I could tell him about more recent experiences and stories from what is happening in Germany today (e.g. politics etc.). He was very knowledgeable about things happening in Australia so we could exchange information. He could see differences between the two systems. We could share our migrant experiences and stories.

One Chinese participant (male, 82), however, appeared more speculative about his involvement. While he acknowledged that it was good to have opportunities to talk to young people and to find out more about Australia, he said that he felt too old to participate in such a programme.

For a Spanish female participant (age 67), it was especially important to know that 'young students are interested in knowing about my language, our language ... It makes me happy that kids are interested in learning my language'. She was 'delighted to discover that [name of student] was interested in working with the Spanish community'. Likewise, another Spanish participant appreciated being able 'to emphasise the importance of studying a second language, to show them a different view of my country, to enhance their interest in travelling and knowing other cultures' (female, 62). In this case, it appeared that the project provided an opportunity for the older participant to discover that young people enjoy learning about culture and language, and that she can play a role in facilitating the learning process.

Discussion of the Findings

The qualitative interview data has provided rich insights into the value of an intergenerational language programme from the perspective of the older participants themselves. The data strongly suggests that the project was perceived very positively overall and demonstrated encouraging signs that the health and well-being of the older participants were enhanced. These findings support the key role of sustained engagement in social and productive activities to promote successful ageing, as identified by Rowe and Kahn (1997).

In addition, there was evidence that participation encouraged the cultural, linguistic and intergenerational exchange of skills, knowledge and values. While some experiences were expected, others were not anticipated, such as the deep sense of responsibility felt by some Chinese participants to give back to society and the motivation to maintain their language and culture.

There was only limited evidence to indicate that intergenerational stereotypes were challenged in any way, mainly on account of a research methodology that could not identify changes in attitudes. Perhaps more surprising was the evidence indicating the internalised ageist attitudes held by older people themselves about their own abilities, and hence the potential role of such a programme to challenge these negative ways of thinking within their own generation.

By drawing only on the qualitative interview data, as opposed to attempting to quantify the impact of the programme on older participants, we were able to elucidate aspects of the experience that may have otherwise been overlooked. Specifically, the sense of pride and duty that played an important role in deciding to participate in the project perhaps would not have been identified had we relied on quantitative measures alone.

Reciprocity and generativity: Older adults giving back

The intergenerational theories of *reciprocity* and *generativity* are both relevant and useful tools for understanding the value for older people of projects such as ours. They are particularly important for opening up questions about giving and receiving, challenging stereotypes about older people as little more than recipients of care, dependent and a burden. What distinguishes the two theories is that generativity assumes a one-way movement of knowledge from the older adult to a younger generation. Reciprocity, on the other hand, focuses on the exchange occurring between the generations.

Many participants talked at length about how their involvement in the project resulted in gains for themselves, describing feeling more confident, happy and healthy. In our study we summarised these statements as expressions of an increased sense of self-worth. Other participants primarily saw their participation as a duty, as a contribution to the community with minimal acknowledgement of any benefits for themselves. Of interest, however, is that generativity and degrees of self-worth appear to be inextricably linked.

For the participants who did not acknowledge any personal benefits, it was not clear whether there were no benefits to be gained, or whether the participants were simply not attuned to them. There may be cultural and linguistic differences in how interactions with others and group activities are conceptualised. An important consideration is that our project was largely constructed and framed from a Western, individualistic, perspective – seeking to investigate the impact on *individual* participants. However, people in collectivist cultures (such as those from China) perhaps do not necessarily view their experiences through the same (individualistic) lens (asking, for example, 'What did I get out of this experience?'). Rather their assessment may be framed in less self-orientated ways (e.g. It was my duty to impart this information). A sense of duty and responsibility was particularly strong for the Chinese cohort. The desire to be actively involved in continuing a cultural tradition could also be strongly related to cultural background and values, and seen, for example, as a duty.

Importantly, the negative comments of the 78-year-old Chinese woman and the 82-year-old Chinese man quoted above serve as a caution that if the project is not perceived positively by the older participants or if the older participants are not effectively supported in their roles, the experience could be detrimental to their self-esteem. This finding warrants modifications to the design of the project, such as providing more opportunities for feedback during the year, and better matching of conversation partners so that if the older person has limited English proficiency they are able to be matched with a more proficient language student.

Stereotypes and relationships

This study, like many others, counters the stereotype of older people being a burden on society with nothing to offer. Certainly Klaus was a shining example of how participation in the project could enable an older person to move forward after a major life event, increase his sense of self-worth, and proceed to seek out more opportunities to share his skills with the wider community. Whether the students' attitudes about older people had changed as a result of participation was not the focus of our study, but nevertheless would be interesting to explore.

The role of the project in challenging stereotypes of older participants about the younger generation was not made explicit and the study could perhaps have benefited from a more overt investigation. However, there was evidence that participants were generally pleasantly surprised by what they discovered about young people. They observed that most of the students were keen to learn and were hardworking, attributes they had not necessarily expected.

There was a clear appreciation by the older participants of the opportunity to interact and share knowledge with younger people. Indeed, the relationship that formed between the partners was seemingly integral to the success of the project, particularly those relationships that were based on trust and respect and which facilitated the processes of generativity and reciprocity. Feeling respected, being taken seriously and knowing that there was an important job to be done (which was not tokenistic) was clearly significant for the older participants.

Reasons for participation

There was evidence to suggest that some participants were engaging in the study to alleviate their isolation and boredom. Other participants were highly skilled and experienced and sought to pass on their expertise. Still others felt a sense of duty and responsibility to give back to their community and to the younger generation in particular.

In future studies it would be good to collect data regarding participants' reasons for volunteering, their motivations and expectations. After all, one's reason for taking part can often determine how the experience is assessed. For example, if an older participant has volunteered in order to assist the student to get better grades, and there is no objective improvement, the older participant may evaluate his or her participation as a failure. This might have no effect on health and well-being, but there could be a detrimental effect, particularly if the older participant feels responsible for the lack of improvement.

There may have been a desire or expectation amongst participants to enact their cultural beliefs about generativity and to be mentors to the younger generation. Alternatively, participants may have expected to learn new things or to meet new people. Perhaps knowing these reasons and expectations for participation could provide valuable data to inform future iterations of the project.

Methodological limitations

As discussed in the opening sections of this chapter, it was a deliberate decision to draw only on the qualitative data from our study, in alliance with Heydon's (2013) observation that quantifying the impact of complex intergenerational programmes can be problematic. We were also cognisant of the value of hearing the perspectives of older people in their own words, not to mention that this was a cohort of people not born in Australia whose first language was not English. While we stand by this decision, and are confident that this approach tapped into understandings that might have eluded us in a purely quantitative investigation, there were some limitations of this approach.

We relied on the ability of participants to articulate their experiences in relation to the value of the programme, and this was not always an easy exercise. There was the risk that the older participants would feel obliged to please the interviewer and rate the programme positively – a common phenomenon, particularly among the older age group. However, the high rate of participants who continued with the project in consecutive years is good evidence to the contrary.

In order to reduce project costs, participants' responses were translated by each interviewer and recorded as close to verbatim as possible in English during the interview. While the interviews were audio-recorded, it would have enhanced the accuracy if the audio recordings were transcribed and then translated.

Finally, participants were interviewed within a few weeks of their participation in the project. Therefore this study is limited in relation to what it can say about the long-term value of the project.

Conclusion

The data analysed in this chapter has illustrated that there is great value in bringing the 'skipped generations' (Heydon, 2013: 3) together in an environment with specific learning outcomes, particularly when it provides opportunities for engagement in social and productive activities (the third domain identified in Rowe and Kahn's model of successful ageing quoted above). The qualitative data from our study has enabled the identification of some integral aspects of a project such as ours that support older people from culturally and linguistically diverse backgrounds. These include: the opportunities such activities provide to boost self-worth, an outlet to fulfil a sense of duty as older people and citizens, and a platform on which to exchange knowledge, skills and experience with the younger generation. The data supported the relevance of both generativity and reciprocity in understanding the value of intergenerational programmes for older people, most notably the process of generativity for enhancing self-worth. However, the study did highlight the need for caution when selecting and pairing older participants in order to minimise potentially negative experiences resulting in loss of self-esteem. The study also confirmed the complexity inherent in such programmes, and the associated challenges in conducting effective evaluations.

Notes

(1) However, for convenience we use the term 'older participants' for all the native speakers in the project.
(2) All participants' names have been changed.
(3) In presenting the participants' responses in this chapter, the verbatim translations have been edited for fluency.

References

Achenbaum, W.A. (2008) A metahistorical perspective on the theories of aging. In V.L. Bengtson, D. Gans and N. Putney (eds) *Handbook of Theories of Aging* (2nd edn) (pp. 25–38). New York: Springer Publishing Company.
ACMHF [Age Concern and Mental Health Foundation] (2006) *Promoting Mental Health and Well-being in Later Life: A First Report from the UK Inquiry*. London: The Foundation Available at: http://www.mhilli.org.
Aday, R.H., Rice, C. and Evans, E. (1991) Intergenerational partners project: A model linking elementary students with senior center volunteers. *The Gerontologist* 31 (2), 263–266.
AIHW [Australian Institute of Health and Welfare] (2007) *Older Australia at a Glance: 4th edition*. Cat. no. AGE 52. Canberra: AIHW.

Angel, J. and Angel, R. (1992) Age at migration, social connections, and well-being among elderly Hispanics. *Journal of Aging and Health* 4, 480–499.

Angus, J. and Reeve, P. (2006) Ageism: A threat to 'aging well' in the 21st century. *Journal of Applied Gerontology* 25 (2), 137–152.

Atchley, R.C. (1971) Retirement and leisure participation: Continuity or crisis? *The Gerontologist* 11 (1), 13–17.

Bowling, A. and Dieppe, P. (2005) What is successful ageing and who should define it? *British Medical Journal* 331, 1548–1551.

Braun, V. and Clarke, V. (2006) Using thematic analysis in psychology. *Qualitative Research in Psychology* 3 (2), 77–101.

Browning, C.J., Heine, C. and Thomas, S. (2013) Promoting aging well: Psychological contributions. In M.L. Caltabiano and L. Ricciardelli (eds) *Applied Topics in Health Psychology* (pp. 57–71). Chichester, West Sussex: Wiley-Blackwell.

Cumming, E. and Henry, W.E. (1961) *Growing Old, the Process of Disengagement.* New York: Basic Books.

Erikson, E.H. (1963) *Childhood and Society* (2nd edn). New York: Norton.

Feldman, S., Mahoney, H. and Seedsman, T. (2002) Education for positive ageing: A partnership model for effecting sustainable outcomes. *Education and Ageing* 17 (1), 7–23.

Feldman, S., Radermacher, H. and Petersen, A. (2012) The vicissitudes of 'healthy aging': The experiences of older migrant men in a rural Australian community. In A. Kampf, B. Marshall and A. Petersen (eds) *Aging Men, Masculinities and Modern Medicine* 84–104. London: Routledge.

Hatton Yeo, A. (2006) *Intergenerational Practice: Active Participation across the Generations.* Stoke-on-Trent: Beth Johnson Foundation.

Havighurst, R.J. (1961) Successful aging. *The Gerontologist* 1, 8–13.

Heydon, R.M. (2013) *Learning at the Ends of Life: Children, Elders, and Literacies in Intergenerational Curricula.* Toronto: University of Toronto Press.

Hsu, H.C. (2007) Exploring elderly people's perspectives on successful ageing in Taiwan. *Ageing & Society* 27 (1), 87–102.

Kritz, M., Gurak, D. and Likwang, C. (2000) Elderly immigrants: Their composition and living arrangements. *Journal of Sociology and Social Welfare* 27 (1), 85–114.

Lee, M.S. and Crittenden, K.S. (1996) Social support and depression among elderly Korean immigrants in the United States. *International Journal of Aging and Human Development* 42 (4), 313–327.

Litwin, H. (1995) The social networks of elderly immigrants: An analytical typology. *Journal of Aging Studies* 9 (2), 155–174.

MacCallum, J., Palmer, D., Wright, P., Cumming-Potvin, W., Northcote, J., Booker, M. and Tero, C. (2006) *Community Building through Intergenerational Exchange Programs: Report to the National Youth Affairs Research Scheme.* Canberra Department of Families, Community Services and Indigenous Affairs on behalf of NYARS.

Mannion, G. (2012) Intergenerational education: The significance of reciprocity and place. *Journal of Intergenerational Relationships* 10 (4), 386–399.

Matsubayashi, K., Ishine, M., Wada, T. and Okumiya, K. (2006) Older adults' views of 'successful aging': Comparisons of older Japanese and Americans. *Journal of American Geriatrics Society* 54 (1), 184–187.

Ng, T.P. (2009) Determinants of successful ageing using a multidimensional definition among Chinese elderly in Singapore. *The American Journal of Geriatric Psychiatry* 17 (5), 407–416.

Palmore, E.B. (1998) *The Facts on Aging Quiz* (2nd edn). New York: Springer.

Palmore, E.B. (2005) Three decades of research on ageism. *Generations: Journal of the American Society on Aging* 29 (3), 87–90.

Radermacher, H., Feldman, S. and Browning, C. (2008) *Review of Literature concerning the Delivery of Community Aged Care Services to Ethnic Groups*. Melbourne: Ethnic Communities Council of Victoria / Monash University.

Rowe, J.W. and Kahn, R.L. (1997) Successful aging. *The Gerontologist* 37 (4), 433–440.

Sánchez, M., Butts, D.M., Hatton-Yeo A., Henkin, N.A., Jarrott, S.E., Kaplan M.S., Martínez, A., Newman S., Pinazo, S., Sáez, J., Aaron P.C. and Weintraub, A.P.C. (2007) *Intergenerational Programmes: Towards a Society for All Ages*. Social Studies Collection No 23. Barcelona: The 'la Caixa' Foundation.

Seefeldt, C. (1989) Intergenerational programs: Impact on attitudes. *Journal of Children in Contemporary Society* 20 (3/4), 185–194.

Tohit, N., Browning, C.J. and Radermacher, H. (2012) 'We want a peaceful life here and hereafter': Healthy ageing perspectives of older Malays in Malaysia. *Ageing & Society* 32 (3), 405–424.

Ventura-Merkel, C., Liederman, D.S. and Ossofsky, J. (1989) Exemplary intergenerational programs. In S. Newman and S. Brummel (eds) *Intergenerational Programs: Imperatives, Strategies, Impacts, Trends* (pp. 173–180). New York: The Haworth Press, Inc.

Ward, C.R. (1999) The intergenerational field needs more ethnographic research. In V.S. Kuehne (ed.) *Intergenerational Programs: Understanding What We Have Created* (pp. 7–23). Binghamton, NY: The Haworth Press, Inc.

WHO [World Health Organization] (2002) *Active Ageing: A Policy Framework*. Geneva: WHO.

Zeldin, S., McDaniel, A.K., Topitzes, D. and Calvert, M. (2000) *Youth in Decision-making: A Study on the Impacts of Youth on Adults and Organizations*. Chevy Chase, MD: Innovation Center for Community and Youth Development, National 4-h Council.

Part 3

Situated Learning: Enhancing the Opportunities for L2 Students

9 Gaining L2 Self-Confidence in Conversations with Native Speakers

Hui Huang

Introduction

The purpose of this chapter is to examine the effect of the project on students' attitudes to language learning, and in particular on their *self-efficacy*. Motivational and affective factors are understood to be very important for the success of second language (L2) learning. The most commonly discussed in the L2 learning literature are the instrumental and integrative orientations of motivation, originally proposed by Gardner (Gardner & Lambert, 1972; Gardner, 1985). Perceived self-efficacy is documented as a powerful motivational driver associated with performance in several academic areas and as a 'cognitive mediator of action' (e.g. Bandura 1997; Pajares & Schunk, 2001; Pajares, 2003). However, the concept has rarely been discussed in the field of L2 learning. A few recent studies have looked at the relationship between self-efficacy and L2 reading, writing and listening (Chen, 2007; Magogwe & Oliver, 2007; Graham, 2006, 2007; Mills *et al.*, 2006, 2007), but until now the role of self-efficacy in speaking, especially with native speakers in authentic conversations, has not been explored.

We argue in this chapter that promoting positive self-efficacy is very important for language learning in Australia, where decreasing numbers of students are opting to study a foreign language when this is no longer obligatory (Liddicoat *et al.*, 2007). For example, only 3% of Year 12 students in Australian schools take Chinese as a VCE subject, and 94% of students who have learnt Chinese at school quit the subject before Year 10 (Orton, 2008), in spite of the fact that, in the state of Victoria at least, Mandarin is the third most widely spoken language in the home, with Cantonese in fifth place (see Table 1.1). Therefore, we believe it is important to find out whether, and to what extent, our programme of intercultural encounters had a positive effect on the students' self-efficacy in respect of their language learning.

Self-Efficacy

Self-efficacy, as a motivational construct in Bandura's (1986, 1997) social cognitive theory, refers to beliefs about one's ability to perform a given task, attain a certain goal, or act in a particular way. According to this theory, 'What people think, believe, and feel affects how they behave' (Bandura, 1986: 25). In other words, self-efficacy is the *subjective* assessment of one's capabilities rather than a grading based on any external or objective criteria (Mills *et al.*, 2007).

Many studies have provided evidence that a person's judgement about his or her capacity to perform a given task is a better predictor of success than the person's actual abilities. That is, self-efficacy is a critical determinant of behaviour (Bandura, 1997; Pajares & Urdan, 2006; Pajares, 1997; Pajares & Schunk, 2001; Zimmerman, 1995, 2000). These studies found that students with a strong sense of academic self-efficacy willingly undertook challenging tasks (Bandura & Schunk, 1981), showed increased persistence in the presence of obstacles (Bandura & Schunk, 1981), demonstrated lower anxiety levels (Pintrich & De Groot, 1990), displayed flexibility in the use of learning strategies (Bouffard-Bouchard, 1990; Pintrich & De Groot, 1990) and regulated themselves better than other students (Zimmerman *et al.*, 1992). Students with low self-efficacy, on the other hand, chose to complete simple tasks, applied less effort, demonstrated less persistence, or simply avoided completing the task entirely. In short, self-efficacy has been found to affect behavioural, cognitive and motivational engagement in the classroom (Linnenbrink & Pintrich, 2003) which, in turn, affects academic performance.

According to Bandura (1997), a belief in one's own efficacy can be developed through four main forms of influence: mastery experiences (i.e. interpreting the results of one's previous purposive performances in a positive way), vicarious experiences (finding inspiration in the experiences of others' performances), social persuasion (being persuaded by significant others) and one's physiological and emotional state. Teachers, friends and advisers put the greatest emphasis on the first of these, the mastery experience, because prior successes provide the most authentic evidence of what one can achieve (Pintrich & Schunk, 2002). A critical aspect of self-efficacy is that it is domain or situation/task specific; that is, beliefs about one's efficacy in performing a particular task cannot be assumed to apply to a task in a different domain (Schunk *et al.*, 2007). At the same time, mastering a task is impossible if one lacks the necessary skills and knowledge (Pajares, 2003), and here vicarious experiences are important (Bandura, 1997: 86–88). By observing the successes of comparable peers, an individual can learn that a task is manageable and be motivated to develop the necessary skills and knowledge in order to try it for him/herself, sometimes with the additional encouragement of supportive others (social persuasion). One's own perception of the experience (one's emotional state) plays a major role too: namely, that a positive interpretation will strengthen one's sense of self-efficacy, while a negative interpretation will undermine it.

In addition to the four factors identified by Bandura, an increasing body of research has documented the role played by culture in mediating levels of self-efficacy. For example, students raised in Asian cultures, even when they perform well, have been shown to have lower levels of academic self-efficacy than students raised in Western cultures (e.g. Chen, 2007; Eaton & Dembo, 1997), which Chen attributes to 'the common Asian school characteristics' of 'performance feedback focusing on weakness, highlight on hard work and effort rather than ability, and setting higher standards for success' (2007: 28, 27).

Self-Efficacy in the Context of L2 Learning

In recent years there has been a small but growing body of empirical research primarily focused on the interrelationships between students' self-efficacy and second-language proficiency. Much of this research has further supported the view that self-efficacy beliefs 'mediate the effect of other influences, such as aptitude or previous achievement, on subsequent performance' (Magogwe & Oliver, 2007: 341). For instance, Mills, Pajares and Herron (2007) found that grade self-efficacy, or a student's confidence in his or her ability to attain a particular grade, is highly correlated with the academic success of intermediate-level French learners. Similarly, Ching (2002), in the area of teaching English as a second language, found that students with high self-efficacy beliefs were confident about what they could achieve, worked harder to avoid failure, were highly resilient and linked failure with insufficient effort or deficient knowledge and skills which they believed they were capable of acquiring (Henderson et al., 2009: 467). In spite of the small number of studies in this area, a positive relationship between self-efficacy and language proficiency has been reported (e.g. Mills et al.'s 2006 study on intermediate-level French students in reading; Chen (2007) on college-level learners of English in listening skills).

A second group of studies on language self-efficacy has shown that learners' self-efficacy correlates positively with the language strategies they use. On the basis of a series of studies to enhance French learners' self-efficacy in listening through strategy training, Suzanne Graham and her colleague Ernesto Macaro (Graham, 2006, 2007; Graham & Macaro, 2007, 2008) concluded that the strategy training programme improved listening proficiency and learners' confidence in the task. However, Graham also pointed out that effective listening depended on the learner's self-efficacy with respect to aural comprehension, which may be acutely low because it is a less physically 'observable' skill and less controllable, particularly in real-world situations. Our study therefore has as its focus an exploration of students' self-efficacy in authentic conversations with native speakers, the conversations requiring the skills of both listening and speaking in naturally occurring interactions.

Another group of research studies of language self-efficacy that were conducted outside the language classroom (an online learning environment by Lamboy, 2003; and an online virtual world by Henderson *et al.*, 2009, 2012), found that extra-curricular community resources, when combined with an appropriate study design, could be very effective in raising students' self-efficacy beliefs. The face-to-face conversations with native speakers in our project were an attempt to build on these positive findings.

About the Study

Study design

As shown in Figure 9.1, our study had a longitudinal design, with three parallel self-efficacy questionnaires being carried out. These were conducted during the student's first session of the project (pre-study); in the last session of their first year (post-study); and in the first session of their second year (delayed post-study). A background questionnaire and student focus groups provided further statistical and qualitative data. All of these are discussed below.

In designing the study we hoped to address the following research questions:

(1) After the conversation sessions, was there any development in the students' self-efficacy in their general skills of listening and speaking and also in conversing with a native speaker in the target language?
(2) If there was any such development, was the improvement maintained over the next five months during which there were no further conversation sessions?
(3) Did the development differ according to the student's background (i.e. between the Chinese-background and non-Chinese-background groups) and, if so, to what extent?

Self-efficacy questionnaires

The self-efficacy questionnaires were administered to all student participants, but the number of continuing German and Spanish L2 learners was too small (five German and two Spanish) to be of statistical significance in the quantitative analysis. Therefore, only the data of

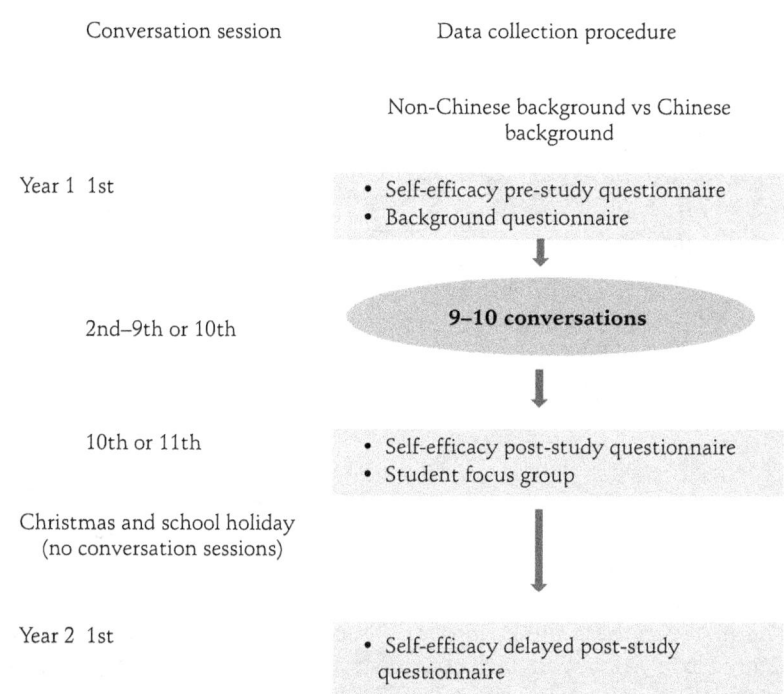

Figure 9.1 Design of the self-efficacy study

the students who were learning Chinese was used. We then matched the pre, post and delayed post data of these Chinese students and limited our analysis to the data from those who had submitted all three questionnaires. Altogether, data from 35 students was used to examine the immediate and long-term effect of the project on their self-efficacy beliefs. The third, delayed post-study questionnaire was administered after a five-month interval during which no conversation sessions had been held in order to gain a longitudinal perspective on the maintained benefits of such encounters.

The three questionnaires were kept the same as a control measure (Table 9.1). Albion's (2001) 5-point scale was employed in constructing the questionnaire, with responses ranging from 1 (least confident) to 5 (most confident). Mean scores above 2.5 represented positive self-efficacy beliefs, while higher results equated to stronger and more positive beliefs. The self-efficacy questions were conceptually organised into two categories: (1) self-efficacy in general language skills of speaking and listening, and (2) self-efficacy in topic management of conversations with a native speaker in the target language. The first category was included in order to explore

Table 9.1 Self-efficacy questionnaire

Skill item		1 least confident ←→ 5 most confident				
1	Speaking	1	2	3	4	5
2	Listening	1	2	3	4	5
3	Conversing with a native speaker in the target language in general	1	2	3	4	5
4	Talking about familiar topics	1	2	3	4	5
5	Talking about unfamiliar topics	1	2	3	4	5
6	Understanding familiar topics	1	2	3	4	5
7	Understanding unfamiliar topics	1	2	3	4	5
8	Initiating a topic	1	2	3	4	5
9	Developing a topic	1	2	3	4	5

the potential impact of the encounters on students' beliefs about more general relevant abilities to do with listening and speaking. The second category was aimed at answering our study questions about the benefits of the project for increasing self-confidence in second-language conversations with native speakers.

The instruction at the head of the questionnaire read: 'Please indicate the degree to which you feel confident that you can do the following aspects well'.

Background questionnaire

The background questionnaire was conducted at the same time as the pre-study questionnaire and was designed to collect personal information about each student such as age, gender, place of birth and language background (Table 9.2). It confirmed that all the students were aged 15–17 and had studied Chinese as a L2 since Year 7. Based on their answers about their linguistic background, these 35 students were categorised as either (1) non-Chinese-background students who were either Australian English monolingual or Australian English and other language bilingual (such as Vietnamese or French); or (2) Chinese non-Mandarin-background speakers (i.e. speaking English and another Chinese dialect such as Cantonese, Hakka, Hokkien). These dialect speakers were included in the study because the Chinese dialects are quite different from the target language Mandarin in terms of pronunciation, semantics and/or syntax. In addition, according to Bandura's theory (1986, 1997), past mastery of a task influences the level of confidence in undertaking a related task. Therefore, one of the purposes of the study was to examine whether and to what extent the students' previous linguistic background in other forms of Chinese would affect their self-efficacy in speaking the target

Table 9.2 Background language of the study group

Students	Male	Female	Total
Non-Chinese background	8	8	16
Chinese background	11	8	19
Total	19	16	35

language of Mandarin with native speakers. We approached our data with the assumption that background speakers would have higher self-efficacy beliefs than non-background speakers in the tested areas of speaking, listening and conversing with native speakers.

Data collection and analysis

All the questionnaire data was matched (unmatched data was removed) and then examined for statistically significant variations using software package SPSS. The data was analysed to examine (1) over-time difference within each group using a Paired T-test; and (2) cross-group difference in different tests using one-way ANOVA. Paired T-tests were conducted within each of the two groups (i.e. background speakers and non-background speakers) between different questionnaires to examine the within-group variations. In particular, analysis of the pre and post questionnaires was targeted at identifying any improvement in students' confidence over the period of the conversation sessions, while the pre and delayed post questionnaires were used to examine how students had maintained their confidence after the five-month non-conversation period. Given the small sample size (both groups < 30), the findings were interpreted carefully, supplemented by the focus group data, and the effect size (eta^2) was used as a main indicator of the significance of the improvement in statistical analysis. Before the analysis, reliability tests were conducted for each test to examine the internal consistency of all items. The results found that all Cronbach's *alpha* coefficients were higher than 0.70 (0.91, 0.83 and 0.86 respectively for non-background speakers in the pre, post and delayed post tests; and 0.94, 0.95 and 0.85 respectively for background speakers). In order to explore differences across the groups, one-way ANOVA tests were processed using 'group' as the fixed factor.

Results and Discussion

Table 9.3 gives the descriptive data for the three questionnaires in each group, while Table 9.4 provides a within-group analysis. All the data was analysed through within-group and cross-group comparisons.

Table 9.3 Summary of descriptive data for each group

		Questionnaires	Non-background speakers (N=16)						Background speakers (N=19)					
			Pre		Post		Delayed post		Pre		Post		Delayed post	
Skill item		Mean* / Standard Deviation	M	SD	M	SD	M	SD	M	SD	M	SD	M	SD
General skills	1	Speaking	2.88	0.89	3.38	0.62	2.75	0.86	3.05	0.91	3.37	0.76	3.00	0.75
	2	Listening	2.88	0.89	3.38	0.62	3.25	0.77	3.47	0.90	3.95	0.78	3.58	0.90
	3	Conversing with a native speaker in general	2.88	0.72	3.19	0.40	3.31	0.70	2.84	1.01	3.37	0.83	3.05	0.52
L2 Conversation skills	4	Talking about familiar topics	3.63	0.81	4.06	0.44	3.63	0.81	3.37	0.83	3.84	0.76	3.47	0.77
	5	Talking about unfamiliar topics	2.19	0.91	2.50	0.52	2.31	0.60	2.37	1.07	2.53	0.77	2.47	0.96
	6	Understanding familiar topics	3.75	0.68	3.94	0.68	3.63	0.50	3.95	0.78	4.05	0.62	3.63	0.76
	7	Understanding unfamiliar topics	2.81	0.66	2.69	0.60	2.56	0.73	3.00	0.94	3.00	1.11	2.89	0.88
	8	Initiating a topic	2.94	0.77	3.06	0.57	3.06	0.68	2.68	1.16	2.95	0.97	3.00	0.67
	9	Developing a topic	2.84	0.68	3.31	0.48	3.25	0.68	2.74	1.10	3.21	0.92	3.05	0.62

* Means are scored are out of 5.

Gaining L2 Self-Confidence in Conversations with Native Speakers   179

Table 9.4 Within-group comparisons

	Questionnaires	Non-background students (N=16)						Background students (N=19)					
		Pre & Post			Pre & Delayed Post			Pre & Post			Pre & Delayed Post		
Skill item		t	p	eta²	t	p	eta²	t	p	eta²	t	p	eta²
General skills	1 Speaking	2.236	0.041	0.39 +++	0.565	0.580	0.02	1.555	0.137	0.15 +++	0.252	0.804	0
	2 Listening	2.236	0.041	0.39 +++	1.861	0.083	0.26 +++	2.141	0.046	0.29 +++	0.567	0.578	0.02
	3 Conversing with a native speaker in general	1.576	0.136	0.18 +++	1.698	0.110	0.22 +++	2.379	0.029	0.36 +++	1.166	0.259	0.08 ++
L2 Conversation skills	4 Talking about familiar topics	2.150	0.048	0.36 +++	0.000	1.000	0	2.964	0.008	0.58 +++	0.622	0.542	0.02
	5 Talking about unfamiliar topics	1.232	0.237	0.11 ++	0.397	0.697	0.01	0.900	0.380	0.05	0.438	0.667	0.01
	6 Understanding familiar topics	1.000	0.333	0.07 ++	−0.696	0.497	0.03	0.622	0.542	0.02	−1.679	0.111	0.14 +++
	7 Understanding unfamiliar topics	−0.620	0.544	0.02	−0.939	0.362	0.06 ++	0.000	1.000	0.00	−0.438	0.667	0.01
	8 Initiating a topic	0.696	0.497	0.03	0.522	0.609	0.02	1.045	0.310	0.06 ++	1.679	0.111	0.17 +++
	9 Developing a topic	2.611	0.020	0.55 +++	2.030	0.060	0.32 +++	2.024	0.058	0.26 +++	1.679	0.111	0.17 +++

+ eta^2 > 0.01 (small effect);   ++ eta^2 > 0.06 (moderate effect);   +++ eta^2 > 0.14 (large effect)

Immediate results

From Tables 9.3 and 9.4 we can see that students in both groups had significantly improved their self-efficacy beliefs at the end of the first year of the project in most tested items. There was a large effect size (eta² >0.14) for items 1–4 and 9 in both groups and a moderate effect size (eta² >0.06) for items 5 and 6 of the non-background group and item 8 of the background group. This can be interpreted to mean that their mastery experiences during the conversation sessions with native speakers enhanced their self-efficacy in the general skills of listening and speaking (items 1 and 2) as well as in most of the other L2 conversational skills. This result was reinforced by the focus group data, in which seven out of nine students said that the biggest benefit for them of participating in the project was an increase in confidence, especially when conversing with a native speaker. One of them confessed that they had thought before the sessions conversing with the older immigrants 'would be very scary'.

Our analysis confirms that *topic familiarity* is an important factor in promoting conversational self-efficacy. The students in both groups perceived their efficacy in talking about or understanding familiar topics to be much higher than their abilities with unfamiliar topics (items 4/5 and 6/7). In addition, students improved their confidence significantly when talking about a familiar topic, but this level of significance was not achieved when they talked about unfamiliar topics or when they listened to native speakers on unfamiliar topics. This finding can be explained by the students' limited lexical and/or cultural knowledge and highlights the importance of 'domain specificity' in academic self-efficacy assessments (Bong, 2006; Pajares, 1997).

We also found that background speakers' self-efficacy in general speaking skills improved over time, but less so than their developing confidence in engaging with a native speaker (cf. items 1 and 3). That is, their self-efficacy in the two different situations of speaking in general and interacting specifically in the target language was not transferrable but varied according to the task and the situation. A careful look at the descriptive data reveals that at the beginning of the study the background students had less confidence when it came to talking with a native speaker (M=2.84) than in speaking in general (M=3.05), but by the end of the year their self-efficacy scores in both these items were the same (M=3.37). In other words, at the time of the pre-study questionnaire the background students were more uncertain about conversing with Mandarin Chinese speakers than about speaking Chinese itself. They lacked the experience of having authentic conversations with native speakers at the beginning of the study, but the opportunity to do so helped to improve their confidence in this activity significantly.

We found that for both groups improvements in self-efficacy in initiating a topic was not significant (item 8), even though there was a noticeable improvement in their confidence in developing a topic (item 9). Again this might be related to the students' limited lexical and/or cultural knowledge compared with that of the older participants. In addition, the young people's unwillingness to cut in or lead a conversation could have been linked to their deference to the older participants, whom they described in focus group interviews as very 'respectful and knowledgeable'. These students, especially background speakers, may also have been influenced by a cultural awareness that initiating a conversation topic with Chinese elders is socio-pragmatically unacceptable, an important consideration in a statistical analysis such as this.

Longer-term results

Students' longer-term confidence in the tested items varied between the groups. Both groups maintained their confidence in conversing with a native speaker in general (item 3) and in developing a topic (item 9), with a medium (eta^2 >0.06) to large (eta^2 >0.14) effect size. However, it is notable that the results were more obvious for non-background students, whose confidence in L2 interactions (item 3) continued to improve after the five-month non-conversation period (M=2.88, then 3.19, then 3.31). This indicates that the experience of conversing with the native speakers in the target language had a durable effect on their self-efficacy with respect to natural talk, and this was confirmed by the focus group data in which they reported that they had 'very rare opportunities to speak Chinese after class'.

The results also showed a lasting impact on non-background students' listening skills. As one student remarked, 'Listening is hard … but you have to understand what the older person says first in order to continue the conversation'. The same level of maintenance was not found in their speaking abilities, however, which, as output tasks, may have higher requirements for vocabulary and sentence construction abilities. Nor did their ongoing confidence in their general listening skills (item 2) transfer to talking about specific topics, whether or not these were familiar (items 6 and 7). It is worth noting too that a maintained improvement in listening skills was not found in the data of the background speakers.

The importance of domain specificity continued to feature in the delayed post questionnaire data. From Table 9.3 we can see that for the students in both groups their self-efficacy in talking with and listening to a native speaker on familiar topics was much higher than when they tried to converse on an unfamiliar topic – a pattern consistent across all three questionnaires. This means that when the topic was familiar, their self-efficacy was higher, while their efficacy was low when conversing on unfamiliar topics. It is important to note that their exposure to unfamiliar topics during the conversation sessions did not have any positive impact on their self-efficacy beliefs, and may even have had a detrimental effect on the students' self-belief in terms of listening to and understanding unfamiliar topics, as shown in the falling figures for both groups (Mean from 2.81 to 2.56 and from 3.00 to 2.89 for non-background and background speakers respectively in item 7) in the delayed post questionnaire. In other words, they perceived the experience of listening to unfamiliar topics negatively and this unhelpfully affected their confidence. One student made the comment, 'I felt more nervous if Mr Zhou was talking about something really beyond my understanding and I even forgot what we were discussing.'

In the delayed post study questionnaire, background speakers had maintained their self-efficacy in starting a topic while non-background speakers' confidence levels in this item were very similar in all three tests. When looking at the descriptive data alone, it is interesting that background speakers started with a comparatively low score (M=2.68) in starting a topic; this was the second lowest score among all the tested items. This may mean that these background speakers were not very confident in their own abilities to start a conversation with a native speaker before they joined in the project. The gradual increase of the score (M=2.68. 2.95, 3.00 respectively), the only tested item to do so in the group, proved that the experience of having regular conversations had a lasting and positive impact on these background speakers' confidence in starting a topic.

Cross-group comparisons

In order to examine whether the student's linguistic background was a variable in self-efficacy levels, all the test data was reprocessed using one-way ANOVA for each of the three questionnaires.

A difference between the two groups was found only for the listening skill (item 2) in the pre- and post-study questionnaires: the background speakers' self-efficacy in listening was significantly higher than that of the non-background cohort ($F(1,33)=3.88$, $p=.057<.1$, $eta^2 =0.105$; $F(1,33)=5.62$, $p=.024<.05$, $eta^2 =0.145$). This means that before and immediately after the study the students with a Chinese family background felt much more confident than their non-Chinese counterparts in the general skill of listening. This might possibly be the result of these background speakers' daily exposure to Chinese, even if not to Mandarin. Such positive self-assessment, however, was found neither in speaking nor in the delayed post-study questionnaire. This indicates that after the five-month holiday break the background speakers' level of confidence in their general listening skills had dropped critically, almost back to its initial score (M=3.47, 3.95 and 3.58 respectively). In other words, their increased confidence in listening was not maintained once the conversation sessions stopped. In contrast, their peers without a Chinese background more or less maintained their confidence in listening in the delayed post-study questionnaire, with scores of 2.88, 3.38 and 3.25 across the data collection period (cf. the within-group comparison). We can conclude therefore that the conversations had a positive immediate effect on the confidence of the background speakers as regards listening, but this effect was not lasting, whereas the positive effect was more durable among the non-background speakers. One explanation for this may be that over the long holiday period the background speakers were likely to have been exposed to other Chinese dialects, and this may have undermined their earlier confidence in listening to Mandarin.

Another observation across the groups was that the non-background group's self-efficacy score was higher in all three questionnaires on nearly all aspects of conversing with a native speaker (items 3, 4, 8 and 9, but not 6), but not on listening to or speaking about unfamiliar topics (items 5 and 7), even if no statistical significance was found. This means that the non-background cohort had a higher perception of their speaking confidence than the students with a Chinese background. By contrast, the consistently higher score of background speakers on unfamiliar topics might be related to their much greater exposure to Chinese (dialects). However, it may also mean that the background speakers set higher goals or standards for themselves. These findings may support the earlier studies mentioned above about the role of culture in mediating mean levels of self-efficacy (Chen, 2007; Eaton & Dembo, 1997). In our study, all the background speakers had a Chinese or Asian family background, while 12 out of the 16 non-background cohort recorded that their family was totally non-Asian.

Conclusion

The study has attempted to evaluate whether and, if so, to what extent the intergenerational project had an effect on students' self-efficacy in L2 oral communication. The analysis documented three main findings. Firstly, the experience of conducting fortnightly conversations with native speakers had a positive effect on the students' self-efficacy in the general language skills of listening and speaking and in conversation-related skills except for the skills of initiating a topic and understanding unfamiliar topics. Secondly, both background speakers and non-background speakers maintained their efficacy in conversing with a native speaker in general and also in developing a topic during the conversation. Thirdly, the students' cultural background was found to have an impact on their perception of confidence. Specifically, all of the students with a Chinese cultural background recorded lower academic self-efficacy scores in many of the items in the questionnaire than students from Western cultures. These findings are further evidence that one's past mastery experiences wield a strong influence on creating a strong sense of efficacy. The results also showed an interplay in the relationship between self-efficacy and domain specificity. For example, the long-term improvement in students' efficacy in conversing with a native speaker did not carry through to their general skills of listening and speaking, especially for the background students. Another example of domain specificity is shown in the students' self-efficacy in relation to their familiarity with conversational topics: their confidence was consistently higher in conversing on familiar topics than in conversing on unfamiliar topics. The interaction between students' cultural background (Asian and non-Asian) was consistently the case in the three questionnaires even though the difference was not statistically significant.

This study is an evaluation study and no causal inferences can be made. However, it has very clear pedagogical and research implications for developing a similar project in the language learning context. Even though it included only a small sample of Chinese language learners, our findings still shed light on the effect of such intergenerational conversational encounters on self-efficacy in L2 learning. Perhaps most significantly, particular attention should be given to the domain specificity principle. That is, conversation topics need to be selected carefully when running a project like this because topic familiarity proved to be a very important factor in the students' self-efficacy. Close collaboration and consultation with school teachers and students will be necessary for effective learning to happen. Moreover, strategies training for all the interlocutors would be helpful in enhancing student confidence. For example, older participants may need to be shown how to introduce unfamiliar topics in a more stepwise manner, while students would benefit from strategies training in conversation management, especially in the initiation of topics. The study has also highlighted that a student's cultural background is an important factor to be considered when interpreting a self-reporting questionnaire such as ours, which was aimed at understanding students' confidence in learning rather than learning itself. Therefore future studies would benefit from objective testing of the students' listening and speaking performance with native speakers and comparison of these findings with their students' self-efficacy beliefs. Inclusion of a control group (i.e. students not participating in conversation sessions) would add weight to the reliability and wider application of the research.

References

Albion, P.R. (2001) Some factors in the development of self-efficacy beliefs for computer use among teacher education students. *Journal of Technology and Teacher Education* 9 (3), 321–347.

Bandura, A. (1986) *Social Foundations of Thought and Action: A Social Cognitive Theory*. Englewood Cliffs, NJ: Prentice-Hall.

Bandura, A. (1997) *Self-Efficacy: The Exercise of Control*. New York: W.H. Freeman.

Bandura, A. and Schunk, D.H. (1981) Cultivating competence, self-efficacy, and intrinsic interest through proximal self-motivation. *Journal of Personality and Social Psychology* 41 (3), 586–598.

Bong, M. (2006) Asking the right question: How confident are you that you could successfully perform these tasks? In F. Pajares and T. Urdan (eds) *Self-Efficacy Beliefs of Adolescents* (pp. 287–305). Greenwich, CT: Information Age Publishing.

Bouffard-Bouchard, T. (1990) Influence of self-efficacy on performance in a cognitive task. *The Journal of Social Psychology* 130 (3), 353–363.

Chen, H.-Y. (2007) The Relationship between EFL Learners' Self-Efficacy Beliefs and English Performance. Unpublished PhD thesis, Florida State University.

Ching, L.C. (2002) Strategy and self-regulation instruction as contributors to improving students' cognitive model in an ESL program. *English for Specific Purposes* 21 (3), 261–289.

Eaton, M.J. and Dembo, M.H. (1997) Differences in the motivational beliefs of Asian American and non-Asian students. *Journal of Educational Psychology* 89 (3), 433–440.

Gardner, R.C. (1985) *Social Psychology and Second Language Learning: The Role of Attitudes and Motivation*. London: Edward Arnold.

Gardner, R.C. and Lambert, W.E. (1972) *Attitudes and Motivation in Second-Language Learning*. Rowley, MA: Newbury House Publishers.

Graham, S. (2006) Listening comprehension: The learners' perspective. *System* 34, 165–182.

Graham, S. (2007) Learner strategies and self-efficacy: Making the connection. *Language Learning Journal* 35, 81–93.

Graham, S. and Macaro, E. (2007) Designing Year 12 strategy training in listening and writing: From theory to practice. *Language Learning Journal* 35, 153–173.

Graham, S. and Macaro, E. (2008) Strategy instruction in listening for lower-intermediate learners of French. *Language Learning* 58 (4), 747–783.

Henderson, M., Huang, H., Grant, S. and Henderson, L. (2009) Language acquisition in *Second Life*: Improving self-efficacy beliefs. In *Same Places, Different Spaces. Proceedings ascilite Auckland 2009* (pp. 464–474). See http://www.ascilite.org.au/conferences/auckland09/procs/henderson.pdf.

Henderson, M., Huang, H., Grant, S. and Henderson, L. (2012) The impact of Chinese language lessons in a virtual world on university students' self-efficacy beliefs. *Australasian Journal of Educational Technology* 28 (3), 400–419.

Lamboy, C.L. (2003) Using Technology in an English as a L2 Course to Accommodate Visual, Kinaesthetic, and Auditory Learners to Affect Students' Self-Efficacy about Learning the Language. Unpublished doctoral dissertation, Nova Southeastern University, Fort Lauderdale, FL.

Liddicoat, A., Scarino, A., Curnow, T.J., Kohler, M., Scrimgeour, A. and Morgan, A.M. (2007) *An Investigation of the State and Nature of Languages in Australian Schools*. Canberra: Department of Education, Employment and Workplace Relations.

Linnenbrink, E.A. and Pintrich, P.R. (2003) The role of self-efficacy beliefs in student engagement and learning in the classroom. *Reading & Writing Quarterly* 19 (2), 119–137.

Magogwe, J.M. and Oliver, R. (2007) The relationship between language learning strategies, proficiency, age and self-efficacy beliefs: A study of language learners in Botswana. *System* 35 (3), 338–352.

Mills, N., Pajares, F. and Herron, C. (2006) A re-evaluation of the role of anxiety: Self-efficacy, anxiety, and their relation to reading and listening proficiency. *Foreign Language Annals* 39 (2), 276–294.

Mills, N., Pajares, F. and Herron, C. (2007) Self-efficacy of college intermediate French students: Relation to achievement and motivation. *Language Learning* 57 (3), 417–442.

Orton, J. (2008) *Chinese Language Education in Australian Schools*. Report for the Victorian Department of Education and Childhood Development. Melbourne: University of Melbourne.

Pajares, F. (1997) Current directions in self-efficacy research. In M. Maehr and P. Pintrich (eds) *Advances in Motivation and Achievement – Volume 10*. Greenwich, CT: JAI Press.

Pajares, F. (2003) Self-efficacy beliefs, motivation, and achievement in writing: A review of the literature. *Reading & Writing Quarterly* 19 (2), 139–158.

Pajares, F. and Schunk, D.H. (2001) Self-beliefs and school success: Self-efficacy, self-concept, and school achievement. In R.J. Riding and S.G. Rayner (eds) *Self-Perception*, 239–266. London: Ablex.

Pajares, F. and Urdan, T. (eds) (2006) *Self-Efficacy Beliefs of Adolescents*. Charlotte, NC: Information Age Publishing.

Pintrich, P.R. and De Groot, E.V. (1990) Motivational and self-regulated learning components of classroom academic performance. *Journal of Educational Psychology* 82 (1), 33–40.

Pintrich, P.R. and Schunk, D.H. (2002) *Motivation in Education: Theory, Research, and Applications*, 2nd edition. Upper Saddle River, NJ: Merrill.

Schunk, D.H., Pintrich, P.R. and Meece, J.L. (eds) (2007) *Motivation in Education: Theory, Research, and Applications*. Upper Saddle River, NJ: Pearson Education.

Zimmerman, B.J. (1995) Self-efficacy and educational development. In A. Bandura (ed.) *Self-Efficacy in Changing Societies* (pp. 202–231). Cambridge: Cambridge University Press.

Zimmerman, B.J. (2000) Self-efficacy: An essential motive to learn. *Contemporary Educational Psychology* 25, 82–91.

Zimmerman, B.J., Bandura, A. and Martinez-Pons, M. (1992) Self-motivation for academic attainment: The role of self-efficacy beliefs and personal goal setting. *American Educational Research Journal* 29 (3), 663–676.

10 Developing Interactional Competence in Dyadic Conversations: Cross-language Evidence

Hui Huang

Introduction

Our thinking about learning, and about language learning in particular, has undergone great changes in recent years from a sociocultural perspective, with particular emphasis now being placed on the individual as a *social* being acting within different contexts. Many studies have drawn on the concepts of 'situated learning' and 'legitimate peripheral participation' put forward by Lave and Wenger (1991), according to which learning is 'changing participation in the culturally designed settings of everyday life' (Lave, 1993: 6) or the process of becoming a member of a certain community (Sfard, 1998). Similarly, language learning can be understood as a situated co-constructed process among participants (Young & Miller, 2004), utilising 'appropriate linguistic forms, registers and sequential routines in appropriate contexts' (Hellerman, 2007: 85), or as changing engagement in 'discursive practices' (Mondada & Pekarek Doehler, 2004: 519). This participationist view holds as fundamental the need for language learners to acquire the skills required to interact in the language of a community and to act according to its particular norms. Central to this view is the notion of interactional competence (IC).

Interactional competence 'involves knowing and using the mostly unwritten rules for interaction in various communication situations within a given speech community and culture. It includes, among other things, knowing how to initiate and manage conversations and negotiate meaning with other people. It also includes knowing what sorts of body language, eye contact and proximity to other people are appropriate, and acting accordingly' (LinguaLinks, 1999).

Since the 1990s, many researchers have argued for the role of interactional competence in second language (L2) learning (e.g. Hall, 1993, 1995; Young, 1999, 2011). He and Young (1998) define IC as

> a knowledge of rhetorical scripts, a knowledge of certain lexis and syntactic patterns specific to the practice, a knowledge of how turns are managed, a knowledge of topical organization, and a knowledge of the means for signaling boundaries between practices and transitions within the practice itself. (1998: 6)

Of great importance for the concept of IC is recognising that it is not static but dynamic, not generally but locally situated in specific interactive activities (Hall *et al.*, 2011). This means that knowledge and interactional skills are local and practice-specific; that is, individual learners do not acquire a general, practice-independent communicative competence; rather, they acquire a practice-specific IC through their participation in interactions. Different from the four components of communicative competence proposed by Canale and Swain (1980), IC includes not merely linguistic knowledge and oral language skills but more importantly familiarity with specific practices and their cultural meanings as well as the capacity to understand how and when these practice resources should be deployed (Hall *et al.*, 2011). Essential to the learning process, therefore, is participation in interactions whereby learners can access culturally framed linguistic or paralinguistic norms, practise with members of the cultural group in particular conversational settings and develop their L2 IC.

Many studies, therefore, have found that the development of L2 IC can be understood and studied within a conversational analysis (CA) framework (e.g. turn-construction techniques, Young & Miller, 2004; sequential organisation of acts, role construction, and change in the participation framework, Cekaite, 2007; diverse methods of doing disagreement, Pekarek Doehler & Pochon-Berger, 2011; an increasingly wider range of repair techniques, Hellermann, 2011) and these studies have helped to increase understanding of the detailed workings of IC by illustrating the wide range of interactional resources L2 speakers utilise in their talk. L2 IC involves the diversification of known methods: that is, learners do not learn anew how to initiate or develop a topic or to express an opinion; rather, they adapt and re-adapt their talk to specific interactive practices by using what they have been practising in L1 or have learnt from previous L2 experience. What they adapt may include linguistic, sequential or prosodic resources. These observables, such as a turn organisation system, repair mechanism or more generally sequential organisation, can be used as indicators of L2 IC. CA, in this sense, has opened a window to examine the changes in IC.

One approach drawn from CA to examine IC development is to study the longitudinal changes of one participant's interactions over time (e.g. Cekaite, 2007; Hellermann, 2008, 2011; Young & Miller, 2004). For example, the well-cited study by Cekaite (2007) explored the one-year development of IC of a seven-year-old Kurdish girl in a Swedish classroom and found that her progress could be attributed to improvements in many skills, particularly the social aspects of understanding how, when and with whom to engage in conversations.

About the Study

Topic management, and longitudinal and cross-language design

Using a CA approach, this study set out to document and analyse improvements in L2 learners' IC over time, with a particular focus on *topic management*, identified as an important interactional skill in a number of IC studies (e.g. topic initiation or opening, Cekaite, 2007; Hellermann, 2007; topic organisation, Gan *et al.*, 2009). The last-named authors, for instance, sought to understand how topic organisation was accomplished among Cantonese-speaking ESL secondary students under assessment conditions using a CA framework, arguing that the ability to stay on topic, to move from topic to topic, and to introduce new topics appropriately was at the core of communicative competence. Their study found that the students were able to pursue, develop and shift topics to ensure the successful completion of an assigned task and to display individual contributions. In Cekaite's (2007) study, the subject's successful self-selection of a new topic was an important indicator of her development of IC in classroom interactions over time. Our study is concerned, therefore, with how the students initiated and developed subjects or themes during their conversations with native speakers, and to what extent they demonstrated competence in topic initiation, shift and pursuit (Button & Casey, 1985). We hoped to find in our data a progression from peripheral to increasingly active participation (Lave & Wenger, 1991) over the months and years of the study.

We were also interested in the assistance and scaffolding provided by the native speakers (Vygotsky, 1978), but the IC of the older participants themselves was not a direct focus of our study. Nor did we make any assessments of changes in the students' IC in L1 over the period of data collection, although we are aware that the communication skills of young people are likely to continue to develop throughout their teens. Finally, the role of gender in conversational dominance was also outside the scope of this study but would reward further research.

As already indicated, a particular methodological consideration of the study was its longitudinal design. Researchers (e.g. He, 2004; Hellermann, 2007) have pointed out that CA's focus on the micro-moments of L2 interaction limits its usefulness in measuring a learner's L2 progress over time. The combination of micro-analyses of data with a longitudinal approach, therefore, allowed us to analyse more fully the student participants' over-time interaction contributions and also enabled us to document the micro-genesis of their IC as located in the changes in their topic management competence.

The cross-language design of our study was a significant innovation. While previous studies have usually been focused on interactions in one language (e.g. Swedish, Cekaite, 2007; English, Hellermann, 2007; Young & Miller, 2004; Japanese, Ishida, 2009; Masuda, 2011), we obtained data in three languages (Chinese, German and Spanish), and this enabled us to explore the possible specificity of each language and/or common discursive practices relating to IC.

Study participants

Three older participant–student dyads were selected for this study, each conversing in one of the target languages: Chinese, German or Spanish. The Chinese and German data covered four recordings over two years, while the Spanish data was taken from two recordings over one year only, owing to restricted arrangements at the school where Spanish was taught. The general background of the participants is shown in Table 10.1.

Table 10.1 Study participants

Language	Student	Older participant (year 1)	Older participant (year 2)
Chinese	Calvin,[1] a 16-year-old boy with a Vietnamese family background. Had been learning Chinese for five years. Participated in the project for two years (2010–2011).	Ms Chu, aged 75 when participating in the project in 2010. A Mandarin native speaker from China with some knowledge of English but not a fluent speaker in that language.	Ms Li, aged 67 when participating in the project in 2011. A Mandarin native speaker from China with some knowledge of English but not a fluent speaker in that language.
German	Graham, a 17-year-old boy with Australian-British cultural origins. Had been learning German and Chinese at school for five years. Participated in the project for two years (2010–2011).	Mr Gabler, aged 76 in 2010. Originally born in East Prussia with a German cultural background. Participated in the project for three years (2010–2012). Fluent in both German and English.	

(Continued)

Table 10.1 (Continued)

| Spanish | Sophie, a 16-year-old girl born in Australia with an Irish family background. Participated in the project in 2010. | Ms Sais, aged 85 in 2010. Participated in the project in 2010 and 2011. Migrated from Argentina and her main language is Spanish. | — |

Data collection and analysis

All conversations were audio recorded and transcribed using Elan software: Recording 1 (R1) in May 2010, Recording 2 (R2) in September 2010, Recording 3 (R3) in March 2011 and Recording 4 (R4) in September 2011. These recordings were then labelled as C-R1, C-R2, C-R3, C-R4 for the Chinese recordings, G-R1, G-R2, G-R3, G-R4 and S-R1 and S-R2 for the German and Spanish recordings respectively. Between R1 and R2 and between R3 and R4 there were about eight or nine one-hour conversation sessions held, and there was a break of five months or so between R2 and R3, coinciding with the end of the school year and the summer holidays. It was expected that all the conversations would be conducted in the target language (i.e. Chinese, German or Spanish) and the recordings were translated carefully by bilingual assistants.

In the analysis, we approached the recorded data from an emic viewpoint, basically using CA methodology. However, in order to have an overview of topic management in the data set from ten recordings over two years in three languages, we included some quantitative observations to back up our CA findings. As noted by previous researchers (e.g. Pekarek Doehler & Pochon-Berger, 2011), quantification using figures is a tricky issue in explaining the details of human actions because it raises the question of whether the quantified occurrences were participant-relevant or not (Schegloff, 1993); that is, whether the actions of items quantified were oriented to doing or being such and such a thing by the participants. We argue, however, that even though details of the progress of each student cannot be identified, some quantitative observations can give a broad overview of their IC in terms of topic management. We specifically classified the topics started by each student and by each older participant separately because we assumed that students might be more knowledgeable about or competent in managing and developing the topics they started themselves. We found that when a certain topic was being discussed, different subtopics (or themes) in relation to the topic emerged, and these were further categorised on the basis of who introduced them. All the transcripts were carefully considered, and each of the student's turns was categorised using a scale of 0 to 3 according to whether and to what extent the student was able to respond to a (sub) topic. In the scaling, 0 means no response to the previous interlocutor's question or statement, 1 denotes a minimum response (including non-lexical backchannel responses like *em, oh* etc. or a simple *yes* or *no* answer), 2 a medium response (referring to very simple answers, generally one- or two-word utterances in response to an interlocutor's question, or phrasal or substantive backchannels which include: (a) brief comments such as *good, okay*; (b) requests for clarification such as *Do you mean...?*; and (c) repetition of the interlocutor's words (Young & Lee, 2004)), and 3 means a maximum response entailing topic elaborations, topic statements and topic introductions, mainly in the target language.

In the process of analysis, we examined the moment-by-moment development of recorded conversation data and asked ourselves 'Why this, in this way? Why right now?' etc. The analytical focus was on the participants' talk rather than on the researchers' categorisation of topics. Accordingly, topic was conceived within this CA framework as something initiated and achieved by the participants turn-by-turn in their talk through repetitions, ellipsis, pronominalisation and deixis rather than as something defined externally by us (Stokoe, 2000: 87). In order to analyse how topicality was accomplished and how topic shifts were managed, therefore, the strategy adopted was to treat a topic as constituted by the way each turn was constructed to display an understanding of and fit with the previous turn (Sacks, 1992). The following case studies illustrate that the development of IC in L2 learning can be usefully understood in terms of changes in the learner's topic initiation, negotiation and management.

Chinese story: Overcoming conversational dominance

Table 10.2 sets out how topics and subtopics were managed during the conversations in Mandarin Chinese between Ms Chu (in 2010) and Ms Li (in 2011) with the student Calvin. We found that the topics were basically led by the older participants in all four recordings and that the student initiated fewer subtopics during each session. In 2010 Calvin initiated more subtopics than Ms Chu when he was developing a topic he had raised himself (5 in C-R1 and 5 in C-R2), but fewer than his partner when she had initiated the topic. He introduced no topics at all with Ms Li in 2011, but did bring up a few subtopics following the older interactant's lead (3 in C-R3 and 4 in C-R4), though still far fewer than her 18 and 10. In developing the subtopics, Calvin gave maximum responses to the topics he had started, except once in C-R1. He only offered about 60% of maximum responses to the topics/subtopics initiated by the older participant in their first recording together (C-R1 and C-R3), but by the end of the year with each older participant (C-R2 and C-R4) he was providing almost maximum responses, except once in C-R4 when Ms Li was talking about Chinese tea culture in a manner much like a monologue. When we scrutinised all the micro-moments during which

Table 10.2 Initiation and development of topics and subtopics by the student in Chinese conversations

Recording	Recording date & length	No. of topics initiated by		No. of subtopics initiated by		Student's development of the subtopics					
						Minimum response No. (%)		Median response No. (%)		Maximum response No. (%)	
C-R1	May 2010 41'29"	Calvin	1	Calvin	5	0		0		5 (100%)	
				Ms Chu	2	0		1 (50%)		1 (50%)	
		Ms Chu	10	Calvin	1	0		0		1 (100%)	
				Ms Chu	24	2 (8.3%)		8 (33.3%)		14 (58.3%)	
C-R2	Sep 2010 43'13"	Calvin	2	Calvin	5	0		0		5 (100%)	
				Ms Chu	4	0		0		4 (100%)	
		Ms Chu	6	Calvin	2	0		0		2 (100%)	
				Ms Chu	14	0		1 (7%)		13 (93%)	
C-R3	Mar 2011 28'27"	Calvin	0	Calvin	0	0		0		0	
				Ms Li	0	0		0		0	
		Ms Li	4	Calvin	3	0		0		3 (100%)	
				Ms Li	18	1 (6%)		6 (33%)		11 (61%)	
C-R4	Sep 2011 30'41"	Calvin	0	Calvin	0	0		0		0	
				Ms Li	0	0		0		0	
		Ms Li	2	Calvin	4	0		0		4 (100%)	
				Ms Li	10	0		1 (10%)		9 (90%)	

Calvin was developing the other-initiated (sub)topics, we found that his employment of all possible interactional resources and strategies to keep up not only the flow of the conversation but also his active participation in it was more obvious in the later recordings with each older participant.

Chinese R1

In R1 of the Chinese data, the conversation is very much like an interview between the older interactant (interviewer) and the student (interviewee) for most of the time, in a question-and-answer format, and the student's peripheral or 'passive' participation is a feature of the recording. In spite of Ms Chu's continuous encouragement in the way of praise and assurance, Calvin does not engage actively overall and his turns are generally very short utterances in the form of acknowledgements, in many instances merely responding with 嗯 (en, *yes*) or 哦 (o, to indicate *I see*) to the older lady's questions. Even when Ms Chu repeatedly praises his good Chinese he expresses his gratitude only once. As a result, the older participant dominates the whole conversation, although it was not her intention to conduct a monologue. She indicates this by completing her utterances on a number of occasions with a rising intonation to check whether Calvin has understand her correctly, and asks 明白吗 (míngbaima, *Do you understand?*) or 是吗 (shìma, *Isn't that right?*), which helps to establish potential turn transition relevance places (TRPs) within the turn-taking system (Sacks *et al.*, 1974). However, these TRPs do not of themselves create speaker transition. That is, Calvin can claim a turn at the TRP if he wishes but he is not obliged to do so. His minimal responses of 嗯 and 哦 are continuer tokens that can yield the floor to the older interlocutor (Schegloff 1981), or signal his recognition that Ms Chu is producing an extended turn, or backchannels to show that he is able to comprehend what she is saying, or all three. In the example below, both the student and the older participant co-construct the asymmetric production of turns even though the older participant, faced with the student's limited initiation of topics, tries to play a scaffolding role. After covering many other topics, she is trying to get Calvin to talk about his childhood, and this leads in fact to an isolated occurrence of Calvin taking the floor.

Example 10.1 'Think about what happened in the past'

Chinese conversation R1: Ms Chu, Calvin

134	Ms Chu	回忆就是想过去的事情是吧是这吧你想讲讲的嗯\ huíyì jiùshì xiǎng guòqu de shìqing shì ba shì zhè ba nǐ xiǎng jiǎng jiǎng de ēn\
		recalling just is think past things yes is this you think talk um\ to recall is to think about what happened in the past yes you can think and talk um

(Continued)

Example 10.1 (Continued)

135	Calvin	嗯
		en
		yes
		yes
136	Ms Chu	慢慢讲慢慢讲
		màn màn jiǎng màn màn jiǎng
		slowly talk slowly talk
		talk slowly talk slowly
137	Calvin	我啊我/我不知道啊我不啊
		wǒ a wǒ/ wǒ bùzhīdào a wǒ bù a
		i ah i/ i don't know i don't ah
		i ah i/ i don't know i don't ah
138	Ms Chu	你是:::/
		nǐ shì:::/
		you are:::/
		are you:::/
139	Calvin	我是从小移民来啊:: 啊::
		wǒ shì cóngxiǎo yímín lái a:: a::
		i am from child immigrate ah:: ah::
		i immigrated when i was a child ah:: ah::
...		
220	Ms Chu	那考试到了你感觉到紧张这是正常的正常明白吗/
		nà kǎoshì dàole nǐ gǎnjuédào jǐnzhāng zhè shì zhèngcháng de zhèngcháng míngbai ma/
		then exam arrive you feel nervous this is normal normal understand/
		then it's exam time and you feel nervous this is normal normal understand/
221	Calvin	[嗯]
		[en]
		[yes]
		[yes]
222	Ms Chu	[正]常就是是这样一回事是这么一回事不是我们也是从读书来的我读书的时候也是
		[zhèng]cháng jiùshì shì zhèyàng yī huí shì shì zhème yī huí shì búshì wǒ men yě shì cóng dúshū lái de wǒ dúshū deshíhòu yě shì
		[nor]mal is is such a thing such a thing no we also from study i study when also
		it's normal to feel nervous about such a thing i also felt like that when we studied too

Up to line 134 of the conversation Calvin has not initiated a topic, but this changes when Ms Chu produces a 'designedly incomplete utterance' (Koshik, 2002) in line 138 that invites him to talk and position his responses as completers. Calvin is then prompted to complete the utterance, and once he takes the floor he becomes very active and goes on to initiate and develop many subtopics, including schooling, religious beliefs, secondary school, friends and feeling nervous during an exam. However, after Ms Chu cuts in in line 220 and tries to explain that it is normal to feel nervous before exams, describing her own experience at school, Calvin returns to his former 'passive' role of providing responses to his interlocutor and does not initiate any more (sub)topics for the rest of the conversation.

Chinese R2

A notable feature of the second recording is the change in participatory structure, with the student now taking an obviously active role in the interaction. There are many occasions on which Calvin self-selects his turn by initiating a question (see Example 10.2) or by seeking further information from Ms Chu in order to develop a topic raised by the older interactant, which never happened during the first recording. In addition, Calvin's high engagement in the conversation is reflected in his attempts to employ other paralinguistic resources, such as laughter at appropriate times or changing intonation.

In Example 10.2 the pair have been talking about which grade Calvin is in, and Ms Chu is explaining the school grade system in China.

Example 10.2 'Is there Prep in China?'

Chinese conversation R2: Ms Chu, Calvin

31	Ms Chu	在这里就是7年级 8 年级 9年级
		zài zhèlǐ jiùshì 7 niánjí 8 niánjí 9niánjí
		here is year 7 year 8 year 9
		here there's year 7 year 8 and year 9
32	Calvin	中国有< E prep E> 吗/
		zhōngguó yǒu <E prep E> ma/
		china has <E prep E>/
		is there <E prep E> in china/
33	Ms Chu	小学:: 小学 <E prim school E> 小学六年小学一年级::
		xiǎoxué :: xiǎoxué <E prim school E> xiǎoxué liù nián xiǎoxué yī niánjí::
		primary schoo::l primary school < E prim school E> primary school six years primary school first gra::de
		primary schoo::l primary school < E prim school E> primary school six years primary school first gra::de
34	Calvin	是一年级吗/
		shì yī niánjí ma/
		is grade 1/
		is it grade 1/

This is a typical example from the second recording in which the student self-selects to talk. In the extract, his initiation of the theme of the Chinese school system is a contribution to develop the topic of the school system in Australia. Such a move is known as a stepwise development (Jefferson, 1984) because the current theme has a connection to what has previously been talked about. Calvin does not simply continue the topic started by the older interactant; rather, he signals his intention to develop the current topic by introducing a new sequence (Sacks, 1992).

Another major feature of the recording is the change in the way Calvin uses backchannels. In C-R1, Calvin's backchannelling was fundamentally non-lexical with 嗯 (en, *yes*) in lines 135 and 221 (Example 10.1), whereas in C-R2 phrasal, albeit brief, backchannels (是吗 (shìma, *is it right?*) or repeated 嗯, 嗯, 是的 (en, en, shìde, *yes, yes, it is*), or more substantial responses such as repeating the older interlocutor's words) (Young & Lee, 2004) have become prominent.

In the next example (Example 10.3), Ms Chu is introducing logographic information about some Chinese characters in order to convince Calvin that Chinese is not as difficult as he thinks. She moves on to the topic of *Hanyu Pinyin*, the romanisation system of Chinese characters.

Example 10.3 '*Hanyu Pinyin*: do you understand?'

Chinese conversation R2: Ms Chu, Calvin

356	Ms Chu	汉语拼音拼音你明白吗/
		hànyǔ pīnyīn pīnyīn nǐ míngbai ma/
		hanyu pinyin pinyin you understand/
		do you understand hanyu pinyin/
357	Calvin	嗯我明白我妈妈以前:
		en wǒ míngbai wǒ māma yǐqián:
		yes i understand my mother in the past:
		yes i understand my mother in the past:
358	Ms Chu	b p m f 对对这叫国音符号 (.) 现在叫汉 (.) 汉语拼音跟英语一样是用26个字母的
		b p m f duì duì zhè jiào guóyīn fúhào (.) xiànzài jiào hàn (.) hànyǔ pīnyīn gēn yīngyǔ yíyàng shì yòng 26 gè zìmǔ de
		b p m f yes yes this is called national sound system (.) now called chinese (.) hanyu pinyin same as english using 26 letters
		b p m f yes yes this is called national sound system (.) now it is called chinese (.) hanyu pinyin very similar to the 26 letters of the english alphabet
359	Calvin	嗯嗯以前他们是用 b p m f
		en en yǐqián tāmen shì yòng b p m f
		yes yes before they used b p m f
		yes yes they used b p m f previously

In this extract, Ms Chu, as always, checks Calvin's comprehension of what she is saying. Calvin does not stop his turn in line 357 by simply backchannelling with 嗯 (en, *yes*); instead, he adds a concise phrasal backchannel 我明白 (wǒ míngbai, *I understand*) to show his comprehension and, more significantly, to extend his turn. Lines 357 and 359 introduce new information by the student, evidence of his active participation in the conversation. His backchannels can be understood as 'change-of-activity' tokens (Gardner, 2001) which simultaneously confirm what his partner has said and prompt further development of the topic.

Chinese R3

After the Christmas/New Year break, Calvin has a new partner, Ms Li, who is less encouraging but more of a teacher than Ms Chu. Despite the older participant's attempts to provide potential TRPs, however, the change of partner seems to have contributed to Calvin's reversion to far fewer non-maximum responses to the initiated topics. For much of the time, Ms Li conducts a monologue with only the occasional minimum response from Calvin. Another change for Calvin is the focus of his new interlocutor's conversation. With Ms Chu the focus was more on content, but now it is on his linguistic performance, especially on his pronunciation and pitch of Chinese words. This too may account for the fact that he does not initiate any topics or subtopics during the session (Table 10.2). The extract below is typical of the many negotiations of pronunciation and the student's repetition of the older interlocutor's words. Nonetheless, these substantive backchannels in the form of repeating what Ms Li has said indicate his high level of engagement in the conversation, which helps him to maintain the floor. In Example 10.4 he is trying to explain why he does not see much of his family.

Example 10.4 'My sister is at university'

Chinese conversation R3: Ms Li, Calvin

945	Calvin	(.) 嗯 ::姐姐\
		(.) ēn ::jiějie\
		(.) ah ::sister
		(.) ah ::sister
946	Ms Li	姐姐::::姐姐 ((focus on the pitch))
		jiějie:::: jiějie
		sister ::::sister
		sister :::sister
947	Calvin	姐姐:::姐姐 ((with better pronunciation))
		jiějie::: jiějie
		sister :::sister
		sister :::sister

(Continued)

Example 10.4 (Continued)

...

987	Calvin	\<E yeah E>::: 我们没有
		\<E yeah E>::: wǒ men méiyǒu
		\<E yeah E>::: we do not have
		\<E yeah E>::: we do not have
988	Ms Li	[自己]
		[zìjǐ]
		[own]
		[our own]
989	Calvin	啊[交谈]
		a[jiāotán]
		ah [conversation]
		ah [conversation]
990	Ms Li	自己忙自己的 (..) [是啊:::]
		zìjǐ máng zìjǐ de (..) [shì a:::]
		their own busy (..) [yes ah:::]
		they are busy with their own (..) [yes ah:::]
991	Calvin	[啊:::是]
		[a::: shì]
		[ah::: yes]
		[ah::: yes]
997	Ms Li	姐姐在上::: 大学/ :::[在上大学啊]
		jiějie zài shàng::: dàxué/ :::[zài shàng dàxué a]
		sister at::: university/::: [the university ah]
		sister is at::: university/::: [the university ah]
998	Calvin	[=她上大学]
		[=tā shàng dàxué]
		[=her university]
		[=she goes to university]

We can see here that the pair overlap each other to gain the floor, which interestingly did not occur in Calvin's recordings with Ms Chu. This overlapping occurs in a very cooperative manner (Tannen, 1993) however, showing that both interlocutors are highly engaged in the discussion (see also Tannen's 'high engagement' style discussed in Chapter 7). The topic is still led and controlled by Ms Li, but Calvin talks along with her, not in order to interrupt but to show his enthusiastic listenership and participation.

Chinese R4

After eight session conversations with his new partner, Calvin seems to be more confident and competent when conversing with the older participant. He works collaboratively with Ms Li and gives maximum responses to almost all the (sub)topics started by her. In this recording, it is still the older participant who selects which of them will take the turn most of the time, but sometimes Calvin cuts in and self-selects as the next speaker to contribute some themes to the topics. C-R4 remains oriented towards language learning, with an emphasis on correcting intonation, and many of the discussions relate to Calvin's detailed study of tea-making. However, his talking along with the older interactant has become very prominent, while Ms Li seems to maintain her speakership by interrupting Calvin more often. These cut-ins and 'cooperative overlaps' (Tannen, 1993) happen on both sides throughout the conversation. In Example 10.5 Ms Li is wondering whether and to what extent Calvin's parents care about him.

Example 10.5 'Do you think your parents care about you?'

Chinese conversation R4: Ms Li, Calvin

251	Ms Li	你觉得父母是不是很关心你呢/
		nǐ juéde fùmǔ shìbùshì hěn guānxīn nǐ ne/
		you think parents is it not very care about you
		don't you think your parents care about you a lot
252	Calvin	啊::
		a::
		ah::
		ah::
253	Ms Li	是很关心但是[会不会觉得说:::]
		shì hěn guānxīn dànshì [huìbùhuì juéde shuō:::]
		very care but [able or unable feel talk:::]
		they care a lot but[don't feel that:::]
254	Calvin	[很:::关心]
		[hěn :::guānxīn]
		[very care]
		[care a lot]
255	Ms Li	哎呀(.) 关心过头了 <@@>
		āiyā (.) guānxīn guò tóu le <@@>
		aya (.) care over <@@>
		yes (.) care too much <@@>
256	Calvin	[噢:::有时:::]
		[o:::yǒushí:::]
		[oh::: sometimes:::]
		[oh::: sometimes:::]
257	Ms Li	[<@@>]
		[<@@>]

(Continued)

Example 10.5 (Continued)

258	Calvin	*我会觉得*
		wǒ huì juéde
		i will feel
		i will feel
259	Ms Li	*会这[样啊*<@@>]
		huì zhè [yàng a<@@>]
		will like th[is <@@>]
		it will be like th[is <@@>]
260	Calvin	[um是啊]
		[um shì a]
		[um yes]
		[um yes]
261	Ms Li	会经常这样会觉得:::
		huì jīngcháng zhèyàng huì juéde:::
		will often like this will feel:::
		it will often feel like this:::
262	Calvin	uhm:::不经常
		uhm::: bù jīngcháng
		um::: not often
		um::: not often
263	Ms Li	不[经常uhm:::]
		bù [jīngcháng uhm:::]
		not [often um:::]
		not [often um:::]
264	Calvin	[但是有时候]
		[dànshì yǒushíhou]
		[but sometimes]
		[but sometimes]

We see the two interlocutors competing for the turn here, especially Calvin, who cannot wait for Ms Li to complete her turn in lines 254, 256, 260 and 264. These overlaps are competitive in nature and indicate Calvin's intention to take the floor. This never happened in the earlier recordings. Interestingly, Calvin's interruptive style is not construed as competitive by Ms Li; instead, the conversation goes on with much rapport with a lot of laughter on both sides.

In summary, a feature of the Chinese data was the older participants' dominance in topic management. Ms Chu in C-R1 and C-R2 and Ms Li in C-R3 and C-R4 led and controlled all the recorded conversations by initiating most of the topics and allocating the turns. In the first recording in particular this may have been partly because the student did not wish or was unable to take the floor, but the stances taken up by the older participants during the conversations generally, including the stance of language instructor, are also highly relevant here (see Chapter 4). However, the over-time analysis found that Calvin underwent great changes in his participatory role during the two-year period, from being a passive interviewee to an active and cooperative conversationalist. In C-R1 his talk was more like the provision of answers in an interview, featuring non-lexical backchannels, yes/no, or one- or two-word answers without any further elaboration, and he could only be drawn on to initiate a topic when presented with a deliberately incomplete utterance by the older participant. In the later recordings, however, he conversed more confidently and competently, even when presented with a new partner and a less topic-driven interaction. He overcame his partner's conversational dominance and took on speakership more often by self-selecting his turn, cutting in or overlapping, and using more expressive backchannels at the level of phrasal responses. He also extended his own turn and held the floor for longer. It was notable that his progress did not cease when he was introduced to a new partner (C-R3), indicating ongoing development of his IC. Importantly, Calvin's transition from peripheral to full participation was achieved in a very collaborative manner with the older interactant as he employed various linguistic and paralinguistic strategies to initiate and develop topics.

German story: Development through translanguaging

As we saw in Table 10.1, the German data was obtained from the same pair over two years. One of the standout findings was the increase in the student's topic initiation, from raising very few topics in G-R1 to introducing all the topics and subtopics in G-R4 (Table 10.3). Another finding was the decline in topic and subtopic numbers over the course of the four recordings, with the highest number of subtopics being initiated by the older participant during the first recording. Interestingly, this was the pattern also in the Chinese and Spanish data (see Tables 10.2 and 10.4). The student Graham gave maximum responses to almost all of the self-started topics, but did not provide responses of 100% to the topics or themes started by the older interactant, Mr Gabler, in some cases offering only a minimal 'ahh', 'ja' (*yes*) or one- or two-word utterances. Another prominent feature of the German data was the extensive use of English by both participants. In some cases, Graham responded to Mr Gabler in English only.

German R1

German R1 covered many different topics and themes, which exposed the student to a wide range of vocabulary. These were introduced primarily by the older participant, while the student tended to contribute to topic development when questioned or encouraged by his partner. He responded frequently in German, but also used English or a mixture of both

Table 10.3 Initiation and development of topics and subtopics by the student in German conversations

	Recording date and length	No. of topics initiated by		No. of subtopics initiated by		Student's development of subtopics			
						Minimum response no. (%)	Median response no. (%)	Maximum response no. (%)	Elaborations in English no. (%)
G-R1	May 2010 39'08"	Graham	4	Graham	3	0	0	2 (67%)	1 (33%)
				Mr Gabler	3	0	0	3 (100%)	0
		Mr Gabler	35	Graham	6	0	0	5 (83%)	1 (17%)
				Mr Gabler	54	9 (17%)	6 (11%)	33 (61%)	5 (9%)
G-R2	September 2010 36'31"	Graham	3	Graham	5	0	0	5 (100%)	0
				Mr Gabler	7	4 (57%)	1 (14%)	2 (29%)	0
		Mr Gabler	10	Graham	2	0	0	2 (100%)	0
				Mr Gabler	22	1 (5%)	2 (9%)	16 (73%)	3 (14%)
G-R3	March 2011 31'25"	Graham	3	Graham	5	0	0	4 (80%)	1 (20%)
				Mr Gabler	3	1 (33%)	0	2 (67%)	0
		Mr Gabler	9	Graham	5	0	0	5 (100%)	0
				Mr Gabler	19	2 (11%)	1 (5%)	8 (42%)	8 (42%)
G-R4	September 2011 7'42" *	Graham	18	Graham	18	0	0	18 (100%)	0
				Mr Gabler	0	0	0	0	0
		Mr Gabler	0	Graham	0	0	0	0	0
				Mr Gabler	0	0	0	0	0

* G-R4 is the last session of the year. After the first session of the conversation, the student asked the older participant to help with his mock Chinese examination. This mock examination was not a conversation and therefore was not recorded.

languages. During the conversation, Mr Gabler dominated the allocation of turns by selecting either himself or Graham as the next speaker. However, like Ms Chu in C-R1 he did not want to hold a monologue, and the following extract shows him prompting Graham to talk. Prior to this, he has been asking Graham what else he would like to know, and Graham asks for clarification of this question and then backchannels that he is thinking of a topic. Mr Gabler repeats his prompt in English and also rephrases the request in German, which is effectively a translation of an English expression. He then asks Graham explicitly to introduce a topic (line 24, Example 10.6).

Example 10.6 'I do a lot of walking'

German conversation R1: Mr Gabler, Graham

24	Mr Gabler	welche fragen würdest du zu mir geben
		what questions would you give me
25	Graham	ja machst du sport (.)
		yes do you do sport (.)
26	Mr Gabler	aeh nicht mehr wie ich jung war ja\
		ah not any longer when I was young yes
27		ich habe auch schi gefahren [und] aeh (.) fechten
		i also did skiing [and] ah (.) fencing
28	Graham	[ja] (.)
		[yes] (.)
29	Mr Gabler	<säbelfechten>
		<sword fighting>
30		und ich habe auch (.) schwimmen und fahrradfahren (.)
		and i did (.) swimming and cycling (.)
31	Graham	<E okay E>
		<E okay E>
32	Mr Gabler	aber jetzt mach ich keinen mehr sport mehr außer ein bißchen schwimmen (H)
		but now i don't do sport any more except for a bit of swimming (H)
33		aeh weil ich <E arthritis E> hab ich weiß nicht wie das deutsche wort heis-
		ah because i have <E arthritis E> i don't know the german word for that
34		<E I got arthritis E> deswegen (.)
		<E I got arthritis E> that's why (.)
35		<<E but E>> ich geh viel spazieren mit (.) ich hab zwei hunde
		<<E but E>> i do a lot of walking with (.) i have two dogs

(Continued)

Example 10.6 (Continued)

36	Graham	ahh=
		ahh=
37	Mr Gabler	=und da geh ich viel spazieren [ja]/
		=and so i do lots of walking [yes]/
38	Graham	[ja] (.)
		[yes](.)

Even though Graham is offered his turn and asks the question in line 25 after Mr Gabler's prompting, his engagement remains peripheral with very brief backchannels (lines 28, 31, 36 and 38). Mr Gabler goes on to talk about his activities past and present in an expansive manner, maintaining the floor with longer turns, and the student's role is minimal.

In fact, many of Mr Gabler's questions in G-R1 are closed, so that Graham only needs to respond with very brief utterances or yes/no answers. His extensive use of non-lexical, phatic expressions is therefore not surprising. This is obvious in the next example from the very beginning of the recording (Example 10.7). Mr Gabler says in English, *We forgot we're recording here*, which suggests the recorder was turned on after the conversation had started.

Example 10.7 'Do you live with your mother and father?'

German conversation R2: Mr Gabler, Graham

3	Mr Gabler	and ae wohnst mit mutter und vater/
		and ah do you live with mother and father/
4	Graham	ja
		yes
5	Mr Gabler	und aha (..)
		and aha (..)
6		und aeh (.) sind die australier (.) deine eltern/
		and ah (.) are they australian (.) your parents/
7	Graham	ja
		yes

In both of these examples in G-R1, Graham's backchannelling can be understood as signals of understanding or of interest in Mr Gabler's topics; however, the framing of the questions does not induce much substantial contribution to topic development.

German R2

After four months of regular conversations with Mr Gabler, however, we find Graham more actively participating in topic discussions, and this is reflected in his ability to provide more maximum responses in the target language to the topics initiated by the older participant (73% in G-R2 compared with 61% in G-R1: see Table 10.3). He also employs longer turns (lines 6 and 7 in Example 10.8) and cuts in to self-select as the next speaker (line 181 in Example 10.9).

Before the conversation begins in Example 10.8, Graham says *We're in business* and Mr Gabler replies with 'Das ist gut' (*That's good*). The older interlocutor then asks him how he liked a book (line 3) and, rather than simply giving a one- or two-word answer such as *good*, Graham uses his reply *Yes it was good* to introduce a subtopic with a long turn, a strategy that occurred very rarely in G-R1.

Example 10.8 'How did you like the book?'

German conversation R2: Mr Gabler, Graham

3	Mr Gabler	und ae sonst wie hat dir das buch gefallen/ (.)
		and ah well then how did you like the book/ (.)
4	Graham	ah ja: (.)
		ah yes: (.)
5	Mr Gabler	es war ein bißchen alt/ (.)
		it was a bit old/ (.)
6	Graham	ja es war gut a: (..) ich habe ein paar idee für wenn
		yes it was good a: (..) i have a few idea for when
7		ich und mein freund gehen nach deutschland (.)
		i and my friend go to germany (.)

Example 10.9 'They should have helped a bit more'

German conversation R2: Mr Gabler, Graham

178	Mr Gabler	*ja* (..) das is- schade na die hätten doch ein bißchen mehr helfen sollen in der beziehung
		**yes* (..) that's- pity well they should have helped a bit more in that regard*
179		daß die leute wissen lassen (.) was los ist oder da haben sie nicht gemacht nein sehr schade (.)
		so that people knew (.) what was going on or they didn't do that no a real pity (.)
180		<@@>
		<@@>
181	Graham	in singapore es war riesig=<@@>
		in singapore it was great=<@@>
182	Mr Gabler	=ah ja
		=ah yes

Prior to this second extract (Example 10.9), Mr Gabler has commented that he could not find any news in Australia about athletic events and continues this theme without any contribution from Graham (lines 178–180). However, Graham's self-selection of his turn in line 181 shows his intention of participating in the conversation, in this case by reverting to the previous topic he had started about Singapore.

Interestingly, Graham's use of English to develop topics has become more obvious in G-R2, and he responds to many (sub)topics started by Mr Gabler entirely in English. Before the extract in Example 10.10 he had been telling Mr Gabler about his activities in Singapore. Mr Gabler comments on how interesting this is, and the student backchannels his agreement before Mr Gabler takes up his turn in line 421.

Example 10.10 'What did you like about Singapore?'

German conversation R2: Mr Gabler, Graham

421	Mr Gabler	und wenn du sprachen sprichst wie du sprichst chinesisch und deutsch
		and when you speak speak languages like you speak chinese and german
422	Graham	mhm
		mhm
423	Mr Gabler	is- es einfach mit anderen leuten zu sprechen
		it is easy to talk with other people
424		auch wenn man nur ein bißchen kann nich- [(.)] es is- sehr gut
		even if you only know a little bit yes [(.)] it is very good
425	Graham	[ja]
		[yes]
426	Mr Gabler	a: (..)
		a: (..)
427	Graham	<E what else is good in singapore E> (..)
		<E what else is good in singapore E> (..)
428		<E a: trying to think E> (....)
		<E a: trying to think E> (....)
429	Mr Gabler	was hat (.) was hat dir gut gefallen <E what did you like about it E> (.)
		what did (.) what did you like <E what did you like about it E> (.)
430 431 432	Graham	<E well the food was <xxx> because it was on a three day cycle by about seventeen eighteen days we got a bit sick of the same thing over and over again [(.)] so the last couple of days we just went to mcdonalds and subway E> <@@>
		<E well the food was <xxx> because it was on a three day cycle by about seventeen eighteen days we got a bit sick of the same thing over and over again [(.)] so the last couple of days we just went to mcdonalds and subway E> <@@>

In line 427 Graham introduces a topic by self-selection, but does so in English by his own choice. In line 429 Mr Gabler provides a prompt to use German, but with a switch to English for clarification, and then Graham pursues the topic of what he liked in Singapore completely in English. In this case, Mr Gabler's prompt (code-switching) triggers a more extensive code-switched (i.e. English) response. This might imply that Graham's limited German prevents him from talking fluently about a subject he is clearly enthusiastic about; however, this translanguaging process is also an effective way to assist with the flow of the conversation (Garcia & Li, 2013) and the pair are clearly enjoying the rapport they have established in the exchange, even if this momentarily overrides the formal goal of improving Graham's German language skills.

German R3

When the two meet again after a five-month break, we find that their conversation features the most English utterances of all four recordings. Indeed, many of Graham's responses are made completely in English (see Table 10.3). This is possibly because Mr Gabler and Graham feel more comfortable with code-switching in order to re-establish their rapport and maintain the flow of conversation, particularly after the long holiday period. However, the older interlocutor's use of English is not new, as Mr Gabler had already invited the student to ask questions in English in G-R1. Because the two interlocutors have a fluent language in common (i.e. English), Mr Gabler has given overt permission to Graham to code-switch, and Graham has adopted this as a useful strategy when he wants to take or maintain the floor. English appears in all of the recordings for German, but Graham's use of English for topic development has become most prominent in G-R3. His reason for this is made quite clear in the next extract. Before moving to a discussion of Graham's Chinese skills in Example 10.11, the two have been talking about what languages the other students in the project are learning.

Example 10.11 'I find Chinese too difficult'

German conversation R3: Mr Gabler, Graham

439	Mr Gabler	ah und sie lernen chinesisch/ ne/ [wie] wie ist dein chinesisch/ <E finished E>/
		ah and they're learning chinese/ yes/ [how] how is your chinese/ <E finished E>/
440	Graham	[ja]
		[yes]
441		<E a:h yeah I am not learning <x> i am learning chinese still but i am not doing the programme anymore= E>

(Continued)

Example 10.11 (Continued)

		<E a:h yeah I am not learning <x> i am learning chinese still but i am not doing the programme anymore= E>
442	Mr Gabler	=aha ok=
		=aha ok=
443	Graham	<E =I find it too difficult because= E>
		<E =I find it too difficult because= E>
444	Mr Gabler	=zu viel arbeit/
		=too much work/
445	Graham	<E yeah and so for example if there is something i might
446		say you are able to correct me and you are able to switch
447		to english whereas ah the chinese people if you don't know something you are not gonna get it E> <@@>
		<E yeah and so for example if there is something i might say you are able to correct me and you are able to switch to english whereas ah the chinese people if you don't know something you are not gonna get it E> <@@>
448	Mr Gabler	ah ja
		ah yes

Graham explains entirely in English why he decided not to continue with Chinese in the project. Here it is hard to tell why he shifts to English when responding to Mr Gabler's question in German in line 444. It might be linked to his lack of vocabulary (which is the case for many of the examples in previous recordings), but alternatively he may have chosen to convey his opinion in English in order to avoid any misunderstanding by his listener. In the example, Mr Gabler's use of English is minimal (*finished*, in line 439); however, this one word may still have been a trigger for Graham to respond in English (Clyne, 1980). Possibly his use of English reflects his mood or interest in the subject, although affective aspects of code-switching are difficult to determine conclusively here. It is notable that the code-switched segments produced by Graham in response to Mr Gabler's questions are contextually appropriate, indicating that he has understood his interlocutor's German, and that he is able to develop the topic, albeit in L1 English.

In fact, English is used by Graham on many occasions for different functions, such as requesting clarification, expressing his feelings or conducting meta-talk about the conversation tasks, as in the following example. In their turns prior to Example 10.12 the pair have been talking about the type of car Graham's mother and Mr Gabler's son own and drive.

Example 10.12 'My aunt has a Volkswagen too'

German conversation R3: Mr Gabler, Graham

173	Mr Gabler	=und dann ah will er er will wieder einen volkswagen kaufen=
		=and then ah he wants he wants to buy a volkswagen again=
174	Graham	meine tante <habt> hat auch ein volkswagen=
		my aunt <has> has a volkswagen too=
175	Mr Gabler	=auch mh was für einen/
		=too mh what sort/
176	Graham	ah ein golf aber es ist ein wagen <E so its got a long back in the end E>=
		ah a golf but it's a wagon <E so it's got a long back in the end E>=
177	Mr Gabler	=oh <E a station wagon E>=
		=oh <E a station wagon E>=
178	Graham	=<E yes station wagon E>
		=<E yes station wagon E>
179	Mr Gabler	sehr gut mein sohn hat einen passat < als> <E station wagon E> ja
		very good my son has a passat <as> <E station wagon E> yes
180		und der ist sehr sehr gut [sehr gut]
		and it is very very good [very good]
181	Graham	[ja] mein nachbar hat ein [ja <x>]
		[yes] my neighbour has a [ja <x>]
182	Mr Gabler	[ja was] für eine farbe/
		[yes what]sort of colour/
183	Graham	was für ein/ <E sorry E>
		what sort of/ <E sorry E>
184	Mr Gabler	farbe/ <E what colour E>
		colour/ <E what colour E>
185	Graham	ah silber=
		ah silver=
186	Mr Gabler	=silber/ gut ja
		=silver/ good yes
187	Graham	<E boring but E> <@@>=
		<E boring but E> <@@>=
188	Mr Gabler	=<x>=
		=<x>=
189	Graham	=<E boring but ah well E> <@@>
		=<E boring but ah well E> <@@>

In this extract, we see that Graham and Mr Gabler work very closely to develop the topic and in doing so introduce a number of potential subtopics about their families: *aunt, son, neighbour*. Interestingly, when Graham struggles to explain what a station wagon is in German and resorts to English (line 176), Mr Gabler responds 'Oh, a station wagon', which is both the English and the German term for such a vehicle. English is utilised extensively by both interactants for elaborations, clarifications or explanations (line 184) or for making comments (lines 187, 189).

German R4

German R4 is the shortest conversation of the four where Graham uses well-formulated German utterances to open and develop the topics, basically about Mr Gabler's life and opinions, even though sometimes his utterances are not grammatically correct. English is used very minimally in two turns only at the very end of the conversation. One striking difference between this conversation and the previous ones is the change of conversational role taken on by each interlocutor. In G-R1 in 2010, Mr Gabler acted as the primary topic initiator, whereas in G-R4 in 2011 we find the conversation controlled by the student. In fact, the student functions solely as a topic initiator while the older participant collaborates as a topic responder.

In addition, Graham demonstrates that he has learnt the appropriate linguistic convention for speaking with an older person (the formal 'Sie' rather than the informal 'du'), which is an essential cultural and grammatical consideration in German. He contravened this convention twice in G-R1 (see line 25 of Example 10.6, for instance, where he asks the older interactant 'Machst du Sport?', rather than 'Machen Sie Sport?), but in fact he did not make this error in any other sessions. In G-R4, when he asks all the questions, he consistently addresses Mr Gabler correctly by using the formal 'Sie' (you, plural) (see line 25 in Example 10.13). Of particular interest for our study, we find that, when initiating or developing the topics, Graham now adopts one of Mr Gabler's own strategies, namely backchannelling to the previous topic before introducing the next one.

In the following exchange in Example 10.13, Mr Gabler is answering Graham's question about his relationship with his sisters.

Example 10.13 'I get along very well with my sisters'

German conversation R4: Mr Gabler, Graham

24	Mr Gabler	oh mit meinen schwestern verstehe ich mich sehr gut (..)
		oh i get along very well with my sisters (..)

(Continued)

Example 10.13 (Continued)

25	Graham	ah sehr gut u:nd haben sie noch kontakt mit mit ihrer familie in deutschland/
		ah very good a:nd do you still have contact with with your family in germany/

In line 25, Graham briefly but positively backchannels to Mr Gabler's previous response before asking him a new question. Mr Gabler has frequently used this utterance combination of comment-plus-introduction of a new (sub)topic as a means of encouraging Graham's participation (e.g. line 179 in Example 10.12). Graham's own well-timed and appropriate usage of this format in line 25 indicates that he has identified and acquired a new interactional strategy; that is, he has found that a strategy used and learnt in one situation can be applied in other similar situations (Hellermann, 2007).

In fact, expressing an opinion is a feature of Graham's talk, especially in this later recording. A number of examples have already been cited above, including 'In Singapore es war riesig' (*In Singapore it was great*) in G-R2 (Example 10.9) and 'Boring, but ah well' in G-R3 (Example 10.12). In these instances, however, the comments are stand-alone and do not function to further introduce or develop a topic. In contrast, his *Ah, very good* in Example 10.13 is a token of acknowledgement and approval of his interlocutor's talk, but also and more importantly, an effective change-of-activity token (Gardner, 2010) that enables him to extend his turn.

A striking finding from our over-time analysis was the significant increase in Graham's topic initiation, from minimal initiation in G-R1 to leading all the topic discussions in G-R4. Correspondingly, the interlocutors changed their participatory roles. Graham moved from being a topic responder to being a topic initiator, while the opposite occurred with the older participant. In G-R1 Graham tried to remain active in the talk by providing non-lexical backchannels, but these did not make any substantial contribution to topic development and served only to indicate his legitimate but peripheral participation. His developing IC was reflected in his correct use of 'Sie' rather than 'du' in the later conversations and in his well-timed and appropriate adoption of backchannels that commented firstly on the utterance of the previous speaker and then gave him the floor to introduce a new topic so that he could extend his turn. This strategy was observed in Mr Gabler's turns and was acquired by the student specifically through talk-in-interaction with the native speaker.

Prominent throughout G-R2 and G-R3 was the student's extensive code-switching to English when he made requests or comments or conducted meta-talk for the purpose of taking the floor or maintaining speakership. However, his use of English was much reduced in G-R4 and he conducted the conversation mainly in the target language. Interestingly, the scaffolding strategy provided by the older interlocutor was also largely one of code-switching, as in 'Wie ist dein chinesisch? Finished?' in Example 10.11. This type of linguistic accommodation facilitated extended topic development in both languages, but also, as we saw above, may have encouraged the student to continue the conversation in English, with possibly a negative impact on his L2 development (Antón & DiCamilla, 1998).

Spanish story: Topic shifting

Table 10.4 shows that the older participant, Ms Sais, initiated most of the topics and subtopics in both conversations. The student, Sophie, was also active in initiating and contributing new themes to the topics, although interestingly far fewer in S-R2. A general observation is that Sophie provided more maximum responses to self-initiated (sub) topics than to older interactant-started (sub)topics. This was especially prominent in the second recording, where her responses to the topics and subtopics she initiated herself were 100%, but her follow-up to topics initiated by Ms Sais continued to be a combination of minimum, medium and maximum responses, albeit with more maximum responses in S-R2. In the Spanish data, as in the Chinese and German, it was the case that fewer topics (themes) were introduced and discussed in S-R2 compared with S-R1.

Spanish R1

In Spanish R1, many of the topics were oriented solely by the older participant with very little contribution from the student. This occurred frequently in spite of Ms Sais's attempts to encourage Sophie to talk by repeating her own utterances or Sophie's answers (e.g. lines 113, 118 in Example 10.14) or by suggesting her turn (line 111). However, many of Ms Sais's questions were also closed, merely requiring yes/no or one-word answers from the student (e.g. lines 108 and 116), and this would partly explain Sophie's non-maximum responses and inability to develop the topics fully. In fact, Sophie's responses in S-R1 were generally short, favouring non-lexical backchannels such as 'mmm' (line 109), yes/no answers (lines 112, 115, 119) and one- or two-word answers (line 117). Her limited linguistic and interactional competence in this early recording would also account for these minimal replies. In the extract below, Ms Sais has just asked about the days that Sophie goes to school and then continues the topic by asking Sophie whether she likes school.

Table 10.4 Initiation and development of topics and subtopics by the student in Spanish conversations

	Recording date & length	No. of topics initiated by		No. of subtopics initiated by		Student's development of the subtopics				
						No response no. (%)	Minimum response no. (%)	Medium response no. (%)	Maximum response no. (%)	Elaborations in English no. (%)
Recording 1	May 2010 37'55"	Sophie	6	Sophie	13	0	1 (8%)	0	12 (92%)	0
				Ms Sais	10	0	2 (20%)	1 (10%)	6 (60%)	1 (10%)
		Ms Sais	10	Sophie	10	0	0	1 (10%)	9 (90%)	0
				Ms Sais	42	5 (12%)	21 (50%)	6 (14%)	10 (24%)	0
Recording 2	September 2010 31'22"	Sophie	1	Sophie	1	0	0	0	1 (100%)	0
				Ms Sais	1	0	0	0	1 (100%)	0
		Ms Sais	10	Sophie	5	0	0	0	4 (80%)	1 (20%)
				Ms Sais	35	1 (3%)	12 (34%)	5 (14%)	17 (49%)	0

Example 10.14 'Do you like school?'

Spanish conversation R1: Ms Sais, Sophie

108	Ms Sais	sí (.) te gusta la escuela/
		yes (.) do you like school/
109	Sophie	(..) mmm (.) [umm]
		(..) mmm (.) [umm]
110	Ms Sais	[mmn]
		[mmn]
111		es un poquito difícil=
		it's a little difficult=
112	Sophie	=sí=
		=yes=
113	Ms Sais	=un poquito (..) difícil <E understand E> [difícil] sí (..) un poquito
		=a little (..) difficult <E understand E> [difficult] yes (..) a little
114		difícil
		difficult
115	Sophie	[<E yeah E> sí]
		[<E yeah E> yes]
116	Ms Sais	eh tú (.) en qué año estás/
		eh you (.) in what year are you/
117	Sophie	um estoy en (.) año ah once
		um i'm in (.) year ah eleven
118	Ms Sais	once
		eleven
119	Sophie	sí
		yes

Ms Sais's dominance in the conversation is also featured in her role as language instructor, making corrections to Sophie's grammar, vocabulary or pronunciation. Line 30 in the next extract is a good example of the older interactant recasting the student's mistaken use of 'una' (the feminine indefinite article *a* in Spanish).

In Example 10.15, after talking about going to the movies, Ms Sais asks about another activity (going to the park) with a closed question. Sophie responds negatively, but then shifts the topic to her work.

Example 10.15 'Yes, takeaway food'

Spanish conversation R1: Ms Sais, Sophie

22	Ms Sais	(.) sí (.) e:::hm (..) e:::h fuiste e:::h (.) algún parque/
		(.) yes (.) e:::hm (..) e:::h did you go e:::h (.) to a park/

(Continued)

Example 10.15 (Continued)

23	Sophie	(..) uhh (.) no
		(..) uhh (.) no
24	Ms Sais	no/=
		no/=
25	Sophie	=no
		=no
26	Ms Sais	[no/]
		[no/]
27	Sophie	[umm] <E i E> (..) trabajo
		[umm] <E i E> (..) i work
28	Ms Sais	(.) tú/
		(.) you/
29	Sophie	<ten> tengo una trabajo
		<i ha> i have a job
30	Ms Sais	no es así (.) tengo= (.) =un trabajo
		it's not that way (.) i have= (.) =a job
31	Sophie	(...) =tengo=
		(...) =i have=
32	Ms Sais	(.) <E where E> dónde/
		(.) <E where E> where/
33	Sophie	(.) um en (..) un (.) comida (..) rápido/
		(.) um in (..) a (.) food (..) fast/
34	Ms Sais	(.) ah comida rápida no no sé cómo se llama esto comida bueno comida
		(.) ah fast food no i don't know what it's called this food rightly food
35		rápida (.) eh (.) en español (..) se dice comida (.) al paso
		fast (.) eh (.) in spanish (..) one says food (.) to take away
36	Sophie	(..) umm=
		(..) umm=
37	Ms Sais	=paso
		=takeaway
38	Sophie	(.) <E okay E>
		(.) <E okay E>
39	Ms Sais	sí comida al paso(.) umm (.) cómo está tu papá y tu mamá/
		yes takeaway food (.) umm (.) how are your dad and your mum/

The recordings revealed that both interlocutors resorted to English in order to maintain the flow of the conversation, especially in S-R1. In spite of her own limited English, Ms Sais frequently translated the Spanish into English, mostly to facilitate Sophie's comprehension of the vocabulary (e.g. line 32 above). However, Sophie's use of English was also very pronounced in this conversation, either to elaborate her utterances or to question her interlocutor (16 times) or to code-switch to one or two English words sporadically (23 times; e.g. line 27 in Example 10.15).

Among the three case studies, and compared with Calvin and Graham, Sophie was the student who introduced the most (sub)topics in the first recording, initiating about one-third even though the conversation as a whole was led by her older partner. She did so, in many cases, by self-selecting her turn (e.g. line 27 in Example 10.15), showing her (intention to maintain) active participation in the conversation. In S-R1 she used the strategy of introducing new topics eight times in order to take or to maintain the floor. For example, in line 27 she is clearly feeling pressured to explain why she did not go to the park, as Ms Sais seems to express surprise or disbelief at her negative response with an upraised tone ('no?', line 26). Sophie does her best to accommodate this rather forceful yielding of the floor by introducing the new topic of her work, although she does not have the linguistic or interactional capacity to make explicit that her work prevents her from going to the park, and Ms Sais does not pick up on this fact. In the next few lines the two interlocutors continue their talk on the theme of Sophie's work until line 39 when Ms Sais changes rather abruptly to another unrelated topic, asking about Sophie's parents, without explicit completion of the previous topic (cf. line 245 in Example 7.7). This is a typical example of topic shift in S-R1, perhaps explained by both participants struggling to talk any more about takeaway food.

The concurrence of topically disengaged utterances (represented by repeated *no*, lines 23–26, and Sophie's *umm* or *okay* in lines 36 and 38) are sufficient to give the other speaker the opportunity to embark on a new topic (Drew & Holt, 1998), and topic shift in both cases is an obvious strategy to keep up the flow of the conversation. However, these topic shifts are quite disjunctive, involving the introduction of a markedly different topic from that of the prior turn (Jefferson, 1984). Frequent disjunctive topic introductions are, in fact, a measure of a 'lousy conversation' (Sacks, 1992: 352) and may, at least partially, account for why more (sub)topics were raised in this recording.

Spanish R2

In the second Spanish recording, conducted four months after S-R1, Sophie gave more maximum responses to both self- and older-interactant-initiated topics but did not initiate as many topics as in S-R1 (Table 10.4).

Ms Sais asked longer questions of more variety and introduced fewer closed questions (see for example lines 145–148 in the next example, 10.16), allowing Sophie more development options. The student, in her responses, gave more complete, comprehensible answers (e.g. lines 149, 153) and used English less than she had previously (to elaborate or ask a question: 12 times in S-R1 and 16 times in S-R2, and sporadic use in sentences: 15 times in S-R2 and 23 times in S-R1). There was a tendency on Sophie's part towards slightly longer turns and more turns without the older interactant's prompting (e.g. lines 167, 169 below).

The pair have been talking about friendships and a number of subtopics. Having exhausted these, Ms Sais appears to consult some notes and begins a new unrelated topic about the holidays.

Example 10.16 'Where would you like to go on holiday?'

Spanish conversation R2: Ms Sais, Sophie

145	Ms Sais	buena buena (.)= ((writing noise)) =a ver (.) DÓNDE te gustaría vivir
		good good (.)= ((writing noise)) =let's see (.) WHERE would you like to live
146		(..) no dónde te gustaría viajar en tu- próxima- vacacione- en tu (.) cuando (..)
		(..) no where would you like to travel for your nex- holi- day- for your (.) when (..)
147		cuando (..) finalice- la el año las clase- (..) dónde te gustaría (.) ir
		when (..) finish- the the year the classe- (..) where would you like (.) to go
148		de vacacione-
		on holiday-
149	Sophie	(..) oh umm (..) me::: ahh me gusta:::ría (.) a viajar/
		(..) oh umm (..) i::: ahh i would like (.) to travel/
150	Ms Sais	viajar
		travel
151	Sophie	(.) sí (.) ahh (.)
		(.) yes (.) ahh (.)
152	Ms Sais	europa/
		europe/
153	Sophie	sí y sudamérica
		yes and south america
...		
167	Sophie	y umm (.) me gusta viajar a irlanda
		and umm (.) i like to travel to ireland

(Continued)

Example 10.16 (Continued)

168	Ms Sais	irlanda/
		ireland/
169	Sophie	porque mi familia (..) [es]
		because my family (..) [is]
170	Ms Sais	[son] irlandeses/
		[they] are irish/
171	Sophie	sí
		yes
172	Ms Sais	ah qué bueno tu hablas el idioma de ellos/
		ah how nice do you speak their language/
173	Sophie	a::::hm (.) un poco
		a::::hm (.) a little
174	Ms Sais	un poquito
		a little bit
175	Sophie	*<E yeh E> sí*
		<E yeh E> yes
176	Ms Sais	un poquito
		a little bit
177	Sophie	un poqui[to]
		a little bi[t]
178	Ms Sais	[PO]CO (.) poquito
		[LITT]LE (.) little bit
179	Sophie	oh <E okay E>== =<@@>
		oh <E okay E>== =<@@>
180	Ms Sais	=<@@>=
		=<@@>=

In line 149, when Sophie tries to answer Ms Sais's elaborate question about where she would like to travel, she provides an answer, which, interestingly, is very similar to a response she provided in S-R1. The only difference is that Sophie's answer is now grammatically correct. In the first recording, her answer 'umm but I'd like to travel to umm un- una viaje' was half in English, probably due to her inability to use the conditional tense, and contained uncertain use of the indefinite article 'un' or 'una' for 'viaje' (*trip*). Her linguistic improvement, as exemplified in this extract, has certainly contributed to the comprehensibility of her statement and the flow of conversation in Spanish. This may be one reason why the amount of English Ms Sais uses in S-R2 is negligible compared with S-R1. In the next few lines, they continue to talk about places to travel in South America, and the student then switches to a new subtopic, travel to Ireland, in a very smooth manner. After an attempt at a more elaborate description of her family, however (line 169), she falls back on a typical short response in line 173 (to confirm that she speaks Gaelic a little). In line 174 Ms Sais repeats Sophie's response by adding a diminutive, which the student copies. Ms Sais then corrects her again, prompting laughter from both of them and signalling the rapport that has developed between the pair.

Several themes have been developed collaboratively by the two interlocutors in this example. The topic moves from travel in general, to travel to specific places, and then to Ireland where the student's family comes from. It subsequently moves again to speaking Gaelic (the first official language of Ireland). The exchange involves multiple topic transitions and the typical stepwise shifts (Jefferson, 1984) of a smooth interaction. Every theme builds on the previous topic and, at the same time, makes it possible to take the conversation forward. Without any overt termination of the prior topic, such stepwise moves introduce new sequences that connect with the previous ones and indicate the collaborative work of the speakers. As Sacks has observed, the 'flow' from one topic into another is the best way to organise topics (1992: 566) and we can see here that Ms Sais and Sophie take pleasure in learning from and about each other when their contributions to topic development are a naturally evolving feature of the conversation.

Although our study included only two Spanish recordings, in May and September 2010, there was a demonstrable improvement in the student's interactional competence over this time, from using many non-lexical backchannels and code-switching in S-R1 to participating more actively in the target language in S-R2. The older interlocutor continued to introduce most of the topics and subtopics, but in the second recording the student was providing maximum responses of 49% to the older-interlocutor-initiated topics as compared with 24% four months earlier (Table 10.4).

Discussion

The three longitudinal case studies we have described allowed us to document the changes in IC of L2 students of Chinese, German and Spanish in conversation with native speakers using a CA analysis framework. We were particularly interested in topic management and how the students learnt to employ resources and strategies acquired during the conversation sessions or from similar situated discursive practices such as L2 classroom interactions. Specifically, we documented their capabilities in topic initiation and development, turn allocation, employment of interactional strategies, diversification of strategies and changes to the conversational framework.

Not surprisingly, a prominent feature of the first recorded conversation of each pair was the minimal or peripheral participation of the student and the leading role of the native speaker. The students initiated fewer topics themselves and provided less than maximum responses to the topics initiated by the older interlocutors. Ms Chu conducted her first conversation with Calvin very much like an interview, while Mr Gabler dominated his first session with Graham. Sophie was the most active student among the three in R1, but was unable to develop the many subtopics she introduced with Ms Sais owing to her limited language skills.

Over time, however, each student acquired the skills to engage more actively in the conversation and to contribute in different ways. Calvin learnt how to self-select his turn, and to cut in and overlap Ms Chu while maintaining rapport with the older participant. Sophie's improving Spanish enabled her to shift topics in a more stepwise manner to maintain the flow of the conversation, and Graham began to address the older interlocutor correctly in German and to use code-switching less often when he wanted to make a request or comment or conduct meta-talk in order to take or maintain the floor. All of these improvements in the students' IC were achieved with the older partner's encouragement to become more active participants, through repetitions, corrections, scaffolding and compliments.

Another common feature of developing IC among the three languages was the way the students began to adopt the backchannelling strategies of their partners. In the first recordings their backchannels were very minimal, basically occurring only as non-lexical terms, but in the later recordings they used more phrasal lexical items or substantive expressions such as brief comments. Thus we saw Graham copying Mr Gabler's common strategy of backchannelling acknowledgement before shifting to a new (sub)topic (Mr Gabler's 'Sehr gut. Mein Sohn...' in G-R3; Graham's 'Ah, sehr gut. Und haben Sie...' in G-R4), and Sophie and Calvin repeating the previous utterances of their partners. The immediate feedback provided by the native speakers in these situated interactions allowed the students to model the older participants and develop their IC skills in moment-by-moment exchanges.

A consistent finding among all three language pairs was the reduction in the number of (sub)topics initiated over time. This was due partly to the closed question format of many of the older participants' questions in the first recordings and their attempts to initiate topics the students could respond to. We also noted Sophie's extensive but inappropriate use of many disjunctive topic shifts in her first session with Ms Sais as she tried to remain an active participant in the conversation. Hand in hand with fewer (sub)topics, however, was an increase in the number of maximum responses the students were able to provide. In other words, as the students took the floor more often and extended their turns, the interactants stayed on the one (sub)topic for longer, made appropriate stepwise shifts, and the exchanges became smoother.

Although there was great variability in each participant's conversation experience as demonstrated above, the study has, in general, evidenced the improvement of IC among the three young language learners in the project. The over-time analysis has revealed their developing deployment of all possible interactional resources, linguistic, sequential, prosodic and paralinguistic in the initiation and development of topics. Through their regular conversation sessions with native speakers they may have acquired the ability to identify or recognise context-specific patterns by which turns are taken, actions are organised and practices are ordered. The common trajectory among the three students was the change in their participation patterns from minimal or peripheral to full engagement in the conversations, during which they interpreted and co-constructed their interactional micro-moments according to context.

Hall (1995: 218) suggests that becoming a participant involves three processes: discovery of interactive patterns in the practices of engagement; observation of and reflection on the participatory moves of others and responses to these; and the participant's own active constructions of responses to these patterns. The move from periphery to centre entails therefore not merely acquiring knowledge of interactional resources but also developing the sociocultural competence to use these resources familiarised through previous instances of the same practice. As 'experts' in the target language, the older native speakers were able to acquaint the young learners with the vocabulary as well as the linguistic and paralinguistic tools and resources needed to discuss a range of topics, while the regular conversation sessions were designed to allow the students to consolidate their skills, compare their progress over time, and generally improve their IC.

Conclusion

The findings of this study have clear implications for the utilisation of such dyadic conversations as both a research tool and a learning and teaching resource to raise the IC of L2 students in a way that can hardly be achieved in classroom learning. However, we conclude with a few observations that could benefit future projects. Firstly, greater attention should perhaps be paid to the role and contributions of the native language speakers. As we have stressed in this chapter, IC is acquired in situated interactions, not developed by an individual in isolation, like mastery over linguistic forms or processes of reasoning. In the conversations of our study, it was the older participant's implicit yet appropriate co-construction that allowed for growth on the part of the students. Thus, the use of closed questions, which discouraged the students from taking the floor with an extended turn, should be replaced with open questions when possible. Also, when native speakers are made aware of how to scaffold rather than dominate a conversation, they will generally help to maximise the chances for students to interact more competently. The extensive use of English in the German conversations also raised the issue of the need to find a balance between rapport-building and language practice when these two equally important components become disjunctive.

Finally, caution should be taken when interpreting these results because they were based on three case studies only. Our analysis has focused on changes in topic management using a CA framework with an emphasis on the contingently adaptable micro-moments that unfold in context. Therefore, future research should be conducted with more informants in combination with other research instruments. This will facilitate probing further into the psychological and social factors that affect the development of IC.

Note

(1) All participants' names have been changed.

References

Antón, M. and DiCamilla, F. (1998) Socio-cognitive functions of L1 collaborative interaction in the L2 classroom. *Canadian Modern* Language *Review/La revue canadienne des langues vivantes* 54 (3), 314–342

Button, G. and Casey, N. (1985) Topic nomination and topic pursuit. *Human Studies* 8 (1), 3–55.

Canale, M. and Swain, M. (1980) Theoretical bases of communicative approaches to second language teaching and testing. *Applied Linguistics* 1, 1–47.

Cekaite, A. (2007) A child's development of interactional competence in a Swedish L2 classroom. *The Modern Language Journal* 91 (1), 45–62.

Clyne, M. (1980) Triggering and language processing. *Canadian Journal of Psychology/ Revue canadienne de psychologie* 34 (4), 400.

Drew, P. and Holt, E. (1998) Figures of speech: Figurative expressions and the management of topic transition in conversation. *Language in Society* 27, 495–522.

Gan, Z., Davison, C. and Hamp-Lyons, L. (2009) Topic negotiation in peer group oral assessment situations: A conversation analytic approach. *Applied Linguistics* 30 (3), 315–334.

Garcia, O. and Li, W. (2013) *Translanguaging: Language, Bilingualism and Education*. New York: Palgrave Macmillan.

Gardner, R. (2001) *When Listeners Talk: Response Tokens and Listener Stance*. Amsterdam: John Benjamins Publishing.

Hall, J.K. (1993) The role of oral practices in the accomplishment of our everyday lives: The sociocultural dimension of interaction with implications for the learning of another language. *Applied Linguistics* 14, 145–166.

Hall, J.K. (1995) (Re)creating our worlds with words: A sociohistorical perspective of face-to-face interaction. *Applied Linguistics* 16 (2), 206–232.

Hall, J.K., Hellermann, J. and Pekarek Doehler, S. (eds) (2011) *L2 Interactional Competence and Development*. Bristol: Multilingual Matters.

He, A.W. (2004) CA for SLA: Arguments from the Chinese language classroom. *Modern Language Journal* 88, 568–582.

He, A.W. and Young, R. (1998) Language proficiency interviews: A discourse approach. In R. Young and A.W. He (eds) *Talking and Testing: Discourse Approaches to the Assessment of Oral Proficiency*. Amsterdam and Philadelphia: John Benjamins.

Hellermann, J. (2007) The development of practices for action in classroom dyadic interaction: Focus on task openings. *Modern Language Journal* 91, 83–96.

Hellermann, J. (2008) *Social Actions for Classroom Language Learning*. Bristol: Multilingual Matters.

Hellermann, J. (2011) Members' methods, members' competencies: Looking for evidence of language learning in longitudinal investigations of other-initiated repair. In J.K. Hall, J. Hellermann and S. Pekarek Doehler (eds) *L2 Interactional Competence and Development* (pp. 147–172). Bristol: Multilingual Matters.

Ishida, M. (2009) Development of interactional competence: Changes in the use of *ne* in L2 Japanese during study abroad. In H. Nguyen and G. Kasper (eds) *Talk-in-Interaction: Multilingual Perspectives* (pp. 351–385). Honolulu: University of Hawaii, National Foreign Language Resource Center.

Jefferson, G. (1984) On stepwise transition from talk about a trouble to inappropriately next positioned matters. In J.M. Atkinson and J. Heritage (eds) *Structures of Social Action: Studies in Conversation Analysis* (pp. 191–222). Cambridge: Cambridge University Press.

Koshik, I. (2002) Designedly incomplete utterances: A pedagogical practice for eliciting knowledge displays in error correction sequences. *Research on Language and Social Interaction* 35 (3), 277–309.

Lave, J. (1993) The practice of learning. In S. Chaiklin and J. Lave (eds) *Understanding Practice: Perspectives on Activity and Context* (pp. 3–32). New York: Cambridge University Press.

Lave, J. and Wenger, E. (1991) *Situated Learning: Legitimate Peripheral Participation*. Cambridge: Cambridge University Press.

LinguaLinks Library (1999) Electronic resource published by SIL Publications. See http://www-01.sil.org/lingualinks/languagelearning/otherresources/gudlnsfralnggandcltrlrnngprgrm/WhatIsInteractionalCompetence.htm.

Masuda, K. (2011) Acquiring interactional competence in a study-abroad context: Japanese language learners' use of the interactional particle *ne*. *Modern Language Journal* 95, 519–540.

Mondada, L. and Pekarek Doehler, S. (2004) Second language acquisition as situated practice: Task accomplishment in the French second language classroom. *Modern Language Journal* 88, 501–518.

Pekarek Doehler, S. and Pochon-Berger, E. (2011) Developing 'methods' for interaction: A cross-sectional study of disagreement sequences in French L2. In J.K. Hall, J. Hellermann and S. Pekarek Doehler (eds) *L2 Interactional Competence and Development* (pp. 206–243). Bristol: Multilingual Matters.

Sacks, H. (1992) *Lectures on Conversation*, 2 vols. Oxford: Blackwell.

Sacks, H., Schegloff, E.A. and Jefferson, G. (1974) A simplest systematics for the organization of turn-taking for conversations. *Language* 50 (4), 696–735.

Schegloff, E.A. (1981) Discourse as an interactional achievement: Some uses of 'uh huh' and other things that come between sentences. In D. Tannen (ed.) *Analyzing Discourse: Text and Talk* (pp. 71–93). Washington, DC: Georgetown University Press.

Schegloff, E.A. (1993) Reflections on quantification in the study of conversation. *Research on Language and Social Interaction* 26 (1), 99–128.

Sfard, A. (1998) On two metaphors for learning and the dangers of choosing just one. *Educational Researcher* 27 (2), 4–13.
Stokoe, E.H. (2000) Constructing topicality in university students' small-group discussion: A conversation analytic approach. *Language and Education* 14, 184–203.
Tannen, D. (1993) The relativity of linguistic strategies: Rethinking power and solidarity in gender and dominance. In D. Tannen (ed.) *Gender and Conversational Interaction* (pp. 165–188). Oxford: Oxford University Press.
Vygotsky, L.S. (1978) Interaction between learning and development. In M. Cole, V. John-Steiner, S. Scribner and E. Souberman (eds) *Mind and Society: The Development of Higher Psychological Processes* (pp. 79–91). Cambridge, MA: Harvard University Press.
Young, R.F. (1999) Sociolinguistic approaches to SLA. *Annual Review of Applied Linguistics* 19, 105–132.
Young, R.F. (2011) Interactional competence in language learning, teaching, and testing. In E. Hinkel (ed.) *Handbook of Research in Second Language Teaching and Learning* 2, 426–443.
Young, R.F. and Lee, J. (2004) Identifying units in interaction: Reactive tokens in Korean and English conversations. *Journal of Sociolinguistics* 8, 380–407.
Young, R.F. and Miller, E.R. (2004) Learning as changing participation: Discourse roles in ESL writing conferences. *Modern Language Journal* 88, 519–535.

11 An Innovative Model for Second Language Learning and Social Inclusion

Hui Huang, Marisa Cordella, Colette Browning and Ramona Baumgartner

A Multi-Dimensional Model of Co-construction

The model described in this chapter (Figure 11.1) offers a framework for the collaborative utilisation of community language resources to enhance second language learning. The model's fresh approach lies in its multi-faceted design, which integrates at least four dimensions and situates language learning within the broader objective of social inclusion. These dimensions can be summarised as: (1) second language learning; (2) cross-cultural understanding and multiculturalism; (3) development of intergenerational empathy; and (4) engagement of older people in community life. The model is built on a foundation of co-construction, in which the L1 speaker and the L2 learner work together to develop the conversation in the target language for their mutual benefit. Each of these aspects is considered below.

L2 Development. The model's primary purpose is identified in its first dimension. That is, it complements classroom language teaching by offering language students the opportunity to participate in regular, authentic, one-on-one conversations with an older native speaker. The model recognises that classroom teaching rarely exposes young language learners to natural, everyday use of the language and that students have very limited opportunities to develop their interactional skills. Further, the classroom environment may impose certain constraints on a student's motivation or sense of identity (Duff, 2012), while a different scenario can help boost the learning process. In this book we have shown that conversation sessions between L1–L2 pairings did indeed have a positive effect on the students' self-efficacy (Chapter 9) and also led to improvements in their interactional competence in terms of turn-taking, negotiating meaning, developing a topic and so on (see Chapter 10). Our model fits well with Australian National and State language curricula and initiatives to increase

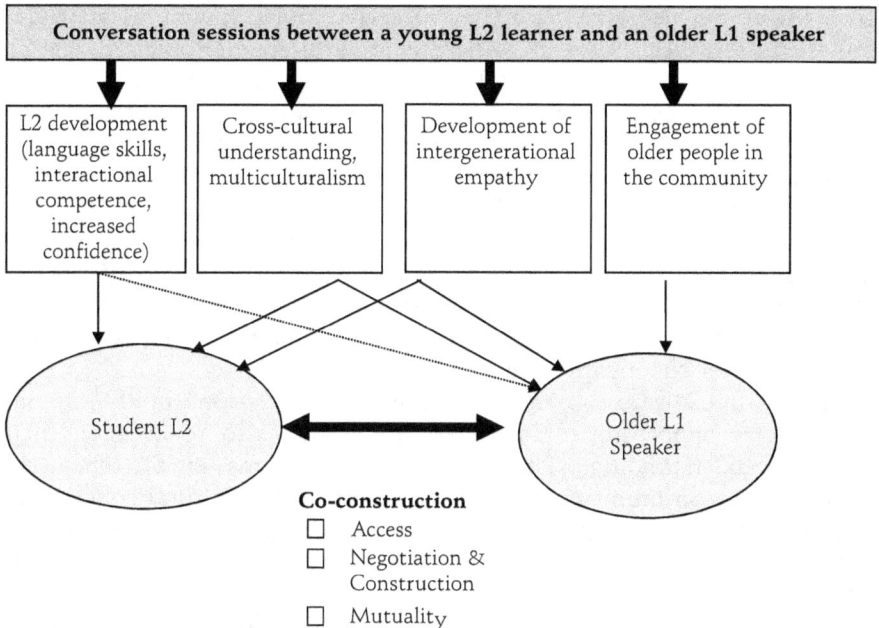

Figure 11.1 An intergenerational, intercultural model of language learning and social inclusion

participation in language studies and increase connections to real speakers. For instance, the guiding principles in the *Victorian Government's Vision for Languages Education* (2013) emphasises 'encouraging partnerships among settings and sectors, and with ... *community* groups and other partners to support quality and continuity of languages learning, increased time on task and opportunities for *real-world* language use' (emphases added).

In addition, the model has been shown to be of value in improving the second language skills and confidence of some of the *older* participants. During our project, recent arrivals among the older migrant group commented that the conversation sessions had helped them with learning English and understanding Australian society (see Chapters 4, 5 and 8). Thus, there are *reciprocal* benefits of this approach to language learning, in that it facilitates situated learning for both the young L2 learner and the older L1 speaker.

Cross-cultural Understanding. The second dimension of the model accords with Australia's official Multiculturalism Policy (*People of Australia,* 2011) and recognises that a culturally and linguistic diverse society is more cohesive when people from different cultural backgrounds are given opportunities to meet, understand and learn more about each other. Open communication between cultures helps to break down negative cognitive, affective and behavioural attitudes and fosters respect for and tolerance of difference (Robinson, 1992). Further, as Scarino explains (2010), interaction with another culture challenges and even transforms one's own identity and values. For students learning another language, the 'intercultural orientation' they experience as they converse with an older native speaker helps them to 'decenter' from their own linguistic and cultural world (2010: 324). Intercultural capability is developed in the act of communicating, as the students must move between their own world view and that of their partner in order to convey meaning in the target language. The model recognises that it is culture itself that provides the contextual framework for the meaning presented in the exchange.

As with L2 learning, the cross-cultural connections built into our model offer opportunities for older immigrants also to broaden their cultural understanding. The conversation sessions enable them to experience a community activity outside their own cultural cohort, not only by meeting immigrants from other cultural groups involved in the project, but also by meeting young people from a wide variety of linguistic and cultural backgrounds.

Intergenerational Empathy. We consider this third dimension of our model a significant innovation. The tensions created by the media's relentless focus on youth and the reality of an ageing population have been recognised by the UN and the Australian Government, the latter appointing its first Age Discrimination Commissioner in 2011 and publishing a number of guides for people in later life as well as a video awareness campaign, 'The Power of Oldness', in 2013.[1] These commendable initiatives are designed to break down the stereotypes which are at the root of ageism and to promote positive images of older people. We argue, however, that the message needs to be taken into the community in real and practical ways, that intergenerational understanding and empathy are born from personal encounters between the generations. The parallels with the second dimension of our model, multicultural exchange, will be obvious. The conversation sessions bring together people from different generations to build communicative links, and in so doing, assumptions, attitudes and prejudices about young and old can be confronted and revised.

Engagement of Older People. We have shown in this book that older people can be a *resource* for the younger generations by sharing their language, cultural and life skills as well as their accumulated wisdom. At the same time, the model offers a stimulating and educational experience for the older participants. Lifelong learning has been identified as a way of retaining cognitive skills, emotional resilience and mental health (Hammond, 2004; Narushima, 2008), while ageism, which would deny older people these opportunities, has been reported as a key barrier to well-being in older life and can even impact on mortality rates (Angus &

Reeve, 2006; Levy *et al.*, 2002; Nelson, 2004). Our model provides one way for older people to engage with the wider community in meaningful and rewarding ways, and recognises that a healthy society embraces healthy ageing and opportunities for older people to enhance their quality of life.

All four dimensions of the model function to meet the broader objective of *social inclusion*, defined by the Australian Social Inclusion Board as all people having the resources, opportunities and capabilities to

> Learn (participate in education and training); Work (participate in employment, unpaid or voluntary work including family and carer responsibilities); Engage (connect with people, use local services and participate in local, cultural, civic and recreational activities); and Have a voice (influence decisions that affect them) (ASIB, 2012: 12).

Co-construction

The key to the model is *Co-construction*, the 'joint creation of a form, interpretation, stance, action, activity, identity, institution, skill, ideology, emotion, or other culturally meaningful reality' (Jacoby & Ochs, 1995: 171). In our model, co-construction implies an equal role for the Student L2 and the Older L1 in each conversational pair in the tasks of language learning, negotiating meaning, establishing and maintaining rapport, (re)constructing identity, and developing intercultural and intergenerational understanding. The interaction will be a successful one when the co-construction is cooperative and supportive.

Co-construction has three implications. The first of these is *Access*. Quite simply, the conversation meetings make a diverse group of people – young and old, from different linguistic and cultural backgrounds – *available* to each other. We recognise that access to the different strands of society, even in an openly democratic and multicultural society like Australia, is not always easy. In fact, young language students may be made aware of the local community of the target language for the first time, and this community is made accessible to them through their conversations with the native speaker. For their part, the older immigrants are able to gain access to a different cohort while still making use of their own language and cultural knowledge. This can be of great value for more recent immigrants who have not had the opportunity to engage in social activities outside their immediate families, and for older people who have been left feeling isolated or marginalised following retirement, illness or a change in family circumstances.

The second implication of co-construction is *Negotiation and Construction*. In order to communicate successfully, each speaker in a conversation must go through a sequence of discovery, observation and negotiation, as well as making their own contributions to actively co-construct the exchange (Hall, 1993). As they converse, they discover and observe the patterns of interaction and the interactive style and participatory moves of their partner(s), and learn which patterns are considered important or acceptable for a successful social engagement. The conversation is co-constructed as the first speaker's intentions and meaning are modified according to the many contingencies that are specific to the context. This is particularly true of young L2 learners in conversation with native speakers, as they are dependent on the negotiation of meaning for a clear understanding of the other's intentions in terms of linguistic tokens, cultural concepts and interactional patterns. Because of this, their responses are a form of hypothesis testing in which they test not only the patterns and moves of their partner but also their own sociolinguistic output (Swain, 1985, 2005). Once their hypothesis is confirmed they are in a position to develop their own sets of responses and interactional strategies, consciously or unconsciously. Alternatively, they can modify their strategies or employ other (or more) linguistic and non-linguistic resources to support their interactive activities. The model therefore provides opportunities for young language learners to negotiate and construct meaning in the target language in real time, which they accomplish with the joint creation of appropriate linguistic forms, registers and sequential routines.

Similarly, the older participants will negotiate meaning in their conversations with their young partners when cultural concepts, topics or lexical items are new to them. The ongoing topic shifts and stance repositioning reflect the dynamic nature of the exchange.

Important for understanding the process of negotiation and construction is the idea of *agency* (Deters *et al.*, 2015), which describes an individual's motivation, initiative, autonomy and so on in relation to a task. From a sociocultural perspective, agency is mediated through the individual's cultural background, experiences, emotions, ideologies and identity, and as a result there are 'culturally diverse interpretations of what constitutes agency and empowerment' (Wray, 2004). Conversations, in this view, are dynamic social activities which bring into focus the contingent and dialectic nature of language in the discourse, while the agency and identity of an individual are always situation-dependent. Our model seeks to give agency to each participant by providing a context in which the contributions they make are valued and valuable not only for second language learning but also for their role in promoting intercultural and intergenerational understanding.

The third feature of this process is *Mutuality*. Interactions between an L2 learner and an L1 speaker provide a locus for mutual affective, cognitive and behavioural development. Linguistic, cultural and social knowledge is exchanged in the dyadic interactions, and this exchange constitutes a pivotal but enriching experience for both parties. The contribution during the conversation is not a one-way process. Rather, it is mutual: both parties work closely together to negotiate meaning, and to mutually help or support each other for the purpose of meaningful interaction. This mutuality is something shared by both interlocutors, who make contributions as adequate to the purpose and the situation as possible in the process of conversations with many 'mutual contingencies' (Jones & Gerard, 1967: 715). In a mutually beneficial exchange, each interlocutor may contribute to the conversation what the other may lack, and offer experiences derived from their generational and/or linguistic/cultural background. The mutual benefit for the speakers, in this sense, is reciprocal and complementary, but not necessarily symmetrical; that is, it may be biased in one direction or the other at different times (Graumann, 1995).

Mutuality also describes the benefits to both parties in relation to all of the dimensions described above. That is, through the co-construction of meaning, exchange of ideas, sharing of knowledge and experiences, and development of language skills, there are rewards for all participants in terms of improved intergenerational and intercultural understanding, language skill development, building rapport with a new social group, and a feeling of achievement.

Implementation of the Model: Practical Considerations

Successful implementation of the model requires a co-operative approach. Facilitators, such as project managers, school teachers and community workers, are essential as role models, sources of inspiration or mediators, and must be individuals with high levels of interpersonal and negotiating skills. Their role is to explain the requirements and aims of the project to the students and the older immigrants, managing issues such as expectations, attitudes, language levels, cultural background, levels of commitment and availability to ensure that the participants chosen are able to create a positive, cooperative and supportive learning environment. Facilitators also liaise with the school administration (timetabling, student credits, after-hours access), and handle other administrative requirements (transport for older people, scheduling of meetings). Resources for facilitators have been developed over the course of our three-year project and include a promotional video and brochure as well as a kit with templates.[2]

Older people can be recruited through local councils, ethnic churches or community groups that cater for older people with a non-English-speaking background. They can also be the grandparents or other older relatives of other young people at the school. A local approach is not only efficient in terms of time and costs but also helps to enhance the older people's sense of belonging to their neighbourhood, of which the school is a part. If the model were widely accepted as a supplement to classroom teaching in schools, it would be desirable to set up a national database listing all the community organisations of different ethnic groups that could be approached for volunteers, and to keep this resource up-to-date.

The language students and older multilingual speakers give freely of their time, and it is therefore important to acknowledge their involvement. For example, their contribution can be celebrated during community festivities or school events. Certificates of participation or appreciation should be presented to the older participants, such gestures serving to reinforce their understanding of the importance of social inclusion in the project. For the students, a certificate will provide proof of their commitment to second language learning and document the social skills they have developed through their participation. Recognition and celebration of the project at public events and in the media not only help to promote awareness of this approach to second language learning but also encourage a positive attitude towards older adults and people from a migrant background in the wider community.

An important finding of our project was the need to work more closely with language teachers in the preparation of topics. Topic selection featured as a significant variable in the students' self-efficacy beliefs (Chapter 9) and in the ability of both groups to conduct the conversation in a smooth manner (Chapter 10). The encounters are intended to provide a platform to exchange meaning, linguistically and culturally, and so the topics chosen should be ones the participants feel confident and comfortable talking about. Simple questions about hobbies or food can be a good starting point for students to test and apply conversation strategies, while at a later, more advanced stage, abstract topics can be introduced as stimuli for developing a discussion and expressing opinions. The family can also be a suitable introductory topic, but this occasionally involves uncomfortable personal information, as we saw in some of the examples in this book, and the older participant needs to be prepared to activate an empathic topic shift in such circumstances. The topics chosen should also, of course, link to the requirements of the school curriculum.

Extra-curricular activities are another way for language students to tap into local community resources. These could include, for example, a visit to a Chinese museum, eating out at a Spanish restaurant, or watching a German film during an international film festival. These activities would then provide suitable topics for subsequent conversation sessions and expand the students' understanding of the riches available to them in their multicultural society. Social activities involving all the project participants in its early stages can also help to broaden inter-ethnic understanding and provide topics for discussion (see below).

The opportunities for co-construction were also limited when the older participants' talk tended to take the form of closed questions (Chapter 10). While the stances they adopted in the interactions were always appropriate, some guidance could be given to the formulation of their utterances so that the students were prompted to give fuller responses to open questions and to initiate topic development to achieve a more balanced dialogue. Ensuring that the older participants were fully aware that they were primarily involved in a language-teaching activity would be likely to improve the quality of the conversations and also give the immigrants a stronger sense of purpose. Indeed, allowing them to 'have a voice' – the fourth criteria for positive ageing in the ASIB report quoted above – by helping to develop the topics would also give them agency. However, the guidelines should not be prescriptive, as this would interfere with the authenticity of the conversations and with the natural stance-taking acts of the participants we observed in Chapters 5 and 6. In addition, opportunities for older people to tell their life stories to a sympathetic audience and to share their knowledge and wisdom have been shown to be meaningful activities which promote their sense of well-being (Trentham, 2007), and are valuable in 'passing on important life messages to current and future generations and in fulfilling the generativity or social contribution functions associated with old age' (25). We have included a number of extracts in this book in which the older immigrant is clearly appreciating the opportunity to share past experiences with the student whether these were happy ones (e.g. Example 4.5) or more difficult ones (e.g. Example 5.6). These narratives also added to the students' understanding of the migration experience and to the challenges faced by older people in society. Further, the extended turns of the native speakers exposed the students to a realistic use of the language that is less commonly encountered in textbook and classroom learning. All of these benefits align with the aspirations of the model.

The Model in Action

Our model has attracted the attention of state education departments, and language teachers throughout Australia have expressed an interest in introducing similar projects into their curricula at primary, secondary or tertiary levels, for both week-day and weekend community schools. During the project undertaken in Melbourne the research team provided guidance and expert knowledge to educators setting up their own projects elsewhere, with particular attention to adapting the model to the specific constraints and resources available locally. In addition to the continuation in wider Melbourne (e.g. Tintern School and McKinnon College and Xin Jin Shan Chinese Language and Culture School), a smaller-scale application of the model has been carried out successfully in south-eastern Queensland as part of the project 'Language and Cultural Learning: An Intergenerational Approach', funded by Independent Schools Queensland. The project took place at Moreton Bay Boys College in 2013 and paired Spanish language students enrolled in Year 10 with older Spanish-speaking migrants for a series of weekly 50-minute conversations over a 10-week period. A notable difference between this project and the Monash one was that the student cohort was from a mainly Anglo-Celtic background and had had limited exposure to other ethnic groups.[3] In order to help build rapport between the participants, a number of social activities were arranged during the first three weeks of the project. Both the older people and the students were invited to show their talents, play guessing games, sing songs and share their favourite traditional meal with the group. These activities were found to be of real value for initiating conversation topics, which were set by the researcher and the students' teacher.

The benefits of the project for the Brisbane students echoed those of their Melbourne counterparts, and included: (1) increased confidence in speaking Spanish: 'This is the first time that I have put together a sentence in Spanish. I feel great'; (2) an improvement in the conversational skills required to engage with a native speaker; (3) increased awareness of their own cultural heritage and an insight into the cultural and life experiences of the Spanish-speaking immigrants; (4) increased awareness of the concept of healthy ageing; (5) increased awareness of the contribution that older people can make to society through their volunteer work.

Also funded by Independent Schools Queensland in 2013, the project 'Connecting Classroom 2 Community (CC2C)' was carried out from Toowoomba to Townsville during 2013, and included eight independent schools.[4] Participants were students in Years 7 to 12 (roughly 12–18 years of age) who were learning one or two of the following languages: Chinese, French, German, Japanese, Indonesian and Spanish. This project introduced a series of activities to the language curricula to enrich the students' experience and engagement with the language they were learning. Regular meetings with native speakers was not always feasible due to a limited number of L1 speakers in some of the regions, therefore identification of the community resources available to each of these schools was essential for the success of the project. Various opportunities for excursions were made available to the students depending on the community resources of the region. Examples of the activities the schools carried out over a one-year period included going to restaurants to try iconic dishes from other countries, ordering the meal in the language of the restaurant, cooking with Chinese ingredients previously unfamiliar to most students, interviewing a Spanish native chef about Latin American cuisine, interviewing German native speakers about their experiences in Australia, and going to festivals and celebrations. These activities played a major role in shaping the students' attitude to language learning and were rated 'highly satisfactory' by both teachers and students. Students were involved with the language of study at first hand, and were also asked to reflect on their learning experience through their preparation of a group magazine, which was presented to the rest of the class at the end of the year. The following main outcomes were identified: (1) establishing a link between the classroom and community to provide students with authentic exposure to the target language and culture; (2) improvement in the students' confidence and speaking abilities after using the target language outside the classroom with native speakers, which led to greater confidence in spontaneous speaking tasks and a desire to use the language more frequently and fluently in class. Some students' grades improved after their participation in the project; (3) students' greater awareness and appreciation of cultural differences and customs, and greater enthusiasm to experience these cultural practices in authentic settings; (4) development of the students' range of vocabulary and writing skills in a variety of genres and modes which gave them scaffolding and collaborative opportunities. Students were able to recall language, facts and history from their experience and reflect on them in written tasks; (5) awareness of how immersion in the culture positively impacts language proficiency. Among the students who had previously had some in-country experience, many indicated a strong desire to return to that country in the future; (6) a platform for teachers to encourage collegial learning, planning, networking and the sharing of teaching strategies.

In Melbourne the model is being used in a primary school, where Year 5 and 6 students regularly visit an aged care facility for German speakers to chat, play games and sing with the residents. This has inspired discussion at another aged care facility with a view to involving secondary school students. Elsewhere there is a trial of linking primary school students with a grandparent via the internet to practise language learning, opening up new possibilities for access to the model.

All of these projects highlight the benefits of utilising the human resources available in our suburbs and towns to build stronger, more connected communities. The model can be implemented at any year level in any education system and embraces and supports any language taught in schools. We would like to see our model become an integral part of the language curriculum in Australia (and beyond) so that different generations and language groups can continue to learn from each other and build a more inclusive society.

Notes

(1) Australian Human Rights Commission, 'Power of Oldness'. See https://www.humanrights.gov.au/news/stories/power-oldness.
(2) Monash University, Intergenerational, Intercultural Encounters and Second Language Development. Available at: http://artsonline.monash.edu.au/intergenerational/.
(3) This reflects the broader results of the 2011 national census in which 9.8% of Queenslanders were reported to speak a language other than English (LOTE) at home, compared with 23.1% of Victorians.
(4) Fraser Coast Anglican College; John Paul College; Montessori International College; Saint Stephen's College; St Aidan's Anglican Girls' School; The Lakes College; Toowoomba Grammar School and Townsville Grammar School.

References

Angus, J. and Reeve, P. (2006) Ageism: A threat to ageing well in the 21st century. *Journal of Applied Gerontology* 25, 137–152.
ASIB (2012) Australian Social Inclusion Board. *Social Inclusion in Australia: How Australia is Faring*. Canberra: Australian Government.
Deters, P., Gao, X., Miller, E.R. and Vitanova, G. (eds) (2015) *Theorizing and Analyzing Agency in Second Language Learning: Interdisciplinary Approaches*. Bristol: Multilingual Matters.
Duff, P.A. (2012) Identity, agency and second language acquisition. In S.M. Gass and A. Mackey (eds) *The Routledge Handbook of Second Language Acquisition* (pp. 410–426). London: Routledge.
Graumann, C.F. (1995) Commonality, mutuality, reciprocity: A conceptual introduction. In I. Markova, C.F. Graumann and K. Foppa (eds) *Mutualities in Dialogue* (pp. 1–24). Cambridge: Cambridge University Press.
Hall, J.K. (1993) The role of oral practices in the accomplishment of our everyday lives: The sociocultural dimension of interaction with implications for the learning of another language. *Applied Linguistics* 14, 145–166.
Hammond, C. (2004) Impacts of lifelong learning upon emotional resilience, psychological and mental health: Fieldwork evidence. *Oxford Review of Education* 30, 551–568.
Jacoby, S. and Ochs, E. (1995) Co-construction: An introduction. *Research on Language and Social Interaction* 28, 171–183.
Jones, E.E. and Gerard, H.B. (1967) *Foundations of Social Psychology*. New York: Wiley.
Levy, B.R., Slade, M.D., Kunkel, S.R. and Kasl, S.V. (2002) Longevity increased by positive self-perceptions of aging. *Journal of Personality and Social Psychology* 83 (2), 261–270.
Narushima, M. (2008) More than nickels and dimes: The health benefits of a community-based lifelong learning programme for older adults. *International Journal of Lifetime Learning* 27, 673–692.
Nelson, T.D. (ed.) (2004) *Ageism: Stereotyping and Prejudice against Older People*. Cambridge, MA: MIT Press.
The People of Australia: The Response to the Recommendations of the Australian Multicultural Advisory Council. Canberra: Australian Department of Immigration and Citizenship, 2011.
Robinson, G. (1991) Second culture acquisition. In J. Alatis (ed.) *Linguistics and Language Pedagogy: The State of the Art* (pp. 114–122). Washington, DC: Georgetown University Press.

Scarino, A. (2010) Assessing intercultural capability in learning languages: A renewed understanding of language, culture, learning and the nature of assessment. *Modern Language Journal* 94, 324–329.

Swain, M. (1985) Communicative competence: Some roles of comprehensible input and comprehensible output in its development. In S. Gass and C. Madden (eds) *Input in Second Language Acquisition* (pp. 235–253). Rowley, MA: Newbury House.

Swain, M. (2005) The output hypothesis: Theory and research. In E. Hinkel (ed.) *Handbook of Research in Second Language Teaching and Learning* (pp. 471–483). Mahwah, NJ: Lawrence Erlbaum Associates.

Trentham, B. (2007) Life storytelling, occupation, social participation and aging. *Occupational Therapy Now* 9 (5), 23–26.

Wray, S. (2004) What constitutes agency and empowerment for women in later life? *The Sociological Review* 52, 22–38.

Index

Aboriginal Australians
    culture 27
    languages 7–8, 14
ageing
    healthy ageing 33–34, 150–151,
        228–229
    of first-generation immigrants 27–28,
        151
    of populations 25
    see also generational intelligence, older
        people
ageism 26, 82, 111, 145, 159, 162, 228
agency xxiii, 159, 230, 233
alignment
    of speakers 52, 53, 60, 61
    with a group 86, 94, 108
Asian
    –Australian relations 17
    cultures 86, 160, 173
    languages 15, 16–17
    see also Chinese
Australia
    community languages 14, 37
    immigration policies 7–8, 9–11
    language teaching 14–16, 227
    multicultural society xix, 6, 7–8, 8–9,
        17–19, 88–89, 151
    relationship with Asia xix, 17

backchannelling xxiv, 112, 129, 192, 197,
    198, 205, 207, 211, 212, 213, 221
body language 116, 187

Canada 4, 8, 13
Chinese
    culture 62, 87, 102–103, 157, 159–160,
        162–163, 181, 183
    L1 speakers in Australia 18, 43
    L1 older speakers in the project 43, 89,
        154–156, 190
    language 43, 86, 87, 90, 94, 99, 107, 197
    taught in Australian schools xix, 171
    trade with Australia xix, 15, 17
classroom learning xx, 37, 40, 41, 52, 53,
    55, 111, 226, 233

Clyne, Michael xiii, 15–16, 17, 19
co-construction (in talk) 222, 226, 229, 233
code-switching (translanguaging)
    55, 136–137, 202–204, 208, 209,
    212–213, 217, 223
compliments 112, 121, 123, 125, 127, 132,
    134, 194
conversation analysis (CA) 40, 86, 188,
    189, 192
coordination (in talk) 115, 117, 135–136,
    137, 138, 139, 140, 141, 142–144

domain specificity 172, 180, 181–182, 184

empathy 4, 113, 139, 142, 228
    see also generational intelligence,
        rapport
English
    as L2 for older immigrants 11, 12, 55,
        69, 80, 111, 156, 157
    see also backchannelling, 'monolingual
        mindset'
ethical-moral adviser, stance of 59–61,
    62, 98
ethos of self xxii, 67, 68, 80, 81

face 112, 113, 132
families 19, 26–29, 33, 38, 62, 105, 106,
    132, 232
filters of expressiveness and accuracy 115,
    117, 118, 145, 146
first person pronouns *see* self-referencing
Fraser, Malcolm 9

Galbally Report (1978) 9, 9–10
gender 26, 66, 154, 189
generational intelligence xxii, 63, 82, 152,
    228
generativity 32, 152, 158–160, 161, 162, 165
German
    culture 58, 79–80
    L1 speakers in Australia 18
    L1 older speakers in the project 43, 68,
        73, 81, 89, 154–156, 190
    language 43, 76, 78, 81, 86, 87–88, 90,
        99, 105, 107

Germany 5, 13
Gillard, Julia 12

Hall, Joan Kelly 40
Hanson, Pauline 7, 10
Hatch, Evelyn 39
Howard, John 7, 10

identity
   of immigrants 66–68, 71, 82
   see also ethos of self, the self
interactional competence 187
   and communicative competence 188
   and conversation analysis 188, 189
   in L2 learning 188, 221–222, 229–230
   Monash study 189–223
   studies 188–189, 190
intergenerational
   programmes and studies 29–30, 30, 31, 33, 149–150, 152
   relationships 27–29, 30, 33, 111, 152
   see also generational intelligence

L2 learning 53
   and self-efficacy 171, 173
   as a situated interactional process 38–41
   benefits 16, 17, 19, 228
   extra-curricular programs 37–38, 40, 174
   in families 19, 38, 182
   see also classroom learning
L2 students
   as language instructors 55–56
   as sociocultural guides 59, 76
   as youth ambassadors 63, 125
   in the project xiv, 42, 176–177, 190–191
language instructor, stance of 53–56, 61, 62, 76–77
Latin America
   culture 55, 78
   life in 56–57, 77, 78, 138
   see also Spanish
laughter 76, 120, 122, 129, 131, 135, 196, 201, 220
legitimate peripheral participation see situated learning
Long, Michael 39

mentoring 31–32
migration
   experience 66, 74–75, 80, 125–126, 138–139
   reasons for 56–57, 77, 138

Model for L2 Learning and Social Inclusion xxiv
   design 226–231
   implemented in schools 233–235
   practical considerations 231–232
Model of Verbal Rapport
   see under rapport
Monash Project
   aims 20, 30, 41, 45–46, 149, 152
   conversation topics 43, 45, 61–62, 69, 88, 132, 141, 184, 232
   data collection 43–44, 68, 70, 90, 118, 153–154, 174–177, 191–192
   design 42–44
   interactional competence study 189–223
   limitations 162, 164, 165
   participants see under Chinese, German, Spanish, L2 students
   participant evaluations 156–161, 180–182
   self-efficacy study 174–184
   suggestions for improvement 163, 164, 184, 222–223, 232–233
Monash University xiii, xiv, xxiv, 13, 43
'monolingual mindset' 5, 14, 15
multiculturalism 3–4, 6–7, 8
   negative views 5, 6, 11, 13
   positive views 5, 8, 12
   see also Australia—multicultural society
mutual attentiveness 115, 117, 118–119, 129, 140

older people
   as a language and cultural resource 19, 25, 28
   as caregivers 27
   as ethical-moral advisers 59
   as mentors 31–32
   feelings of isolation xxi, 19, 26, 151, 160, 229
   lifestyles 26
   see also ageing, mentoring, generativity, reciprocity, and under stance

Pica, Teresa 39
politeness 62, 87, 102, 112, 114
positioning see stance
positivity (interpersonal) 115, 117, 120–121, 123, 125, 127, 132–134
   see also compliments

rapport 93, 127, 132, 144, 145, 146
    and stance 114, 116
    definitions 110–111, 112, 113, 115, 117
    importance of 110, 111
    model of non-verbal rapport 115
    model of verbal rapport xxii–xxiii, 114, 117–118, 144–146
    studies 111, 113
    see also coordination, mutual attentiveness, positivity
reciprocity 32–33, 152, 158, 160, 161, 162

scaffolding 194, 213, 221, 223
second language learning *see* L2 learning
self, the xxii, 85–87, 94, 105, 107
self-efficacy 172
    and cultural background 173, 183
    in L2 talk 180–184
    Monash study 174–184
    studies 171, 172, 173–174
self-referencing 70, 85, 86–87, 107
    as everyone 98–99
    as I, myself 99
    as speaker + listener 90, 92–93
    as speaker + others 93
    Chinese and German usage compared 90, 91, 93–94, 99, 107
self-selection 189, 196, 197, 200, 202, 206, 207, 208, 217, 221
situated learning 38–39, 40–41, 41–42, 187
social capital 30
social inclusion 6–7, 19–20, 229
sociocultural guide, stance of 56–59, 61–62
sociolinguistics xxi, 26, 66, 67, 86, 112, 144

Spanish
    L1 speakers in Australia 18
    L1 older speakers in the project 43, 68–69, 74, 81, 154–156, 191
    language 43
    see also Latin America
stance 51–52, 116, 117
    affective stance 72–73, 77, 79
    and rapport 114, 116
    comparative stance 72, 79, 81
    contextual stance 71, 78
    epistemic stance 71–72, 73, 78, 79
    expert stance 70–71, 73
    of ethical-moral adviser 59–61, 62, 98
    of language instructor 53–56, 61, 62, 76–77
    of sociocultural guide 56–59, 61–62
stance-taking *see* stance
stance triangle (Du Bois), 51, 69

Tannen, Deborah 112, 137
Tickle-Degnen, Linda 111, 114, 115, 117, 119
topic management 125, 131, 132, 135, 136, 193, 203, 214, 233
    as indicator of interactional competence 188, 189, 201–202, 212–213, 220–222
    self-efficacy in xxiv, 175–176, 178–184
    see also Monash Project—conversation topics
translanguaging *see* code-switching
turn in talk 112, 113, 115, 188, 192, 194

White Australia Policy 7, 8

Young, Richard F. 39, 40

For Product Safety Concerns and Information please contact our EU Authorised Representative:

Easy Access System Europe

Mustamäe tee 50

10621 Tallinn

Estonia

gpsr.requests@easproject.com

www.ingramcontent.com/pod-product-compliance
Lightning Source LLC
Chambersburg PA
CBHW070558300426
44113CB00010B/1301